Apostles of Certainty

Oxford Studies in Digital Politics

Series Editor: Andrew Chadwick, Professor of Political Communication in the Centre for Research in Communication and Culture and the Department of Social Sciences, Loughborough University

Apostles of Certainty

DATA JOURNALISM AND THE POLITICS OF DOUBT

C. W. ANDERSON

OXFORD
UNIVERSITY PRESS

Oxford University Press is a department of the University of Oxford. It furthers
the University's objective of excellence in research, scholarship, and education
by publishing worldwide. Oxford is a registered trade mark of Oxford University
Press in the UK and certain other countries.

Published in the United States of America by Oxford University Press
198 Madison Avenue, New York, NY 10016, United States of America.

CIP data is on file at the Library of Congress
ISBN 978-0-19-049234-2 (pbk.)
ISBN 978-0-19-049233-5 (hbk.)

9 8 7 6 5 4 3 2 1

Paperback printed by WebCom, Inc., Canada
Hardback printed by Bridgeport National Bindery, Inc., United States of America

Contents

Acknowledgments

This book took a long time to write, but it would have taken far longer without the help and support of many colleagues and friends along the way. The bulk of the final draft was completed while on sabbatical at the University of Southern California's (USC) Annenberg School for Communication in the spring of 2017; many thanks to Mike Ananny and Christina Dunbar-Hester for the invitation and for their friendship and to Sarah Benet-Weiser for helping to make my visit so enjoyable. Thanks go out to the Department of Media Culture at the College of Staten Island and my chairs David Gerstner, Ying Zhu, and Cindy Wong who created a most welcoming work environment in which to write a long book. Special thanks go to the School of Media and Communication at the University of Leeds, where the book was completed, and to my heads of school Bethany Klein and Kate Nash who helped make sure it made its way across the finish line. As I began the arduous (and occasionally quite terrifying) process of moving jobs and continents while still finishing this book, a number friends in Leeds helped ease the difficult transition. There are too many to name here, but thanks to all of you.

Many thanks, too, to the staff at the Rockefeller Foundation Archives in Tarrytown, NY, whose support and genuine interest in my project were a welcome surprise. At one point it was hard for me to believe anyone would be interested in this book, but never doubt archivists. All of the individuals who allowed me to interview them or who shared their personal archives with me have earned my eternal gratitude, but I want to single out Philip Meyer for special thanks. He and his wife Sue not only met with me all day but graciously opened their Chapel Hill home to me and my probing questions, which made the entire experience really a delight. Thanks also go out to Bill Adair (of Politifact) and David Caswell who allowed me to poke around the Structured Stories New York City summer project in 2015 and whose thoughtful conversations really helped me figure out how to finish this book.

I was lucky enough to present parts of this book at various symposiums and seminars, including the Mary Junck Research Colloquium at the University of North Carolina, the 2012 Hackers on Planet Earth (HOPE) Conference in New York City, the Matter Matters Conference at the University of Lund, the 2013 National Conference on Media Reform in Denver, the University of Haifa Conference on Cultural and Media Production, the 2014 Rebele First Amendment Symposium at Stanford University, the Conference on Media and Capitalism at the School of Journalism and Communication at Renmin University of China, the 2015 International Symposium for Online Journalism at the University of Texas-Austin, the first Data + Power Conference at the University of Sheffield in 2015, the Yale Information Society Project's Conference on Algorithmic Power in 2016, and the 2017 Annenberg Research Colloquium at USC. Deep thanks to all who invited me to speak, and who facilitated my attempts to wrestle with these ideas in public.

A number of kind colleagues read parts of this book in various stages of completion: many thanks to Mike Ananny, Christina Dunbar-Hester, Lucas Graves, Paula Chakravartty, Cynthia Chris, Jinee Lokaneeta, Maggie Gray, Dave Karpf, Matthew Powers, Pablo Boczkowski, Gina Neff, Simon Braune, and Michael Shapiro for their generosity, or masochism, or both. A special debt of gratitude is owed to Rasmus Kleis Nielsen and Daniel Kreiss, who read the entire manuscript and who contributed some key insights that shaped the final draft. Thanks of course also go to two anonymous reviewers at Oxford University Press and to Andrew Chadwick and Angela Chnapko who contributed thoughtful editorial advice and helpful suggestions. It should go without saying that none of these kind souls is responsible for the final product that is now in your hands.

I've been lucky to be friends with a number of journalists, reporters, and editors whose practical, real-world wisdom kept this book from sliding completely off the rails into irrelevance. Carrie Melago, Jonathan Lemire, Jacqui Maher, Paul Rissen, and Jessica Lee—thank you all a tremendous amount for your friendship and advice. Jessica Kaufman was a gracious and supportive presence throughout the very long production of this book. My family, finally, deserves special thanks, particularly my parents, Thomas and Nancy Anderson, my brothers, Matt and Tom, and their spouses, Jessica and Laura.

Parts of chapter 2 appeared in a different form in C.W. Anderson. 2017. "Social Survey Reportage: Context, Narrative, and Information: Visualization in Early-Twentieth-Century American Journalism." *Journalism: Theory, Practice, Criticism* 18(1): 81–100.

A small section of chapter 3 appeared in C.W. Anderson. 2014. Early-Modern Journalism and Its Boundaries: Between Theory and Belief. In Carlson, M. and Lewis, S. (eds.) *Boundaries of Journalism*. Abingdon-on-Thames: Routledge, 201–217.

Parts of the appendix appeared in C.W Anderson. 2015. Between the Unique and the Pattern: Historical Tensions in Our Understanding of Quantitative Journalism. *Digital Journalism* 3(3): 349–363.

Apostles of Certainty

1

Introduction

This is a book about objectivity, uncertainty, and the role played by facts and doubt in the practices of journalism and democratic life. It mounts an argument that since the middle of the twentieth century, journalists have engaged in an increasingly successful effort to render their knowledge claims more certain, contextual, and explanatory. In large part, they have done this by utilizing different forms of evidence, particularly evidence of the quantitative sort. These changes can also be understood by looking at journalism's relationship with social science, which has been a key and often overlooked player in the professional history of news reporting. Nevertheless, the book concludes that this heightened professionalism—and the increasing confidence of journalists that they are capable of making contextualized truth claims—has not always had the democratic outcomes that journalists expect. Modern American political discourse has tried to come to grips with the uncertainty of modernity by engaging a series of increasingly strident claims to certitude. Professional journalism has not solved this dilemma; rather it has exacerbated it. To better grapple with the complexity of the modern world, journalism ought to rethink the means and mechanisms by which it conveys its own provisionality and uncertainty. If done correctly, this could make journalism more like modern science rather than less.

The idea for this book began with the notion that it might be useful to historicize the current mania behind the growth of data journalism in digital news production by looking at how data had been mobilized, as a form of factual evidence, over the course of American journalism's history. In other words, while the existence of a thing called "data journalism" might be new, the use of data in journalism is not, and analyzing how the understanding and interpretation of quantitative evidence in journalism has changed over the course of the last century would provide citizens and journalists with insights into changes in journalism as well as changes in what it means to use "data" to construct truthful narratives. I hope this book can tell us not only about journalism, but also about knowledge production practices in general. It is meant to be a contribution to both journalism studies and science and technology studies (STS) and is part of a broader movement to link media and journalism research more closely into the STS tradition (Boczkowski 2004; Gillespie, Boczkowski, and Foote 2014; Graves 2016).

To tell this story I focus on three key moments in the history of data use in news reporting and construct chronological linkages between them to develop an overarching narrative about the relationship between journalism and practices of quantitative truth building. I should note here that this book does not claim to be a complete analysis of all journalism everywhere and throughout all time, but rather a story of three key "crystallizing moments" in the history of quantitative news reporting. As a model we could point to a book like *The Averaged American* by Sarah Igo (2008), which tells the story of the development of large-scale quantitative surveys in the United States. Like Igo, I don't pretend to chronicle the entire history of a particular cultural movement, but I do try to focus on key moments that narrate the history of a particular socio-political era.

The first of these "crystallizing moments" lies in the late nineteenth and early twentieth centuries, when social movements in the United States (the so-called progressives) agitated not simply on behalf of a raft of social and political reforms (change in labor laws, prohibition of alcohol, reform of municipal and state governments, etc.) but also began to argue that certain forms of fact generation—based on empirical, numerical evidence—provided greater access to social reality than others. This mania for "data collection" would infect a variety of early-twentieth-century causes and would have a glancing but meaningful impact on practices of journalism.

The second key moment centers on the invention of "precision journalism" in the early 1960s and the manner through which this "social science in a hurry" evolved into computer assisted reporting (CAR) and the data journalism we know today. Precision journalism took advantage of the increased computational firepower available to journalists and the growing accessibility of government databases containing a wide variety of statistics about the US population and social life more generally—databases that had once been compiled on a voluntaristic and ad hoc basis by religious reformers earlier in the century. But it also drew on a growing professional self-confidence on the part of journalists themselves, at least a few of whom found themselves capable of imagining an occupational world where they could operate like social scientists. These precision journalists became "computer-assisted reporters" and later "data journalists," with each change in nomenclature reflecting a larger shift in the idea of what it meant to use data to tell stories.

The third key moment takes place in the present day, drawing upon what we might call a "post-data" tendency within a few advanced journalism institutions. Rather than using databases to tell stories, "computational journalism" conceives of the narrative world as composed of structured information and thus turns stories into databases. Computational journalists extract syntactical items like nouns, verbs, and objects from real-life narratives and place them in spreadsheets with which they can manipulate the relationships between these items. The process of data journalism is, as it were, reversed. The databases themselves are, in turn, grounded in online semantic structures that lend data a form of immaterial solidity. These developments mark a further transformation of both journalistic objectivity and the tools available to journalists to tell stories in new ways. They also mark a shift in more generalized understandings of what data means for social scientists and other empirical knowledge workers.

This book thus takes two oblique turns in an attempt to shed new light on old problems of knowledge and epistemology. The first is its attempt to draw journalism more tightly into the analysis of knowledge generation practices on a comparative level. Journalism is an odd and overlooked form of knowledge work. Rather than making journalism uninteresting or unworthy of study, I argue that the profession's very oddity makes it a useful heuristic device through which to understand epistemology more generally. Journalism makes claims that are both incredibly modest (it simply reports the news of the day, quickly) and incredibly wide ranging (it possesses methodological techniques that allow it to objectively parse social reality) (Anderson and Schudson 2008). This combination of simplicity and hubris can therefore help us understand other professions that are less torn between epistemologically modest and epistemologically extreme claims. The second turn is the book's focus on elite, data-oriented forms of news reporting. The cases discussed here do not claim to cover the entire length and breadth of journalistic work. They are, in many ways, examples of journalism operating at its highest level and as such exclude tabloid newspapers, Fox News, many blogs, social media, and a variety of other important (perhaps even more important) forms of news work. They also exclude most forms of news that are not American. In my earlier research (Anderson 2013a) on local news ecosystems it was important for me to discuss the length and breadth of journalism in a single city without pre-judging what actually constituted news. My historical strategy here has been somewhat different, but I hope this book will leave readers in the same uneasy place. Drawing on Rasmus Kleis Nielsen's distinction between journalism as "acquaintance with" and journalism as "knowledge of," I wanted to focus on a type of knowledge which has been largely absent from many discussions of journalism—knowledge of the world, but a knowledge driven largely by quantitative (not oral or qualitative) facts. This entire book, in some ways, might be seen an empirical elaboration on Kleis Nielsen's evocative essay (Kleis Nielson 2017). Like my previous work on subaltern forms of journalism (Anderson 2013a), I again focus on marginal or emergent practices in order to assess new questions about the profession of journalism at large. In other words, I try to problematize an elite form of news that many of those reading this book might assume to be perfectly natural and simple "common sense."

Embedded in this narrative are two additional threads that I hope readers will also appreciate as they make their way through the book. The first thread is the relationship between objectivity and passion. We tend to think of objectivity as an emotionless practice adopted by cold, logical people, people somehow capable of eliminating excess feeling from their professional lives in pursuit of the truth. One of the things that I hope this book makes clear is the fact that the avoidance of passion in factual analysis is itself a passionate endeavor. The drive to "be objective" is itself an emotional commitment, freighted with beliefs, hopes, standards and conventions, and political commitments (Wahl-Jorgensen forthcoming; Kennedy et al. 2016). One of the goals of this volume has been to probe the values that lie beneath the drive to separate facts from values. A second narrative thread is the relationship between crisis and objective knowledge—by which I mean political crises, epistemological crises, and the reaction of journalism to these crisis moments. Since at least the early twentieth century the response of journalism to moments of crisis has been to double down on its commitment to objectivity, often shifting definitions of what objectivity means but holding fast to its ideal and even, in many cases, struggling to become more objective rather than less (Schudson 1978). This professional response is not foreordained; the social upheaval of the early twentieth century or the tumult of the 1960s and 1970s, and their accompanying crises of epistemological certainty could have called forth a more subjective press, a more narrative-driven press, or a more post-modern press (as indeed they did in certain segments of the American academy). Instead, journalists, for the most part, sought to raise the bar by which they could act as professional arbiters of truth. They have embraced professional certainty in an uncertain moment, with complex consequences.

In Lieu of a Model, Inspirations

In the last few years, the scholarly study of the relationship between so-called big data, "computational thinking" (Wing 2006), and journalistic practice has become something of a growth industry. Starting from only a few professionally oriented articles in the early 2010s (Cohen et al. 2011; Turner and Hamilton 2009) recent publications have examined the early years of the New York Times technology department (Royal 2010; Usher 2016), the routines and ideologies of data journalists in Chicago (Parasie and Dagiral 2012), rhetorics of technology in American newsrooms (Powers 2011), the relationship between data journalism and open source discourse (Lewis and Usher 2013), and possible theoretical frameworks for undertaking a "sociology of algorithms" (Anderson 2013c). Much of this fertile growth was captured in a special issue of *Digital Journalism* edited by Lewis (2015), which documented the state of the field and in Nikki Usher's magisterial overview of data journalism and interactive information practices in the early twenty-first century (Usher 2016).

But while we have begun to glimpse the historicization of data techniques and practices (particularly in Parasie and Dagiral 2012 and Powers 2011), we have yet to see the emergence of a full-fledged genealogy of data journalism and computational thinking in a true Foucauldian sense. For Foucault, genealogy was a "form of history which can account for the constitution of knowledges, discourses, domains of objects, etc., without having to make reference to a subject which is either transcendental in relation to the field of events or runs in its empty sameness throughout the course of history" (Foucault 1980, 117). In other words, the object of study contains few, if any, pre-determined characteristics, and its meaning changes—in not entirely intended or pre-determined ways—over the arc of its existence. One of the inspirations for this book, then, is the work of Foucault and the related notion that understanding data journalism requires us to conduct a genealogy of epistemological assemblages. That is, we ought to study the process by which journalism engages in a form of public "world building"; the way that a variety of processes, technologies, and evidentiary objects contribute to this crafting of publics and public issues; and the manner in which these materialities and discourses have been loaded with different meanings at different times. From this perspective, "big data" might be seen as another object of evidence that enters the journalistic bloodstream at a particular moment or moments. The question would then be why these moments? This genealogical perspective can, in turn, shed light on why the relationship of journalism to data matters in a more normative sense.

Foucault, clearly, carries a great deal of intellectual and historical "baggage," often serving as a stand-in for arguments that a certain strain of post-modern thinking has reduced all truth-claims to the exercise of power. Other historians of ideas in traditionally less contentious disciplines have also probed the macrostructures that allow certain ideological constellations to congeal, be spoken of, and manifest themselves in society. Along these lines, a second source of inspiration for this study can be found in the work of the "Cambridge School" of political philosophy represented by historians such as Quentin Skinner (2012), J.G.A. Pocock (1970), and others. Rather than studying the ideas of "great men" in isolation (the writings of Hobbes, for example, disconnected from any larger social context), Skinner and Pocock, as well as their followers "have both been associated with a program of remodeling the history of political thought as political discourse."

The study of a specific thinker may focus on establishing the particular language or languages in which he wrote, as a prelude to discovering what he actually said, intended, or conveyed ... in civilizations employing complex literary traditions, patterns of language and thought outlive the authors who utter them in specific texts, and reappear in specific texts or contexts ... they consist, in part, of kinetic and paradigmatic structures, which act on the intention using them and the consciousness they express, and modify the world just as the world modifies them. (Pocock 1981, 50–52)

To understand how journalists thought about data, and how that thinking had political consequences, we must study not only what journalists said about data but discover the larger social and historical context that allowed what they wanted to say to be speakable.

Finally, there are two interrelated difficulties with the work of both the Foucauldians and the Cambridge School in the context of the study of professional knowledge in general and journalism in particular, difficulties that have led me to additional methodological inspirations. Both Foucault and Skinner largely ignore the materiality of knowledge production—the fact that the discourses, ideas, and ideologies they study did not simply emerge out of nowhere but must be produced as actual things and depend on other things for the specific forms that production takes. Ideas and ideologies, in other words, need paper, the printing press, or some other form of materially grounded infrastructure for their dissemination if not for their outright inspiration. The web of speech acts traced by such scholars as Skinner and Pocock do not exist without being "embodied" somewhere. Fortunately, several generations of STS (Daston and Galison 2010; Dunbar-Hester forthcoming; Shapin and Shaffer 1985) and Actor–Network Theory (Hemmingway 2005; 2008; Latour 2010a; Loon and Hemmingway 2005; Plesner 2009) have taught us to analyze the intersection of materiality and ideology in ways that supplement the discourse-focused scholarship of Foucault and the structuralist historians of the Cambridge School.

A second difficulty arises from the particular object of study—journalism, specifically—as a form of knowledge. In addition to the oddity of journalism as an epistemological form, referenced earlier, journalism is also a rapid and regular producer of its own media material. In other words, journalism generates the materiality of its own existence as part of its professional raison d'etre. So, in addition to analyzing discourse and technology we must also make use of the regular and classic tools of communication, such as the content and discourse analysis of traditional media studies.[1]

This book thus stands as an attempt to sketch out a particular genealogy of data and its relationship to journalism. There is no entirely unproblematic understanding of big data; its history is not determined by its purpose and use, but rather its purpose and use is enabled by its entangled history. As Nietzsche noted, in a passage from the *Genealogy* of Morals that held particular resonance for Foucault:

> the "development" of a thing, a practice, or an organ has nothing to do with its progress towards a single goal, even less is it the logical and shortest progress reached with the least expenditure of power and resources. Rather, it is the sequence of more or less profound, more or less mutually independent processes of overpowering that take place on that thing, together with the resistance that arises against that over-powering each time, the changes of form which have been attempted for the purpose of defense and reaction, as well as the results of success-ful counter-measures. Form is fluid; the "meaning," however, is even more so. (Nietzsche 1887)

Overview of the Book

These inspirational models underpin each of my empirical chapters. Chapter 2, "The Idea of Data, Documents, and Evidence in Early-Twentieth-Century Journalism," launches our story in the early twentieth century, a moment in which the settled practices of journalistic evidence gathering were being chal-lenged by the rise of social science, the emergence of new objects of evidence, the professionalization of a variety of "knowledge disciplines," and a new mania for representing social facts in graphic form. The chapter aims to chronicle the manner in which a reform-oriented social movement attempted to mobilize the public through the deployment of quantitative facts by looking at a long forgotten Progressive Era reform movement, the Men and Religion Forward Movement (MRFM). This group attempted to advance progressive and reform-ist goals by documenting a variety of social conditions, such as church attend-ance, poverty, and alcohol consumption, feeding these statistics to news outlets, and using these news outlets as a way to gain publicity for their cause. In so doing, they helped advance a form of "data journalism" in the service of liberal reform. The MRFM was part of the larger Social Survey Movement (SSM), a kind of journalistically oriented social science tasked with the goal of reform-ing society. The MRFM, organized in part by a charismatic minister turned social "scientist" turned advertising executive, has left us a particularly rich set of documentation about exactly how these reformers envisioned their relation-ship to the press and how they saw the use of surveys and informational graphics as both a knowledge-creating and a publicity-generating reform strategy. One poorly understood aspect of the larger Progressive Era (the political context in which the MRFM emergences) is its attempt to "democratize data"—or at the very least attempt to turn data toward public, transparent purposes. This, in turn, involved using journalism as the popular medium of publicity par excellence, one that could be used to advance movement goals. I call one particular figure in the movement out for special attention: the Reverend Charles Stelzle, who was responsible for both the group's statistical work and its focus on the public relations benefits of well-displayed "charts and graphs" that could help visualize the movement's findings. To probe the relationship between the epistemological work undertaken by the MRFM to the type of objectivity practiced by reporters at daily US newspapers, chapter 2 focuses on four particular "object of evidences"—(1) the survey blanks and statistical notebooks employed by Stelzle and the Presbyterian Bureau of Social Service; (2) the seven volume *Messages* of the MRFM, along with the book *American Social and Religious Conditions*, written by Stelzle and drawing on the recently compiled survey data; (3) the actual data visualizations themselves and the manner by which the MRFM used the technologies and display practices of the time to advance what they believed to be an objective, empirical, and publicly captivating view of the social world; and (4) newspapers and how they used movement data to craft their own news stories. The chapter concludes with a discussion of how the particular materiality of early-twentieth-century journalism combined with a particular constellation of journalistic practices and cultures to create particular patterns of news coverage and what this tells us about journalistic and social scientific knowledge practices in the early days of social science. Early sociology made little distinction between the deployment of quantitative information for the purposes of science, for the purposes of reform, and for the purposes of publicity; in essence, the social survey movement acted as a big tent that housed pre-professional sociology, elements of the progressive movement, and journalism. For publicity's sake, they collected and displayed urban data that allowed them to claim to display the "whole of the population" before the public in order to encourage social activism and political change. They hoped that these unusual displays would catch the eyes of editors and journalists, who would use them in their daily news stories. Journalists, however, made little use of this patterned, visual, and contextual information, and were far more likely to cover individual events in which quantitative data was displayed, such as survey exhibitions and dinners where survey results were discussed. The event-focused nature of daily newspaper reports, along with technological difficulties in easily laying out and printing information graphics, contributed to these failures of journalism to focus on patterns as opposed to individual events.

Chapter 3 steps back from the granular analysis of the MRFM to examine the evolution of early-twentieth-century newspaper journalism and twentieth-century social science in more general terms. As chapter 2 shows, from the turn of the twentieth century well into the 1930s the line between a journalistic and a sociological ontology was far from straightforward. This chapter explores the processes of boundary work by which academic sociology and journalism were constructed as separate professions in this three-decade period, decades that happened to coincide with the formative period of professionalization across a wide range of knowledge disciplines. Drawing on theories of knowledge that understand professional expertise as both material and networked, this chapter moves between an analysis of the processes of boundary drawing (in which clear divisions and well-articulated categories and temporalities of evidence are reified) and an analysis of a messy, hybrid world of journalism/sociology (in which clear occupational divisions are both rhetorically unsettled and repeatedly transgressed in practice). The chapter begins by briefly recapitulating the socio-technical context of the early twentieth century, a world in which journalistic and sociological practice were deeply entangled. The second section is a qualitative discourse analysis of the *American Journal of Sociology*, the *American Sociological Review*, the *Columbia Journalism Review*, and *Editor and Publisher* in order to examine the techniques through which this entanglement began to be sorted out through the deployment of rhetorical boundaries. The chapter zeroes in on the different ways that sociology imagined and represented journalism within its scholarly journals. Through this discourse analysis, we can see a remarkable shift taking place—from a world in which the evidentiary practices and commitments of journalism were admired, even embraced, by many budding sociologists to a world in which they were scorned, dismissed, and rejected out of hand as inferior forms of knowledge work. This rejection occurred for many reasons, as I outline in the chapter (journalists used largely qualitative not quantitative methods, they wrote particularly clearly, and so on), but the main reason can perhaps be summarized in the claim that journalists were too embedded in the cut and thrust of public life. Journalism, for social scientists, could never be a real science because it busied itself too much with public affairs rather than with formulating abstract models of social life in the service of building theory. Journalism, for its part, came up with its own justifications for simultaneously dismissing social science in general and sociology in particular.

This analysis of sociology's construction of journalism and journalism's construction of sociology can be considered the "bookends" of chapter 3. In between these analyses I look at the more general process through which sociology expelled a variety of suddenly non-scientific reformers from its ranks, including many of the participants in the social survey movement discussed in chapter 2. Paradoxically, just as sociology was denigrating journalism for its lack of empirical value, journalism was becoming increasingly visual and contextual and concerned with reporting the "why" and "so what" of events. I consider this development by looking at the rise of contextual journalism, the career of the small journal the *Survey Graphic*, and the evolution of the display of graphical information on the front pages of the *New York Times*. Journalism was, in short, becoming more scientific—but the definition of what it meant to be a science had itself changed. While this is something of an exaggeration, we might say that social science was now for theory building and quantitative modeling and the more disconnected it was from reality the better. By the new standard of mid-twentieth-century social science, journalism was found wanting. The social survey movement had united journalism, science, and advocacy on behalf of the public, but the collapse of the "big tent" of progressive-era reform would see publicity claimed by journalism, the science of society claimed by sociology, and a more explanatory, public-facing type of scholarly communication left an orphan. The easy link between making confident fact claims and mobilizing the public on behalf of certain political goals broke down. It was clear that the public could be activated in a variety of ways, but that this public would always be partial, provisional, and already inclined to engage in certain particular political actions. The progressive public could no longer be mistaken for the public writ large. I describe this process in detail in chapter 3.

Sociology and political science, in other words, dismissed increasingly common visualization techniques in favor of the rigor of statistical techniques and a reliance on scientific method. Additionally, they rethought their understanding of what it might mean to be a publicly relevant social science, leaving activism behind and embedding themselves more firmly within the post-war policy-making apparatus, seeking to influence the direction of society through expert advice and access to political decision makers. The role played by journalism in this evolution is key: it was the primary institutional entity that stood between social science, government, and the public and as such, was increasingly tasked with explaining the ramifications of social change to an increasingly overwhelmed public. Chapter 4 begins by discussing the cultural status of social science in the post-World War II years through an overview of how mainstream sociology was portrayed in popular culture during this time, as well as the work of the Russell Sage Foundation (RSF)'s Social Science in the Professions project, a project that tried to unite social science methods with professional practices in the law, social work, and journalism. The most important output of this now forgotten project was Phil Meyer's book *Precision Journalism*, published 1973, which is considered by many to be the founding text of the data journalism and CAR movements. In it, Meyer argued that journalists not only needed to forge a closer working relationship with sociologists, but that they could even take on some of the tasks of sociology in political science—that journalism could become "social science in a hurry." Meyer, in other words, launched an attempt to reunite the fractured domains of sociology and journalism and to do so on the terrain established by mid-twentieth-century sociology by incorporating variables, surveys, and new forms of objectivity into journalistic work. For Meyer, journalism ought to concern itself with questions of method rather than stance; it should worry less about whether or not it ought to have a point of view and worry more about how it could justify the truth claims it did make. In pushing journalism to state with authority what the truth was, Meyer made a particular professional claim upon journalistic certainty and argued that journalists, indeed, could state clearly the facts of the matter and render professional judgment on what was and what was not. For Meyer, science had already taken this step and there was no reason why journalism could not as well.

In the earliest days, however, Meyer's arguments found few supporters. The pre-publication reviews of *Precision Journalism* show just how hard it was for both journalists and social scientists to conceive that they might have anything at all to say to one another—this despite the fact that a mere fifty years earlier there was little to distinguish much of sociology from journalism in any case. Over and over, reviews complain that working journalists won't have the time or interest to absorb Meyer's techniques, and in any case, they would fit poorly into daily news routines. Social scientists, these reviews continue, will see the arguments of *Precision Journalism* as overly simplistic and lacking the nuance necessary to be really accurate or useful. "Who is this book even for?" one perplexed reviewer asked in some dismay. Russell Sage itself declined to publish the book, perhaps expressing tacit disapproval about how far Meyer had strayed from their basic proposition that what journalists needed to do was forge a tighter relationship with social scientists in order to explain their work. The idea that journalists themselves should embrace the techniques of social science was seen, by many who first read Meyer's book, as a step too far.

In retrospect, these concerns seem overblown. *Precision Journalism*, while it did not fundamentally transform everything about the news business, managed to foster a thriving insurgent reform movement within the journalism profession itself, one that would lead to the invention of CAR and eventually the rise of interactive and data journalism. What led to this change, which took less than twenty years? In most accounts, digitization and the rise of computers are identified as the reasons why data journalism has emerged. In more nuanced histories, Meyer is given credit as the individual responsible for "inventing" data journalism and evangelizing for its use in newsrooms. We certainly see the importance of his role in chapter 4.

In chapter 5, however, I expand the lens of the commonly received history. While neither the personal nor the technological explanation is wrong, per se, chapter 5 shows just how much the use of digital technologies depends on the evolution of an already existing journalistic culture. This chapter also stresses the degree to which the diffusion of Meyer's basic insights was only made possible through the existence or invention of a variety of institutions, some of which were only orthogonally interested in data journalism. Part of the reason for the embrace of data journalism lies in an emerging vision of computers, and especially of databases, which allowed them to be integrated into journalistic work. The rise of data journalism was also facilitated by changing notions of what was meant by "investigative reporting" in the 1970s, the founding of the National Institute for Computer Assisted Reporting (NICAR), and a long-term crisis in notions of journalistic objectivity in the 1960s, in part prompted by the emergence of "new journalism" at about the same time.

Chapter 5 begins by delving more deeply into the text of *Precision Journalism* itself and takes advantage of the fact that the book went through four editions, three of which were substantially different from one another. By reading *Precision Journalism* hermeneutically, I argue that we can see an evolution in the larger ideologies and structures surrounding data, reporting, and notions of objectivity. I also show the dynamic relationship between precision journalism and the narrative journalism of Hunter S. Thompson, Tom Wolfe, and Jimmy Breslin, which also emerged in the 1970s and in many ways functions as precision journalism's ideological enemy. Both narrative journalism and precision journalism were grappling with a larger crisis of journalistic method. Each sought, in Meyer's words, a way to ground journalistic reportage in a particular location that transcended the uncertainty of traditional objectivity. One answer was to ground it in the romantic mind of the novelistic reporter, while another answer was to ground it in the methodologies of science. The scientific processes, and the various forms of evidence upon which science drew, would reduce situational uncertainty and allow journalists to become more objective.

For this larger transformation to be conceivable, two additional developments needed to also take place. The first involved the development and implementation of journalistic databases and particularly a change in the way journalists imagined what the database was capable of contributing to journalistic work. While it might seem natural to identify the major technology behind the rise of CAR as "the computer," I argue in this chapter that the computer was actually secondary. What the computer did was make journalistic work more efficient. But in material terms, the primary shift occurred with the growth and digitization of governmental databases. Along with this change was a related one, in which the meaning of what it meant to do "investigative reporting" evolved in order to incorporate more contextual, social-scientific, and explanatory modes of reportage. Sitting at the center of both these shifts was NICAR, which acted as an organizational container for CAR projects and helped guide journalistic use of data in the direction of investigative reporting. With the rise of NICAR, both CAR and data journalism gained increasing institutional prestige. One of the consequences of this prestige, ironically, was that it made the use of numbers and social-science methods seem increasingly opaque, elite, and outside the area of interest for average everyday reporters, even as it also claimed to make the truth more certain and factually clear. These developments—the growth of NICAR, the accessibility of databases, the growth of interactive news, and continued shifts in understandings of journalistic objectivity in the field of data journalism—have combined to create the varieties of quantified, contextual journalism we recognize today.

The final empirical chapter, chapter 6, turns the discussion to an emerging form of quantified journalism, one that may represent a fundamental shift in the manner by which journalists mobilize objective facts on behalf of the public. Under this model, facts can be certifiably true if they exist in a digital database and can be placed in a semantic relationship with other facts. The narrative of this book, from roughly the third through fifth chapters, chronicles the emergence of a particular form of data journalism that made use of particular evidentiary objects, combined with an evolving idea of what journalistic objectivity ought to mean. This journalism had a specific relationship with social science, first as an outsider and then as an adopter of specific sociological methods. But there was a moment—the years of the social survey movement, for instance—before this particular constellation of objects, ideologies, and material affordances came into being. Rather than focusing directly on data journalism, chapter 6 provides a history and overview of what is called "structured" journalism, journalism that grapples with a different conception of journalistic facts and the means by which these facts can be strung together to create news stories. Instead of using databases and social science methods to craft narratives, so-called computational or structured journalism turns narratives into databases; it creates structured data out of unstructured events and uses that structure to inform journalistic work and produce new news products. Chapter 6 describes the findings of a field research project that looked the computational journalism project Structured Stories, a structured journalism experiment in New York City, and then compares that experiment with similar projects at the BBC and with fact-checking organizations in the United States. It discusses the operations, ideologies, and institutional routines of Structured Stories, and analyzes the underlying computational cultures that seem to intersect with the larger belief patterns of traditional journalism. It details some of the ways that a deeper understanding of the work routines of structured journalism might help us understand general trends, tensions, and critical junctures common to digital news production in general. The chapter focuses on four aspects of Structured Stories worthy of note: the ontologies of evidence imagined by Structured Stories, the changing epistemologies of journalists participating in Structured Stories, the manner in which notions of journalistic professionalism might be changing in a world of structured journalism, and finally, the economic imperatives driving work in Structured Stories.

This discussion of structured journalism highlights a few important areas that are worthy of final consideration. One is the continued role of the database in thinking about journalistic narrative, though it is a database "with a twist." Structured journalism represents the fullest extension of computational thinking into the journalistic process. Rather than taking data and turning it into a story, as both Phil Meyer and Tom Wolfe urged (though with diametrically opposite areas of emphasis), structured journalists take narratives and turn them into data(bases) rendering them accessible to computational and algorithmic analysis. As the database becomes the operational object at the center of the journalistic process, I argue that this starts to change the very notion of journalistic objectivity, turning it into what I call "second order" objectivity. The most important anchor point for journalism in this model—to use Phil Meyer's phrase—becomes the database itself. A fact is true, in other words, if it exists in the database. Although there is indeed some sort of link between "the world" and "the database," the primary task in the case of structured journalism becomes the creation of the database itself for computational purposes. This, in turn, may be leading to a rebirth of the "naïve empiricism" discussed by Michael Schudson and other scholars of news (Schudson 1978). The journalist is now a compiler of discrete, individual facts whose truth or falsity is ultimately knowable and transparent. The professional work once carried out by the journalism organization to mediate the inherent uncertainty of the world has, in turn, been farmed out to the computer. While I may be exaggerating somewhat, the full impact of computational thinking on traditional notions of journalistic process and objectivity are most visible in journalism experiments like Structured Stories, experiments which demonstrate the tenuous nature of most modern notions of objectivity, including those guiding precision journalism, data journalism, and CAR.

In chapter 7, I compare the work of MRFM, the Detroit Riots reporting of Phil Meyer, and the journalism of Structured Stories. This brief overview chapter, comparing three journalistic ways of understanding the city, helps to summarize the developments chronicled in these pages and point us toward this book's conclusion. In chapter 8, finally, I leave both history and theoretical models behind to speculate more openly about how the story told in these pages helps us understand political, social, and communicative events of the present day. The election of President Donald Trump in the United States, and other events such as Brexit in the United Kingdom, seem to clearly demonstrate that we have reached another crisis point both for Western political structures and the empirical knowledge professions more generally. Journalism, traditionally, has responded to these crisis moments by doubling down on objectivity, whether in the embrace of contextual journalism, precision journalism, CAR, data journalism, or today's structured reporting. The difficulty, however, is that the language of science and scientific fact no longer seem to assemble a public in any meaningful sense. Rather, they divide and even polarize that public. In the early twentieth century, facts, data, reform, and publicity were unproblematically unified. How ought one mobilize a public for the purpose of political change? The answer was clear: through fact, data, and graphic visualization of society. As the failures of the Progressive Era became apparent after World War I, different elements of the progressive vision were claimed by different knowledge professions: sociology and political science would become the scientists of society, while journalism would be tasked with speaking to the public about matters of political concern through objective methods. How ought the public understand the larger social and contextual processes that drove that society, however? Although social science and journalism sought to answer that question in different ways, the twentieth-century response was increasingly through a fusion of the two—through a public sociology or through a contextual, data-oriented journalism. The passion that lay underneath the journalistic and sociological love of objective fact could be turned to public purposes without further commitment to actual political principles or to public beliefs.

Nevertheless, the politicization of fact has occurred without journalists and social scientists being asked for their views on the matter (Graves 2016). Moreover, the very visual language of fact appears to be seen by many as simply another strand of elitist discourse, alienating at best, offensive at worst. "Facts" are now just another type of narrative power, one wielded by the elite against the ordinary for the purposes of bamboozlement and control. Populism responds to these claims of factual certitude by invoking its own anxiety-reducing modes of truth and attempts to turn journalistic objectivity into just one more assertion or order among many. How ought journalists deal with this latest epistemological, political, and cultural crisis? This book demonstrates that they will most likely respond by raising the bar, yet again, on what it means to be objective. However, this might not be enough. There is nothing wrong with being passionate about objectivity. The fault lies with the belief that a love of facts alone can save the world, or at the very least, save democracy. The argument I mount in the conclusion of this book is that uncertainty, rather than certainty, is the common human predicament and that anxiety must be turned toward progressive political purposes. What unites us? Our fear of the future and the inherent provisionality of all truth claims. Journalists should want to grapple with this situation by becoming more humble and more willing to admit the complexity and uncertainty of more situations, rather than by aggressively shouting about their own professional confidence in the face of doubt.

2

The Idea of Data, Documents, and Evidence in Early-Twentieth-Century Journalism

Introduction: Journalism, Sociology, and Cultures of Data

Imagine the following situation for a moment: you are a middle-aged, religiously minded church volunteer (probably a woman) alive at the dawn of the twentieth century. You look around you and are bewildered by all the new faces you see crowding a city that once seemed safer, cleaner, and filled with more people "like yourself." You know that many of these new city dwellers are poor, but unlike your parents, you don't think that this poverty is simply their fault. Rather, larger systems also play a role in creating poverty. You think that the church of which you are an active member can help alleviate that poverty, but not only by providing charity. It can document the number of poor people that exist, map them in visually arresting ways, publicize these poverty conditions in the newspapers, write journalistic stories about your work, and help bring these new city dwellers to church. So you go house to house, counting the number of people who live in each one. You count the number of saloons and churches on each street, trying to understand if there is a relationship between the number of bars and the levels of poverty. You bring those numbers to a fellow church member, who plots them on maps of the city streets. You take those maps to the lobby of the local newspaper, or to a reporter you know, and try to convince someone to run stories on the poverty, the maps, and the counting you have done. What are you? A journalist? A sociologist? A social worker? An activist? Something else?

Professional occupations all originate somewhere, and they all have a history. For scholars who study professional knowledge, as well as researchers in the field of science and technology studies, this might be a self-evident observation. Most outside observers, however, rarely stop to consider the fact that what it meant to practice law, medicine, science, accounting, and even journalism or sociology was once different than it is today and that it might be different again in the future. One of the stories that scholars of the professions and occupations tell is a story in which once-unified occupational bodies merge, split, and differentiate themselves from other bodies with which they might have once been more closely aligned. The history of any knowledge occupation is often tied up with the history of its professional "other."

Most often, the story of the birth and professionalization of sociology considers its professional other to be the discipline of social work. Bound together uneasily in the late decades of the nineteenth century, a loose confederation of empirically minded social reformers concerned with the behavior of groups and "associational life" would diverge in the early twentieth century into the case-oriented, ameliorist profession of social work and the university-housed, theoretically driven, objective discipline of sociology. The story of the relationship between sociology and social work contains within it both standard narratives and far more critical narratives pointing to the gendered, racial, and political origins of this split (Lengermann and Niebrugge 2007) but either way, the story of early sociology is often a story of sociology and its relationship with social work.

The following two chapters complicate this narrative by adding a third occupation to the mix, one far more "professionalized" than either social work or sociology in the early twentieth century: the occupation of journalism. Despite the fact that many of the earliest sociologists and social settlement workers had also worked as journalists—Robert Park, Franklin Giddings, W.E.B Dubois, Ida Wells-Barrett—the relationship between journalism and sociology is usually overlooked in most histories of professional knowledge (though for an exception, see Linder 2006). In order to understand the way social science would impact journalistic "cultures of truth," however, and the way that the growing use of "data" and "facts" challenged journalistic notions of objectivity, we must pay particular attention to sociology and social work at the moment these professions came into being. The following chapters thus inevitably bump up against the standard professional history of sociology and social work from a somewhat oblique angle. In their attempts to use empirical research methods, first, to advance the cause of social reform and second, to draw on the fullest range of publicity methods in order to make their empirical data "do work" in the world, the earliest social scientists embraced journalistic work in either an explicit or implicit fashion. Turn of the century social science was often journalism, or at the very least concerned with *publicity* in a particular and important way. However, journalism itself was still recognizably *journalism* in terms of its methods, its understanding of objectivity, and its reliance on the incidental framing of news events. The complex relationship between these cultures of truth is essential for understanding the use of quantitative information in journalism prior to the crucial decade of the 1960s during which the thing we now call "data journalism" was first given a name.

Journalists, as we will see, reacted ambiguously to the pressures on them to embrace a more scientific certainty in the early twentieth century. They preferred to largely dismiss the availability of contextual quantitative information and continue to focus on chronicling the myriad "incidents" that created the fabric and texture of American life. But journalists also had their own bulwarks against doubt, even in this "pre-scientific" era. What united the social scientists, surveyors, and religious activists was an embrace of what Michael Schudson has called "naïve empiricism," or the belief that the single pieces of easily graspable "facts" were transparent, real, and understandable by all people. This, in turn, led to what we might call the first "big data" moment in the United States. The ways that journalists and sociologists reacted differently to this data explosion provide essential contextual grounding for the history that follows in later chapters.

One final note about my analysis of the MRFM in this chapter and its use as a stand-in for early-twentieth-century social science more generally. There are certainly more famous, successful, and scientific surveys I might have discussed here, such as the Pittsburgh Survey or other surveys carried out under the aegis of the Charities and the Commons. What is most interesting about the MRFM, however, is the fact that it openly and explicitly grappled with the relationship between journalism, data-gathering, and scientific work, going so far as to write an entire volume about its dealings with the press (discussed extensively later in this chapter). The MRFM is perhaps more ameliorative and journalistic than social scientific, but in a book about journalism I can think of no better example from the early twentieth century than a movement run by someone who began life as a printer and ended it as a Madison Avenue public relations man.

The Context

Reading US newspapers from the years immediately prior to World War I is an odd business. In many ways, the world on display in these articles is our own: a world of teeming urban spaces, rapidly accelerating technologies, often banal political speechifying, publicity and public relations, social dislocation, and churning capitalism. In other ways, though, the polity represented in these news stories appears distinctly foreign. And while news organizations had begun to develop their own understanding of what was meant by a specifically *journalistic* objectivity, they were also enmeshed in larger social and political currents that pulled the news business in a variety of often contradictory directions. Out of this heterogeneous mix of forces would arise a hybrid style of journalism/

academic writing/public relations I call "social survey reportage." While news organizations had been using data, documents, statistics, and infographics for decades, our investigation into journalism's empirical cultures of truth—in their truly modern sense—begins here, in the first years of the twentieth century. The constellation of social factors that gave birth to social survey reportage was both explicitly religious and aggressively rational; deeply concerned with social justice but also utterly enthralled with the self-obvious efficiency of the reforms needed to enact this justice; obsessed with data and data visualization but seemingly lacking any of the basic social science techniques that we would consider essential to the proper analysis and display of this data. Most importantly, perhaps, it saw no contradiction between public enlightenment through empiricism and the deployment of public relations techniques for the purposes of manipulating the daily press. By analyzing a variety of Progressive Era reform movements and journalistic practices—the SSM, the MRFM, public relations professionals, and social survey reportage—this chapter aims to document some of the earliest intersections of data, documents, statistics, and the news industry.

The chapter proceeds as follows. The first part, drawing on historical research conducted at a variety of archives and through a close reading of the secondary literature on social reform movements in the early twentieth century in the United States and the United Kingdom, places the SSM, progressive-era journalism, and the MRFM in their historical context. The literature on the history of sociology is replete with analyses chronicling the intersections between social surveys and the emerging discipline of sociology (Bateman 2001; Bulmer et al. 1991; Claussen 1998; Greenwald and Anderson 1996). There is a third strand to this intellectual excavation however—the relationship between sociology, the social survey, and *journalism* as it was practiced in the early twentieth century. Understanding how surveyors understood their relationship with journalism, and how journalists reported on the survey, is essential if we are to understand the forms of boundary work engaged in by journalists and sociologists and chronicled in the next chapter.

The second section of this chapter, primarily drawing on qualitative content analysis, looks at the different forms of data generated by the MRFM, and examines how this data was reported (or not) by urban newspapers between 1911 and 1912. The third part, again drawing on archival research, analyzes the ways that the MRFM brought its data visualizations to the public *in the absence* of widespread newspaper coverage of its quantitative work, a strategy which in turn fed back upon news organizations and led them to engage in additional (highly idiosyncratic) coverage of the movement. The final part concludes by discussing some of the boundaries (or rather, the relative *lack* of boundaries) that lay between the different quasi-professions in the early 1900s, and the way that different institutional understandings of what it meant to deploy objectivity in support of the assertion of fact would begin to shape the form of the more well-bounded knowledge professions which emerged more fully by mid-century. Specifically, I investigate the manner in which social survey was itself adopted—or not—as an object of early-twentieth-century journalism (Anderson and de Maeyer 2015). How, in short, was the particular vision of the public constructed by the MRFM adopted, translated, or ignored by those working in a journalism industry that was one of the purported targets of that movement? How, to return to the language of chapter 1, did the particular materiality of early-twentieth-century journalism combine with a particular constellation of journalistic practices and cultures to create particular patterns of news coverage? What does this tell us about journalistic knowledge practices at the turn of the century?

For readers who have picked up this book in order to understand data journalism, computational reporting, the internet, and digital technology—well, for those readers, all of this might seem like a strange detour. The next dozen pages or so are about a great many things, but all of those things are old, few of them are journalistic, and very little of them directly tie into discussions of technology per se. Where, you might want to ask, are the data journalists? Where are the journalists, period? While all of this will become clearer in the next chapter, it is important to begin in the bowels of the early decade of the twentieth century because that era is both simultaneously close and remote from our own. The simultaneous closeness and remoteness of this era to ours is more easily grasped when we consider that the SSM was made up of a group of men and women, nearly all of them religious and many of them volunteers, who shared a deep-seated belief that the plagues of poverty and social unrest could be ameliorated in part through the simple gathering of granular statistical data about the actually existing urban social conditions. In 1911 little of this information—whose ubiquity we often take for granted today—was accessible. Much of it did not even exist in any written form. In today's era of big data and voluntaristic, "crowd-sourced" information gathering, the spirit behind this distributed collection of statistical information might resonate with your average "networked" citizen. But the SSM also shared a uniquely progressive-era belief that making this data public would almost inevitably result in progressive social change, and that enacting this change would also help fulfill the mission of god on earth and lead to the increased temporal power of institutional religious belief. Decentralized data collection, the progressive promise of statistics and the scientific method, the religious tenor of this faith in efficiency and transparency—all of these things might seem both familiar and strange to us today. It is this combination that makes the SSM a good opening case study in this attempt to probe the relationship between data, facts, and journalistic practice.

The SSM in Context

To place the cluster of early-twentieth-century techniques, technologies, and political commitments I am calling social survey reportage in context, I conducted research in a variety of archives between 2013 and 2015, including the Charles Stelzle Collected Papers at Columbia University and the RSF archives housed at the Rockefeller Foundation Archives in Tarrytown, NY. As already noted, primary source documents contained in these archives included *The Church and the Press* Volume VII, *Messages of the MRFM*, the "Sociological and Religious Survey of Seventy American Cities" produced by the Bureau of Social Service of the Presbyterian Church in the United States, and "The ABCs of Exhibit Planning" by the RSF. I also drew heavily on the large amount of published, secondary literature on the history of social science, sociology, and the so-called knowledge professions in the early-twentieth-century United States and United Kingdom. I found *The Social Survey in Historical Perspective* (edited by Kevin Bales, Kathryn Sklar, Martin Bulmer), *Pittsburgh Surveyed* (edited by Margo J Anderson, Maurine Weiner Greenwald), and *Sociology in America: A History* (edited by Craig Calhoun) to be particularly valuable in providing an overall historical structure through which I could interrogate my specific findings on data production and journalistic production.

Social survey reportage, as we will see, is a phenomenon that stands at the crossroads of a variety of important epistemological paths: a progressive and ameliorative thrust in segments of the larger US political culture, a belief in the importance of collecting on-the-ground empirical evidence, and an obsession with counting and with the power of numbers to illuminate important truths. At the moment social survey reportage emerged, the boundaries of a variety of knowledge-generating occupations were also in flux, with the professions as we understand them today only beginning to emerge. For several decades, in other words, the dividing lines between journalism, social reform, data gathering, and social science were far less solid than they were for most of the later twentieth century. Consequently, aspects of survey reportage were scattered across many fields and disciplines in ways that often make little sense to our modern eyes. To the degree they clustered at all, social survey reportage was focused around particular journals, such as the *Survey Graphic*, as well as around social movements, rather than particular fields or occupations. In general, the SSM

(1) believed in the inherent and unproblematic truth of quantitative data
(2) understood the visual power of graphical representation of statistics
(3) thought that these graphics and data needed to be placed in a popular format in order to reach the people

(4) believed that journalism had become the most powerful moral voice in society, and

(5) saw no contradiction between social science, public relations, journalism, and social reform.

Where did the SSM come from, and how did it spawn both the MRFM and the quasi-journalistic techniques I am calling social survey reportage? We can begin by asking the following seemingly simple question: how many people in 1880s London lived in poverty? To answer this question today we might use Google or Wikipedia. A few decades ago we might have used an atlas or consulted news reports for the answer. But the most interesting aspect of this query is simply that, in the 1880s, very few people could do anything more than guess at a possible answer. While the regular decennial census of the United Kingdom contained figures about employment and the distribution of workers into a variety of occupational categories, the quality of the data on work and poverty was, in general, mediocre (Bales 1991, 71).[1]

Thus, without an answer to even the most basic of questions—*how* many people in London were poor?—answers to the far more socially and politically vexed questions of *why* some people were poor and *what* could be done about it were unanswerable through empirical methods. And answering these questions was of vital social and political importance, particularly to an English middle class that had come of age in the nineteenth century and was now watching the Victorian economic and social ideals that formed the background nexus to its general worldview challenged on a number of fronts (McGerr 2005). The consequences of the by now century-old Industrial Revolution were no longer new or hidden; by the 1880s, "economic depression had heightened social tensions [and] political groups that had competed in prosperity descended into conflict" (Bulmer, Bales, and Sklar 1991, 17). Under pressure from a variety of powerful working-class movements, and with the full impact of industrialization upon urban life now difficult to ignore (the 1886 "Black Monday" and 1887 "Bloody Sunday" riots in Trafalgar Square drew particular attention to the so-called social question and the "problem of the 'East End'"), general concerns with ameliorating a plethora of perceived social ills would only sharpen. At the same time, a number of historians of social science have pointed to the emergence of a second, seemingly tangential movement that would ultimately compliment this interest in the causes of poverty: a growing obsession with statistics and empiricism as the proper lens for understanding society. "One of the impulses that first drove people to measure economic phenomena was an ethical impulse to understand rapidly evolving modern societies . . . it was not primarily a desire to imitate natural scientists that led early [economists] to attempt the measurement of social phenomena, but *rather a moral curiosity to more fully understand the world unfolding around them*" (Bateman 2001, 57, emphasis mine).

Out of this curious mixture of middle-class guilt, unquantified but troubling urban poverty, heightened class conflict, and a general turn toward empiricism stepped the unlikely figure of Charles Booth. A wealthy industrialist, shipowner, and cautious social reformer, Booth was initially attracted to the question of how to measure poverty by a dispute with British socialist leader H.M. Hyndman who claimed in 1885 that 25% of all Londoners were impoverished. Familiar with statistics showing that barely 3% of the population received government relief under the Poor Laws, Booth (among many others) argued strenuously that this could not be the case. But the data, as we have already noted, was faulty and unreliable. Out of this question about the most basic of economic facts was born Booth's seventeen-volume *The Life and Labour of the People of London,* and with it, the SSM.

The basic idea behind *Life and Labour* seems so obvious to us today that it is important to keep in mind that Booth was seen as an innovator by researchers and reformers who agreed with his results and as a controversial figure by those that did not. How could you know how many people lived in poverty in London? Count them—either through first-hand observation and interviews, or through conversations with people who conducted these first-hand observations. There would be no "sampling" used in *Life and Labor.* Rather, volunteers and employees would gather as much granular data as possible before venturing basic hypotheses about the presence or absence of poverty. As described by Booth in a letter to Beatrice Potter outlining his basic research plan:

> We have had two successive evenings with Mr. Mather [of the School Board Visitors] on the School board figures. At the first we got a rough idea of what was to be had; at the second we made a definitive effort at the statement of facts concerning certain streets . . . . Our idea is that having made our classification we should note down *every* occupation we hear of & so make this list in the end a dictionary of employments. What is needed is that the employments should be so arranged as to be capable of research by other means into the facts of income of each class . . . . The plan I suggested is applicable to a complete statement of the whole information touching every street & every house in London. (Bales 1991, 78)

It is important here to point out the differences between Booth's survey methodology, which involved interviewing members of a group known as the School Board Visitors (who were responsible for monitoring households for truancy), and many of the social surveys proper which followed *Life and Labour,* particularly one by Seebohm Rowntree in York in 1899. Booth and his team interviewed School Board Visitors, who themselves carried out house-to-house visits while Rowntree dispensed with the mediating institution of the Visitors and interviewed people directly in their homes:

> Booth had conducted his work on the assumption that the informa-
> tion required was already known to someone other than the house-
> holder himself. Rowntree quickly learned he could not proceed on that
> assumption and he employed a special investigator to undertake house
> to house visits. Freed from a reliance on the School Board Visitors,
> whose knowledge extended only to families with children of school
> age, he embarked on a survey of the total working class population.
> (Hennock 1991, 191)

A second innovation pioneered by these early surveys was the use of color-coded maps showing income levels on a block-by-block or even house-by-house basis. This use of visualization was common in studies that considered themselves part of the SSM, despite variations in their exact data-gathering methodology.

Booth's *Life and Labour* would inaugurate a mania for gathering data about urban living conditions, an obsession that intersected with a deep belief that quantifying the existence of poverty would provide reformers with the tools to end it. Most of these social surveys, carried out in the first three decades of the twentieth century in Europe, the United Kingdom, and the United States, were united by at least a few overlapping methodological characteristics, as described by Bulmer et al. (1991). They:

- involved field work and the collection of information firsthand, rather than relying on secondhand information contained in government reports or other already existing data;
- obtained, or at least attempted to obtain, *complete of information*, rather than either data *samples* or information gathered in a haphazard way;
- were usually confined to a single city or town (necessary, in part, because of the desire to gather comprehensive information at a granular level);
- used individuals, not aggregates, as the level of analysis;
- were quantitative (involved counting);
- were deeply concerned with the policy outcomes that might be generated by the research, and were explicitly normative and reformist in aim.

In essence, to understand the survey, we need to keep in mind that the professional divisions between reform-oriented political movements, empirical social

science, muckraking journalism, and state-oriented policy analysis that we take for granted in the early twenty-first century were far less sharp in the early twentieth. We live, after all, in an occupational world that these progressive reformers created, particularly in their drive to organize a class of experts under the banner of professionalism (Abbott 1991; Haskell 1977). In the early 1900s, however, these distinctions were far from clear. "The survey," wrote Shelby Harrison of the RSF in 1930, "is not scientific research alone, nor journalism alone, nor social planning alone, nor any one other type of social or civic endeavor; it is a combination of a number of these" (Harrison 1930).

Although largely forgotten, the social surveys pioneered in England by Booth and his followers had a major impact on what would later become "academic" sociology as well as on the progressive movement in general. In part they served as a negative example, within a Whiggish epistemological framework, of the kind of "primitive" social research long since transcended by "real" empirical sociology. But they also fostered a more general public discourse about poverty and statistics. These surveys, in short, launched a methodological movement. They became a fad. And their biggest impact would turn out to be on the religiously based, efficiency-obsessed factions of progressive-era America—factions that included a particularly interesting, journalism-focused social movement, the MRFM, which would move the SSM in the direction of conducting a particular form of social survey reportage.

The Social Survey Comes to America

A HETEROGENOUS MOVEMENT

What evidence do we have that the social survey, which developed in the United States out of a trans-Atlantic nexus of settlement-house workers, statisticians, and social reformers (Bulmer et al. 1991), truly became a "fad"? We might begin with the sheer number of surveys: a 1915 bibliography compiled by the RSF lists more than three hundred survey projects carried out between 1909 and 1914 (Potter 1915), while an alternate count shows a jump in the number of surveys from about a dozen in 1904 to more than a hundred and fifty in 1914 (Harrison 1930). "In most of our social movements," noted Paul Kellogg in the 1912 issue of the *Proceedings of the American Academy of Political Science,* "we are under the necessity of starting something going. We must stir up public interest as the first step. The survey movement, if we can call it that, does not seem to be handicapped in this way." The public, it is implied, is already enthused, and all it takes is the deployment of empirical facts in graphical form in order to arouse that public to the fever pitch of action. Kellogg, himself the director of the Pittsburgh Survey and the editor of the magazine *The Charities and the Commons,* would go on to offer a laundry list of completed and potential surveys—in Newark, Sag Harbor, Rhode Island, Illinois, and many other places. "There is," he concluded, "a more spontaneous outcropping of the survey idea the country round than as yet we have any sufficient organization or body of trained workers to deal with" (Kellogg 1912, 3).

In this article, Kellogg is waging a two-front campaign: on the one hand, to unify the explosion of surveys and survey-like exercises carried out in the first decade of the twentieth century under the umbrella of a particular social movement ("if we can call it that"); on the other hand, to construct a typology of more or less "proper" surveys and rank them in an order of most to least "legitimate." The productive tension inherent in the dynamic between creating enough empirical unity to justifiably claim the existence of a collective enterprise of quantitative measurement and the methodological imperative to distinguish properly from poorly done surveys, should remind us that the entire notion of a "social survey movement" is, to some degree, a construction. While the survey movement might appear, retrospectively, as a unified enterprise, it was actually quite heterogeneous—indeed, it would be strange if this were not so, given the relatively unstructured and pre-professionalized nature of social inquiry in the 1910s. Drawing on information about how survey authors understood their own work, as well as a variety of recent historical overviews of the survey movement, we can usefully compare different surveys along at least four axes: the rigor of the methods they used for data collection, the attitude of surveyors toward notions of "social reform," the breadth of the survey in geographical space, and whether the surveys were carried out primarily by volunteers or by professionals (whether social scientists or otherwise). We can also distinguish the mechanisms by which the results of these surveys were communicated to the broader public at large.

In the methodologically loose and highly ameliorative quadrant of our comparative overview we have the Pittsburgh Survey of 1907–1908, one the most successful surveys carried out in the United States. In his *Proceedings* article, Kellogg claims that the Pittsburgh Survey demonstrates the kind of tasks that a survey can accomplish with a sufficient investment of time and resources. More than seventy researchers were involved in this RSF-funded survey, and the end product consisted of six large volumes on such familiar reformist topics as labor in the steel mills, a ravaged physical infrastructure, and women's work, as well as exhibits, speeches, and articles in popular magazines. The Pittsburgh Survey often stands in for discussions of the general survey movement in many histories of sociology, and it was one of the largest (and certainly one of the most famous) of the US surveys. And yet, for Kellogg, what made the Pittsburgh Survey exemplary was not its strict and rigorous data-gathering procedures. Rather, what made a survey a *survey* was who commissioned it, whether the leading citizen of a city had bought into the process, and whether it made use of local volunteers aligned with professional surveyors (Turner 1994, 37). Indeed, as Turner notes in his critical history of the Pittsburgh Survey "idea," Kellogg heaps scorn upon the "pure scientists .... [Who might] start out [an investigation of a town] without any hypotheses, tabulate every salient fact as to every house, cast up long columns of figures, and make careful deductions, which might and might not be worth the paper they were written on." More important for Kellogg was the role played by the hired social "engineer" who would be familiar with proper community standards and the degree to which the town under observation met those standards or was found wanting, along with the proper way to remedy the defects that were uncovered (Turner 1994).

In another quadrant—the scientific and a-normative quadrant—is *The Philadelphia Negro*, an analysis of the African-American population in Philadelphia's Seventh Ward conducted by W.E.B. DuBois in 1896. Almost entirely ignored at the time it was written, and rarely included in lists of social surveys drawn up in the 1910s and 1920s, DuBois' work has more recently been proposed as one of the founding documents of US sociology. I will return to a longer discussion of its role in sociological boundary work in the next chapter. For now, suffice it to say that *The Philadelphia Negro* was remarkably *different* from the other social surveys being conducted at the time, despite a number of superficial similarities. It is far smaller in scope than either Booth's *Life and Labor* or the Pittsburgh Survey and was carried out not by a team but by DuBois working almost entirely alone. The most important difference, however, was DuBois' attitude toward amelioration and reform. In short, he adopted a far more "scientific" and "objective" attitude toward his data than most of the social surveyors that came after Booth and Rowntree. Compare his cautious discussion about "how to solve the Negro problem" in the conclusion of his monograph—a discussion which is actually the most normative section of his entire work—with the glib and optimistic moralizing of the social surveyors. "We need only to avoid underestimating the difficulties [of the Negro Problem] on the one hand," DuBois writes, "and overestimating them on the other. The problems are difficult, extremely difficult, but they are such as the world has conquered before and can conquer again." The conclusion, the "what to do" is remarkable for its detached and practical tone—very different from the discourse of Kellogg and particularly distinct, as we will see, from the language adopted by the MRFM (DuBois 1967 [1899], 388)

From Social Surveys to Social Survey Reportage

So what was the MRFM, and how did it come to be interested in the kind of empirical study of social problems symbolized by the Pittsburgh Survey and the research of Charles Booth? And why did it push for a closer relationship with the profession of journalism? Today, the MRFM has been almost entirely forgotten. Indeed it might appear, at first glance, to be rather off-topic in a book on data journalism. Because of that, I want to provide a brief, general history of the MRFM before turning to a specific analysis of the relationship between the movement, urban newspapers, publicity strategies, and the incorporation of quantitative data into journalistic reportage.

The church was becoming emasculated—weakened by the Victorian cult of domesticity and the increasing valorization of spiritually flaccid "women's work." Such, at least, was the fear expressed by a group of progressive-era reformers acting as the advocates of what was quickly termed "muscular Christianity" (Putney 2003). As a discourse which emerged, in part, out of a period of deep uncertainty about the proper relations between the sexes (McGerr 2005), proponents of muscular Christianity argued that a particularly masculine version of physical fitness could be linked to an authentically Christian moral health, and thus to the health of US institutions in general. Despite decades of outreach and missionary work, along with the founding of men's and boy's organizations like the Boy Scouts (in 1910) and the YMCA (in 1844), church attendance in 1910 was still running female by a ratio of 2:1 (Putney 2003). For a great many men at the turn of the century, this would not do. "One of the marvels of the Christian religion is the beauty of its womanly virtues," proclaimed Fred B. Smith, the director of the Religious Work Department for the YMCA, "but Christianity is also essentially masculine, militant, and warlike, and if these elements are not made manifest, men and boys will not be found in increasing numbers as participants in the life of the church." Harry Arnold, the secretary of the Maine YMCA, agreed with those sentiments, and in 1910 he went to Smith with a plan to launch a "forward crusade," or massive evangelical effort, to convert or recommit men and boys to the Protestant Church (Putney 2003, 75).

What became known as the "Men and Religion Forward" movement lasted from 1911 to 1912. According to its own reports, it sponsored more than 7,000 meetings involving more than 1.4 million participants (Smith 2000). The movement was both locally organized and centrally controlled. Meetings took place in more than 70 US cities, but the primary impetus for the forward crusade lay with a small group of full-time religious organizers, including Smith, Charles Stelzle, and Raymond B. Robbins, who would travel the country to ensure that local planning went off without a hitch. Despite the participation of Stelzle, who was an active columnist for the labor press and who had, in some quarters, gained a reputation as a radical, the MRFM rested on what Gary Scott Smith has called a "broad evangelical consensus" and often aroused the hostility of organized labor. Yet even with these widely trumpeted meetings and seemingly impressive attendance figures, most historians (and even many contemporary observers) have argued that the MRFM was a dismal failure (Smith 2000, 345). Increases in church attendance were fleeting, the number of men involved in church work continued to decline, and indeed, the entire "social gospel" philosophy upon which the MRFM rested would become outmoded and forgotten as the Progressive Era drew to an exhausted close in the aftermath of World War I.

Despite these manifold failures, I am particularly interested in the attitude of leaders of the MRFM toward the daily press and want to argue that it is the relationship between the MRFM and journalism that makes it particularly relevant for understanding the pre-history of data journalism. The movement sought to activate the public by the deployment of true, objective facts in the press. To understand this combination of "public relations" and "public enlightenment," and the ways that they filtered through early-twentieth-century journalism, I want to briefly examine the career of one of the most compelling figures in the MRFM—the Reverend Charles Stelzle.

THE APOSTLE OF LABOR

Known in his later years as the "Apostle of Labor," the Reverend Charles Stelzle saw himself as a "son of the Bowery," as the title of his biography put it, His second-generation immigrant status and his working-class background would make him relatively unique amongst progressive-era reformers, most of whom hailed from the established middle classes. Stelzle began working in 1877, aged eight, in a tobacco factory, followed by stints in a flower sweatshop killing rats (Curtis 2001, 255). It was as a mechanic working for a printing press manufacturer that Stelzle first began to develop his understanding of unions and working-class life; it is intriguing (though speculative) to wonder if his youthful exposure to the mechanics of the printing press also attuned him to the power of journalism and mass communication. Although it is likely that Stelzle would have continued to climb the shop-floor ladder at the machine factory, he disappointed and perplexed his supervisor by quitting and devoting himself to full-time church ministry in 1893. In 1903, after three years as an ordained minister and a decade after leaving the machine shop, the Board of Home Missions of the Presbyterian Church granted Stelzle "a special mission to workingmen." In that role, which he would hold for a decade, he would be aggressive in his attempts to wean the labor movement away from its embrace of materialism and its creeping atheism, as well as in his attempts to empirically understand the root causes of social dislocation and decay.

Stelzle, according to many contemporary observers, was one of the most electrifying preachers of the social gospel in the United States (Curtis 2001, 338). He also embraced the techniques of social investigation pioneered by the SSM as well as the newly discovered powers of advertising and journalistic "publicity." In this, Stelzle is representative of the larger tendencies within the

MRFM (and indeed, within the SSM) as a whole, although he probably stood at the extreme end of that movement in terms of his attitude toward the value of "press work." Cultural historian Susan Curtis writes that when he founded the New York City Labor Temple in 1910, Stelzle "advocated the use of various promotional techniques so that the 'man on the street and the people in the homes' would come to church and participate in social gospel programs" (Curtis 2001, 260). Stelzle argued that the church " 'had been placed in the position of a solicitor—an advertiser—who must so attractively and so convincingly present his proposition, that it will appeal to those who have a perfect right to buy, or not to buy' " (Curtis 2001, 259). When the Presbyterian Church Board of Home Missions decided in 1913 to reallocate the money Stelzle had been using for his social service and promotional work to other causes, he resigned his church position and went into the advertising business full time—founding his own firm that specialized in church-focused public relations.

Susan Curtis sees Stelzle's metamorphosis from union organizer and lay minister to advertising man as emblematic of a larger tension within the ideology of the social gospel movement between socially meaningful reform and socially meaningful consumption. There is also a third aspect of Stelzle's career—that of an empirically minded survey researcher. Why, after all, would an apostle of labor and a public relations pioneer think it was so important to conduct basic survey research on cities, neighborhoods, and towns? As the MRFM launched its crusade in 1911, how did its members understand the relationship between the press, publicity, and the social survey? For the MRFM, the public could be spurred to action by placing the utterly transparent social world directly in its field of vision. Certainty would drive the public to take the proper steps to both save their souls and minister to the poor. What kept the public from acting was lack of knowledge and an uncertainty about the real facts of the situation. Social science, yoked to the publicity powers of journalism, would shift this balance of power in favor of social action.

Between Social Science and Public Relations: The Objects of the MRFM

TAKING THE SURVEY: OBJECTS OF CLASSIFICATION AND ANALYSIS

In his 1912 article, "The Spread of the Survey Idea," Paul Kellogg dismisses the surveys conducted by the MRFM as "a superficial skimming of facts . . . what we call in the Middle West a lick-and-a-promise":

[They were] limited to passing round and filling our schedules designed to fit any city .... These were not without value in throwing some facts of community life into relief and in showing where released energies might be applied ... [but] they bear about the same relation to a survey that the blanks which a mail order tailoring establishment sends out for self-measurement bear to a thorough-going physical examination. [Of course,] at the other end of the scale we have the sort of survey [like the Pittsburgh Survey]. (Kellogg 1912, 7)

As the moving force behind the Pittsburgh Survey, we might expect some professional jealousy here on the part of Kellogg. The MRFM itself understood that their quantitative work was far from complete, and in a pamphlet urged churches to "make a [more] thorough survey of the local field" and to "make a wider study of social conditions, continuing the investigation made by the social service committee of the Men and Religion Forward Movement." They clearly understood that any attempt to survey the conditions in seventy different cities in a relatively short period of time could never match the scale or the scope of a project like the Pittsburgh Survey.

What's more, an examination of the survey blanks and instructions prepared by the Bureau of Social Service of the Presbyterian Church shows that these data-gathering instruments were often far from primitive. The abridged survey alone, which the MRFM campaigners presumably used in most cases, runs more than a dozen pages and includes population and ethnicity statistics and information on education, government, "social influences," community problems, "the social evil" (i.e., prostitution), "recreation and amusement," and existing social service agencies. Despite this drive for information, however, the questions asked and data called for in the abridged survey require no actual house-to-house visits. The information can presumably be obtained from either government records or city officials.

The extended survey, on the other hand, runs more than fifty pages and is quite obviously concerned with gathering information on the local level. In addition to the plethora of questions, numbering in the hundreds and including queries such as "number of families living in houses the monthly rent of which is (a) $10 and less; $10–$15; $15–$20; $25 and over" and "do foreigners hold themselves aloof or do they participate in the life of the town?" we have a significant amount of documentary material focused on gathering block-level data and mapping that data onto physical space. Two sets of such data visualization devices are presented here: a "community map [whose facts] can be represented graphically by means of dots," and a "location canvass" (Fig. 2.1). "In order to

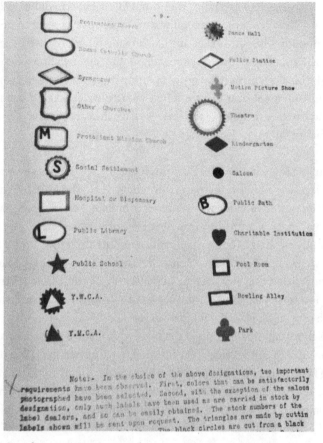

Figure 2.1 Sample canvass instruction sheet

ascertain the exact location of all houses, churches, saloons, etc., referred to in the preceding paragraph," the instructions read

> Make a location canvass of every block in the community. This is of the utmost importance to the reliability of the house-to-house canvass which is to follow, and to the accuracy of the community maps based on it. Divide the block maps among a number of workers (preferably a block to a person) and send them out to secure by actual observation the location of every street number where there is a building of any kind. (Bureau of Social Service of the Presbyterian Church in the United States, 1912, 4)

In the instructions outlining the tasks of the MRFM volunteers, there is an attempt to strike a balance between original investigation and the use of already collected statistics and official knowledge.

In this investigation, care should be taken that no superficial observations are used as the basis of any conclusions, since it is the very purpose of this survey to promote accurate, first-hand knowledge of city conditions . . . . Whenever possible secure facts and statistics from official sources, such as U.S. Census reports [or] city . . . records. But when official sources are not available conduct an original investigation. This will broaden the interest of the citizens in their own city and encourage the starting of new work, or emphasize the necessity of keeping better records. (Messages of the Men and Religion Forward Movement, Volume 7, 1912 (Fig 2.2))

There are, finally, extensive instructions given regarding the house-to-house canvass, along with a sample home visitation card, implying again that home visits were among the potential arsenal of MRFM volunteers and workers. "To no small degree the value of the whole survey depends on the care with which the cards are filled out," the guidelines read.

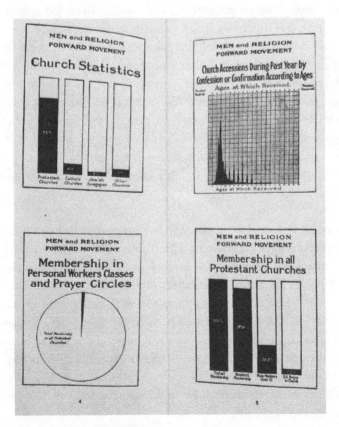

Figure 2.2   Charts used by the MRFM

These are the official guidelines and instructions for how to conduct the MRFM social survey. Is there any way to know how the process actually played itself out in practice? Instructions are one thing, but the actual conduct of the survey may be something else entirely. For other surveys conducted in other places at other times, such as the Pittsburgh Survey and Booth's *Life and Labor,* we have the tally sheets and notebooks into which the data was entered. For Booth's work, we are lucky to have enough historical material to trace changes in the record keeping from the first experimental surveys to the more refined approach taken for the project as a whole (Bales 1991, 72–73). I do not, however, have these data-level products when it comes to the MRFM survey. Comparing Booth's notebooks to the MRFM house-visit cards, we do immediately glimpse a difference in focus. Booth's data records the number of rooms per house, the rent, the occupation of the workers in the house, the age of the children, and a final classification of "position", (i.e., economic status—"poor," "regular comfortable," etc.). The MRFM house cards are not nearly as detailed. Primarily, they focus on the number of men and women in the house and on aspects related to *church attendance*—"church attended" versus "church preference," and so on. Given the religious focus of the MRFM, this difference is not surprising. It does, however, lead me to believe that it would be unlikely that the vast majority of the information asked for in either the abridged or extended survey could have been gathered from house visits alone.

While the lack of pre-aggregated data makes it difficult to know for certain how the MRFM survey was conducted, we can gain some insight from the local news reports filed about the MRFM. A qualitative content analysis of the 409 newspaper articles about the MRFM shows that 57 articles, or nearly 14%, discussed the survey process in some fashion. The July 29, 1911, *Washington Herald* writes that:

> One of the first steps in the social service program to be taken through-out the ninety cities participating is the "survey." This will be done by local committees, and will supply a mass of information regarding moral, social, and religious life in the great centers of population in North America, which will be put in shape for charts and exhibits. It's another "Know-your-city" idea, and the promoters of the movement believe that all the facts that may be known in advance will help the cities apply remedies when the dynamic of those eight-day campaigns will be felt locally. It is said by the leaders that the survey will be the most complete study of social conditions in American cities yet undertaken, barring only the famous Pittsburgh survey.

And the *San Francisco Call* from February 1912 notes:

> "Show me" is [the] motto [of the Movement]. It sends out a corps of investigators who collect facts and figures about every visible and invisible virtue and vice in every city and then makes a map of that city to show it just what its vices are, where they are and the exact ground they cover. Its institutions for good show on the same map.

Most of the coverage is of this more general, highly descriptive variety. Occasionally, a few papers go into greater detail. The *Washington Times*, also in February 1912, describes the survey process as one of "arduous labor . . . [with men] tramping over the outlying districts in search of information." But while it apparently "was the purpose of the canvassers to get the name of every man and boy in Washington . . . owing to the magnitude of the task that was found to be impossible."

To the best I can determine, it appears that the MRFM social survey was far from rigorously conducted (although it possibly was rigorous in places), that it relied mostly on volunteers, that it was primarily concerned with tabulating basic religious preferences and church attendance, that the movement's main methodological claim was the fact that it took place in *so many* different cities simultaneously, and that as a consequence there was a great variety in how the survey was conducted from city to city. To some degree, the movement's social service work was highly variable, and it is even possible that a few cities saw the deployment of the full survey.

Why, then, did the MRFM even *bother* to conduct a social survey? The fact that the survey was poorly done, that it seemed a poor fit with the larger, almost entirely religious goals of the movement, and that it entailed a great amount of work for apparently little benefit does not explain why the social service committee of the MRFM quickly became the most popular aspect of the entire revival. We once again are confronted with the specter of social survey reportage as a particularly American *fad*, one that, moreover, was embraced by reformist tendencies within the larger progressive movement. Why did Charles Stelzle insist that a canvass take place at all? Part of the answer, it seems, can be found when we turn to the *second* object of the MRFM—the seven volumes of findings that summarized the contributions of the movement to the larger American polity.

TAKING STOCK: MESSAGES OF THE MRFM

None of the social surveys we have discussed in this chapter were shy when it came to publishing their findings in bulk. The 2 volumes of Booth's original *Life and Labor of the People of London* would grow to a total of 17 by 1902. The Pittsburgh Survey produced 6 volumes between 1909 and 1914. *The Philadelphia Negro* stood at a comparatively brief 504 pages. And the MRFM published seven volumes of findings.

However, just as there was a variation in the methods by which social surveys gathered their data, there were variations in the final presentations as well. It is useful to compare the titles of the volumes of the Pittsburgh Survey and the MRFM insofar as this quickly demonstrates the differences in focus:

Pittsburgh Survey	MRFM
Women and the Trades (1909)	Congress Address (1912)
Work-Accidents and the Law (1910)	Social Service (1912)
The Steel Workers (1910)	Bible Study & Evangelism (1912)
Homestead: The Households of a Mill Town (1911)	Christian Unity and Missions (1912)
The Pittsburgh District: Civic Frontage (1914)	Boys Work (1912)
Wage-Earning Pittsburgh (1914)	The Rural Church (1912)
	The Church and the Press (1912)

Not surprisingly, the focus of the MRFM is on religious matters, while the Pittsburgh Survey is a classic example of the "muckraking" impulse and pays particular attention to the conditions of labor. The MRFM volumes were published by "The Association Press" and copy-written by the International Committee of the YMCA, while the Pittsburgh Survey was published by the "Charities Publications Committee" with copyright held by the RSF. In the MRFM volumes, there is little of the kind of sociological data we might have expected to see; the second book in the series, *Social Service*, primarily consists of a reiteration of bromides common to social-gospel thinking in general, along with some interesting instructions about how churches might use empirical evidence to address a variety of social ills. There is no data, and there are no charts or maps. Indeed, the vast majority of the actual *results* of the social survey, as popular as the social service committee was with MRFM volunteers, can only be found in a small pamphlet produced by the Bureau of Social Service of the Presbyterian Home Missions. We can assume the primary author of this little volume, which consists of a two-page introduction, twenty-one pages of charts, and a seven-page conclusion outlining some recommendations for different segments of the community, is Charles Stelzle. I will discuss these data visualizations in more detail in the next section.

The most interesting volume of the MRFM series, however, has little analogue in any of the other survey publications we have discussed so far: Volume VII, *The Church and the Press*. This, which today we might read as a public relations handbook, is probably the most truly innovative aspect of the MRFM, and it is what leads me to characterize their work a social survey *reportage*:

> It was by no means unusual for a revival to be well organized . . . . But the Men and Religion Forward Movement had special features that no previous revival had employed. One of these was an explicit effort to use the press as a means of promoting the event. The Committee of 100 in each city was to have a Publicity Committee, whose work was of "the utmost importance," but whose duties were "not to be limited to advertising." Thus, while the Committee was to prepare traditional advertising for such venues as laundry lists, hotel menus, billboards, street-cars, and stationery, it was also to "furnish varied and live copy" (10–11) each week to the local newspapers to insure maximal exposure for the Movement. As the actual event approached, the articles fed to the press were to increase and the Committee was to arrange for daily press coverage during the eight days of the revival. (Bateman 2001, 59)

The drive to fully integrate press relations into the program of the MRFM most certainly stems from Stelzle, who was relentless in his push for more and better copy about church and labor activities. But while we can attribute much of the MRFM's understanding of church–press relations to Stelzle individually, this new way of thinking about the relationship between the church and journalism must also be understood in relationship to larger cultural changes in US society as a whole. Specifically the church, long used to seeing itself as the primary national agent of education and moral uplift" began in the early twentieth century to come to terms with the fact that that role was being usurped by the mass media. Although careful to frame its thinking in terms of the *equivalent power* of the church and the press (Messages of the Men and Religion Forward Movement, 1912, 5), even to grant the press equal say in the shape of American morals and public opinion was a major retreat by the clergy. "A most remarkable developing and readjusting of intellectual attitudes and subtle human forces is proceeding under the inspiration and leadership of the press . . . the everyday man is aware of new mental attitudes and conscious of new forces shaping his thinking. The press more than any other one force has wrought these atmospheric changes in modern life . . . . The church sees this plainer than ever" (Messages of the Men and Religion Forward Movement, 1912, 23). Given that, the volume concludes:

> Religious workers must aid in a very practical way in the gathering and presenting to newspapers materials of positive news value out of the life of the church. No wise newspaperman discounts the value of much that transpires in the religious world. He simply avows his inability to cover

the field. **He must therefore have efficient help.** Not the abstracts of sermons necessarily, but things in the religious world with human interest woven into them; news items that advertise of a community progress and other reading features out of church life . . . . This kind of cooperation is cordially welcomed by newspaper managers, with the understanding that the reporting minister must take his chance with the rest of the staff on his copy meeting the ordinary vicissitudes of the manager's office. **An easy door of efficient publicity service is here opened to the religious worker.** (Messages of the Men and Religion Forward Movement, 1912, 33)

The door is opened, in short, to public relations in the service of the social gospel.

What techniques can best serve the church in its attempt to help newspapermen "cover the field"? *The Church and the Press* helpfully lists several. Emphasize and publicize foreign missionary work, which is always spiced with exoticism and danger (Messages of the Men and Religion Forward Movement, 1912, 52). Make better use of photographs (Messages of the Men and Religion Forward Movement, 1912, 53). Highlight large and unusual gatherings of important men, such as the "dinner of a thousand men" promoted by the MRFM—dinners which not only include illustrious names but are also attended by potential future journalistic sources (54). And tremendous emphasis, finally, is placed the *"power of charts."*

Another phase of the Men and Religion Forward Movement that caught the interest and approval of the city editor quickly was **the social survey and the summarizing of its findings by means of charts. This is the kind of matter live editors like to go after themselves, and to be scooped by a religious investigator and artists is an experience so unexpected that it is fascinating.** Whenever the church comes upon a civic or social festering place and addresses itself promptly and rationally to the eradication of the evil, it can count upon the cooperation of an unshackled press. Its purposes, its performances in that direction make welcome copy, for it is a field in which an unafraid newspaper is operating on its own account generally, and is glad to get help. (Messages of the Men and Religion Forward Movement, 1912, 51)

Herein lies the hinge between public enlightenment and public relations, one possible answer to why a movement so relatively uninterested in empirical sociology would nevertheless embrace and emphasize its social service work and its distributed data-gathering. In a country suddenly obsessed with empiricism and facts, where the social survey had become a fad, social surveys made good copy. Moreover, this was not just any data, but data turned into documents in the style of compelling visualizations. It is not surprising, too, that these tendencies would be united in the figure of Charles Stelzle.

In his description of the illustrious Pittsburgh Survey, touted by Paul Kellogg as a model for what a large, well-funded survey ought to look like, Stephen Turner argues that "the survey commended itself as a method of publicity that emblazons [the needs of the urban worker] upon the public consciousness *without* the occurrence of a catastrophe [like the Triangle Shirtwaist fire]. The journalistic means of bringing these real needs to human terms was the case study method" (Turner 1994 43). It is not surprising, in short, that a far less scientific and far more publicity-savvy reform movement like the MRFM would embrace data and documentary visualization as a way to reach the press. Ultimately, the MRFM had a dual goal: to map the social world using empirical investigatory techniques and carefully assembled documents and to convey that social assemblage to the public through the press. In both cases, these tasks were happily subordinated to the ultimate goal of social reform. Between empirical science and good publicity there need be no contradiction.

To summarize: data gathering took place during the social service portion of the MRFM revival, with volunteers and paid employees questioning local officials and knowledgeable townspeople as to the state of community affairs. Most often this knowledge was stored in paper form, and when it was not immediately available, Stelzle encouraged groups of volunteers to venture into the community, conduct a house-by-house survey, and gather this data for themselves. The data entry forms and the model block maps used for collection were thus extremely important tools in the MRFM's work. In the final instance, the gathered information would be displayed graphically as charts and maps, and these striking visuals would go a long way toward securing needed publicity for the movement.

Our best window into what these 1912 charts looked like comes from the pamphlet "Sociological and Religious Survey of Seventy American Cities" published by the Bureau of Social Service of the Presbyterian Church in the United States. Given the provenance of this pamphlet, we can be fairly sure it was authored by Stelzle, though his name never appears anywhere in the document. The document makes full use of a wide panoply of information display devices in use at the time—primarily bar graphs, line graphs, pie graphs.

From a twenty-first-century perspective the quality of these charts ranges from interesting to somewhat misleading to entirely unhelpful. In the "interesting" category we might include "Nationalities of Parents of Boys Tried in Juvenile Court During the Past Year," a pie chart showing that "Americans" (by which is meant second generation white Anglo-Saxon Protestants) account for 52.3% of all trials in juvenile court.

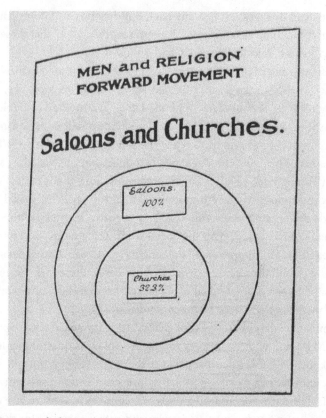

Figure 2.3 Ratio of saloons to churches

When displaying demographic data, these simple pie charts are adequate if not particularly informative. But MRFM information displays seem to have had a harder time when trying to visualize *ratios* as opposed to *percentages*, either over time or at a particular moment, as the charts presented in Figures 2.3 and 2.4 make clear.

A modern reader sees the graphic about saloons and churches and immediately imagines that every building in America (100%) is a saloon, while only 32.3% of these saloons are churches. Likewise, a quick look at the chart on socialists might lead one to believe that 100% of America is now "socialist." Of course, the first chart means to tell us that for every three saloons there is a single church, while the second shows that the number of self-described socialists in the United States has increased five-fold in the past decade. A final category of visualization is neither misleading nor interesting but can uncharitably described as fairly useless, "Vital Statistics: Death Per 1000 Children Under One Year of Age," which appears to show that this number has remained both small and steady for the past decade.

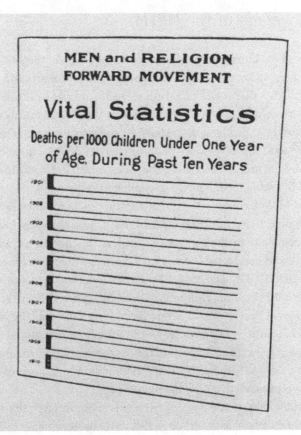

Figure 2.4 Vital statistics

To some degree, the question of visualization quality was irrelevant insofar as the MRFM had already determined that generic data and the visualization of that data could serve as a proper device for the mobilization of the public in support of ameliorative and reformist social ends. First the data had to be gathered, then displayed, and then transmitted to news organizations so it could be publicized more broadly. For these quantitative reformers, "social survey reportage" was a device that *both* represented reality and mobilized the American public to action in support of progressive goals. Because the MRFM straddled the line between journalism, data gathering, and activism, the role quantitative information played in assembling a particular public was effaced—good science made for good visualization, and good visualization would activate the public for political ends, ends which were not in question. Key to all this, however, was the publicity-generating potential of newspapers. How would they incorporate quantitative data into their work? I turn to that question in the next section.

Media Coverage of the MRFM

I have shown how important publicity was to members of the MRFM and the way in which the movement organizers understood that charts and graphs possessed a publicity value as well as a truth value. If coverage by those newspapers mattered so much, how did the data generated by the MRFM find its way into the newspapers of the day? I have discussed how the visually oriented social movements understood the importance of objective facts as a tool to mobilize public opinion and share information about the social world. But how did newspapers understand the same techniques? How much were they influenced by groups like the MRFM? What can we learn about how journalism understood certainty, uncertainty, objectivity, and facts by looking at how newspapers represented data and documents in their pages? To answer this question I went beyond archival work and conducted a qualitative discourse analysis of the newspaper coverage of the MRFM, analyzing 409 articles about the movement contained in the *Chronicling America: Historic American Newspapers* (http://chronicling-america.loc.gov/) project and the *New York Times*. Of those 409 articles, running from 1911 until 1912, a subset of 132 were further analyzed to tease out larger patterns, themes, and nuances of the news reporting, particularly how the quantitative evidence gathered and information visualizations provided by the movement were reflected in daily media coverage.

We can draw several conclusions from this analysis. First, the MRFM *was widely covered on a local level*, although this coverage was highly episodic, scattered, and often consisted of short stories or press releases a few paragraphs long. Nevertheless, the fact that there were over 400 articles about the MRFM printed in less than two years would seem to support the later claim of the MRFM that they had collected "six scrapbooks" each "three inches thick, filled with Men and Religion Forward clippings." I found coverage of the MRFM in papers ranging geographically from the *New York Times* and *New York Herald Tribune*, to the *Washington Herald*, the *El Paso Herald*, and the *San Francisco Call*. There doubtless are many more articles in papers that have not yet been digitized.

Second, the press was willing to publish MFRM press releases, pamphlets, columns, and other materials *verbatim*. While there was no way to determine exactly which clippings were directly taken from materials produced by the MFRM publicity committee, it seems likely that the vastly positive coverage (more than 91% of the articles I analyzed were coded positive) was in part related to this wholesale adoption of MRFM-produced copy. Several pieces in different papers were identical (for instance, an Ohio *News Herald* piece titled "Ministers and Laymen United" is duplicated in at least two papers, right down to the use of a similar picture), meaning they were mostly likely either printed press releases or articles clipped from various newspaper exchanges.

A third finding concerns the question of how the crude empirical techniques, charts, maps, and other visualizations supplied journalists with the material they needed to mount robust factual claims to certitude. In general, I concluded that the *conduct* of the social survey was widely discussed in the daily press, as were the data visualization *techniques* and *products* produced by the movement. There were, however, almost no charts printed in the papers themselves, and the few that were picked up marked the exceptions that prove the rule. The way the survey was conducted garnered regular coverage, but the actual *results* of the survey were rarely discussed. The coverage was almost entirely based on the occurrence of particular events (meetings, presentations, canvass days, etc.), but numerical visualization almost never accompanied the use of numbers. The context that the MRFM sought to incorporate into discussions of poverty had been shorn away by the time its stories reached the daily press.

Discussions of the social survey occurred in fifty-seven articles about the MRFM, or 14% of the total. They ranged from casual mentions to more extensive analyses like this one in the July 29, 1911, issue of the *Washington Herald*:

> One of the first steps in the social service programme to be taken throughout the ninety cities participating is the "survey." This will be done by local committees, and will supply a mass of information regarding moral, social, and religious life in the great centers of population in North America, which will be put in shape for charts and exhibits. It's another "Know-your-city" idea, and the promoters of the movement believe that all the facts that may be known in advance will help the cities apply remedies when the dynamic of those eight-day campaigns will be felt locally. It is said by the leaders that the survey will be the most complete study of social conditions in American cities yet undertaken, barring only the famous Pittsburgh survey.

A second article appearing six months later in another Washington, DC, paper, the *Washington Times*, provides further discussion of the survey: it defines what the survey is, provides a description of the questions asked (what are the amusements of working classes, the housing and labor conditions, the number of telephones in their homes, the number of automobiles they own, etc.). The article is one of the few to mention that answers will be solicited "on blanks provided." Finally, the article tackles the very purposes of the survey—figures, they argue, "have very real value in furnishing data concerning the comparative standard of living."

Nearly all these discussions of the survey failed to include any charts, however, and the few times MRFM charts appeared in the news they largely represented aesthetic failures of data visualization. An article in the *New York Sun* from March 24, 1912, is representative in its unhelpfulness. The last paragraph attempts to explain the map accompanying the article. Since it is one of the few on-record attempts of a daily newspaper engaging in the translation work necessary to incorporate a statistical graph into a news story in the early twentieth century, I will quote it at length:

> Incorporated in this article is a map of the field that has been covered by the Men and Religion Forward Movement up to the present time. The discs indicating the various States when interpreted are: The black space in the discs, according to the census taken by those interested in this movement, indicate the population; the horizontal lines in the discs represent the worshippers in Protestant churches, while the perpendicular lines represent the worshippers in Roman Catholic churches.

We might assume that this article copy has been entirely provided by the MRFM itself, right down to the map.

Far more typical of news coverage of the statistics is an article from the *Washington Times* entitled "Would Place Blame." "Saloons are responsible for much of the poverty and misery of the poor in Washington," it notes:

> The committee has prepared charts for exhibition in the eight day campaign. These, according to members of the committee, show a direct connection between the number of saloons and living conditions, and they believe the charts will be conclusive argument for the regulation of the liquor traffic in the District. Such exhibits, leaders of the movement say, have done much to stir the civic consciousness and lead men to think of means to better their social conditions.

In general, the results of the surveys were rarely discussed at all, and to the degree that they were, it was almost always in the context of survey exhibits (discussed in the next section). Another article in the *Washington Times* discusses survey results (i.e., saloons cause poverty), notes that they were displayed in chart and map form and that these charts are on view at the survey exhibition, and spends a good amount of time talking about what these charts will do to the "public mind." Nevertheless, the charts themselves are not printed, and the statistical results are never interrogated by the newspaper, they are simply reported.

Overall, we should thus conclude that coverage of the MRFM was fairly regular, though scattered, and usually resulted in a few articles in each of the cities they operated in between 1911 and 1912. The coverage was also highly episodic, rarely incorporated contextual information about poverty, and was largely tied to the occurrence of particular discrete events such as public presentations, large meetings, canvass days, and so forth. The stories almost never included charts, graphs, maps, or other visual devices, even in articles where there was an extensive discussion of statistics. The papers that printed them, finally, almost never critically analyzed these statistics. In short, the factual objects so carefully and lovingly assembled by the MRFM never truly played the role in mobilizing public opinion hoped for by the movement organizers. The social survey reportage of the MRFM may have caught the attention of reporters, and it may have prompted the occasional, event-oriented piece of newspaper coverage, but the data assemblage constructed by MRFM out of their canvassing, survey blanks, data sheets, charts, and paper placards were never truly adopted or translated by turn-of-the-century daily newspaper journalists. To the degree that they were, it was through the refracting lens of the survey exhibit. It is to a discussion of these exhibitions and their role in shaping the public mind that I now turn.

From Newspapers to Exhibits to Newspapers Again

The most important reform-oriented data visualization format of the early twentieth century was actually not a publication at all. Rather, it was an **event**, known as an **exhibition**. Here's how the *El Paso Herald* reported a survey exhibit on April 19,1912. "While the convention center of the congress [of the MRFM] will be held in Carnegie Hall," they wrote:

> there are four auxiliary centers in four of the most prominent churches in New York in which many of the meetings will be held. There will be a series of special *exhibits* including moving pictures lantern slides and charts illustrating the conditions revealed by the great social survey which has been made in nearly 190 American cities during the past year. These exhibits show in an indisputable manner evils and abuses of many kinds which religion of a practical kind could largely overcome.

The importance of the social exhibit to the larger survey reportage movement is brought home by the fact that a branch of the powerful RSF was known, in the early twentieth century, as the Department of Surveys *and Exhibits.* In 1918 the Department published a 320-page volume, *The ABCs of Exhibit Planning* as a model to be replicated by other towns doing social survey work. Included in these lengthy, visually nuanced publications (not only is their use of graphics far ahead of many other publications of the time, but they possess a sharp aesthetic sense which would not be out of place in a modern advertising agency) are dis-cussions of the different types of materials that might be included in an exhibit, along with some considerations of the advantages exhibits possessed over other forms of publicity, such as pamphlets and news articles. While we cannot say for certain that the MRFM exhibits resembled any of the models discussed here, it seems likely that they were at least a part of these larger discourses on the public display of visual information. "Social survey reportage," in this example, does not mean physical publishing at all. Rather, it refers to the public display of visual information for the benefit of the public.

One interesting aspect of the RSF discussion of exhibits and visual materi-als is the degree to which they actually downplay the use of pie charts and line graphs, encouraging exhibitors to utilize material which seems far closer to advertising. "Statistical charts, spot maps, and other more or less technical forms that are sometimes referred to as 'graphic material' are of interest and value to special and limited audiences," the author of *The ABCs of Exhibit Planning* writes.

> The showing of percentages by use of colored circles or bars and of comparative statistics by graphs or hills is a favorite device. Diagrams are not equally attractive media of communication to all. To some they represent a disagreeable form of mental effort; one way of making them appear less technical and indeed less dull to such visitors is to invent variations in which the circles or bars or hills have been replaced by successions of concrete items, such as pictures of dollar signs, pictures of human figures, animals, or other appropriate objects. (74)

An illustration in the book comparing a simple pie chart with the use of a more arresting "dollar coin" image gives us an idea of the kind of illustrations being advocated by the RSF.

Among the non-chart objects included in the Springfield Survey exhibit were: three-dimensional models, posters, live "morality plays" (titles include "The Imps and the Children" and "When the Gang Broke Up"), a playground, and a motion picture hall. Nevertheless, it seems clear that charts and maps made up a large part of the printed matter used in many social exhibits, which perhaps was why the author of *The ABCs of Exhibit Planning* was quick to downplay their utility. "Even though they are much used in exhibits intended for popular audi-ences diagrams are more likely to be technical than popular in form."

No matter the exact nature of the visual material being used, why bother mounting an exhibit in the first place? What advantages does the publicity gen-erated through exhibits have over the publicity garnered from newspaper arti-cles and advertisement—which, as we have already seen, formed a large part of the arsenal of the MRFM and men like Charles Stelzle? *The ABCs of Exhibit Planning* points out several:

(1) Exhibits can attract the attention of people who might not read a newspaper.
(2) It is a quick method of information conveyance and appeals to those people who might only skim the news.
(3) An exhibit gains value by the fact that it is presented to multiple people simultaneously; "you have created a sort of group attraction, each visitor feeling the interest of his neighbor and being stimulated to an exchange of talk about the things illustrated."
(4) Exhibitors and social surveyors can do more than vaguely estimate the number of people who are consuming their material, as they are forced to do with newspaper articles.
(5) It stimulates public conversation.
(6) Exhibitors can answer visitor questions in person.
(7) "By means of this new method of telling your story, through pictures, models, objects and other devices, a new life and new force are given to your propaganda." (19)

Exhibits, finally, nicely complimented the tendency of newspapers to focus on single happenings rather than the context in which the MRFM's statistics about poverty were embedded. By displaying their graphical diagrams as part of an *event*, the MRFM could tap into newspapers' natural tendency to engage in episodic event framing about the MRFM. As noted earlier, most newspaper coverage of the MRFM was of meetings, presentations, canvass days, and so on. When these exhibition events featured the statistical representation of poverty information, they could gain a second life in newspapers, both through their spectacular nature and through their existence as a "one-time" phenomenon. While newspapers would often not publish the statistics the MRFM gathered, they would cover an exhibition in which these statistics were presented.

Conclusion

What does this analysis of an obscure and now-forgotten social movement tell us about the boundaries that went into delimiting aspects of quantitative news reporting in the early twentieth century? First, it should be clear that the social and cultural excitement around the power of quantitative data—or even so-called big data—is nothing new. The *idea* of "data" carried within it a powerful symbolic value by the early twentieth century. Data acted as what scholars of science and technology have called a boundary object, in this case a symbolic and material object that mediated between quantitative proof giving and rhetorical persuasion.

Second, despite this general social excitement, both technological affordances and production routines led early-twentieth-century news organizations to de-emphasize the use of data and data visualization in their news stories. I saw few graphical displays of the statistics and chats so painstakingly generated by the MRFM in the pages of newspapers. In part, this is because few newspapers had the technology to produce or reproduce these statistics in their pages, and even those that did largely lacked the ability to generate these charts when they worked within the rhythm of the daily newspaper production schedule. How do we square this finding that data rarely appeared in newspapers with the argument that quantitative information possessed tremendous publicity value? In part, through the analysis of the exhibits and exhibitions discussed above. There were other visual options available to those who wanted to use the visual display of quantitative information for education and reform purposes, options more aligned with the social routines and news production schedules of the time. In turn, stories about these exhibits were also far more likely to run in newspapers than the data sets or the data visualizations themselves. The general society-wide obsession with data and data visualization thus played itself out in the pages of news on a *secondary level*—in stories about the **use** of data rather than the direct use of data **itself**.

Third, the nearly exclusive focus of early-twentieth-century journalism on individuals, interviews, institutions, and events led newspapers to de-emphasize the use of contextual data in their news stories; the lack of contextual data— but the presence of sheer quantitative fact—in the news clips we analyzed was as much about journalistic culture as it was about technological capacity. Interpretive journalism, first discussed in the 1930s, was still several decades away. Newspapers, as Barnhurst and Mutz have demonstrated (1997), were firmly in the breaking news business in the early twentieth century, concerned with reporting on individual events as quickly as possible (see also Fink and Schudson 2014). The news was there to inform not to explain. Ultimately, this journalistic focus on reporting *what happened*—without providing much context or larger explanatory theory—would help fortify the emerging boundary wall between professional journalism and professional social science that solidified in the 1930s, even as that event-oriented focus was first challenged by an emerging form of "interpretive journalism." This paradox—that boundaries between sociology and journalism were strengthened just as the news started to become more "sociological"—will be explored more fully in the next chapter.

Fourth, and finally, it is important to keep in mind that all the events chronicled in this chapter occurred prior to the political and intellectual catastrophe that was the World War I. As Michael Schudson (1978) has argued, the emergence of objectivity (as both journalism and social science envision it today) can only be fully understood in the context of the crisis of empirical faith that followed the war. The role of public relations in selling that war would foster a growing journalistic hostility toward the PR profession. At the same time, sociology would drive out the social reformers who were key to establishing it as a professional discipline in the first place. The idea that it would be simple to mobilize a public through the presentation of certain objective data would prove to be impossible to maintain in the post-war era. The years that followed the MRFM would be years that embraced a hermeneutics of suspicion, leading ironically to social science and journalism that became more assertive and more interpretive in a variety of ways. Future cultural and ideological debates about the relationship between social science, journalism, quantitative information, and objectivity would henceforth take place on radically different terrain. It is to an analysis of that new terrain of the 1920s and 1930s—one in which journalism became more sociological, sociology became more scientific, and both prospered in a state of mutual indifference—that I now turn.

3

Journalism Interprets, Sociology Scientizes

Boundary Work Between Empirical Occupations
in the 1920s and Beyond

Introduction

In 1905, the *American Journal of Sociology* (*AJS*), the official academic journal of the emerging profession of sociology, published a rather remarkable first-person article by George Edgar Vincent. In this article Vincent, who would go on to serve as the sixth president of the American Sociological Association (ASA), described at length how he turned his undergraduate sociology class at the University of Chicago into a full-time news bureau that produced a finished newspaper and gave students "under university auspices, a practical introduction to the technique of newspaper work." Vincent originally conceived the seminar as consisting of both lectures on sociological theory and actual day-to-day newspaper production; journalists would become versed in the science of society and thus become better reporters. But he found that this was actually a terrible idea—sociology had more to learn from journalistic production techniques, he claimed, than the reverse. "The sum of the whole matter," Vincent concluded, "is to bring practical newspaper men into the lecture and seminar room, not for mere general address on the importance of the press to civilization, but for . . . clinical, laboratory work." Perhaps even more shocking than this startling conclusion, however, was the basic notion that a leading sociologist would find it a worthy use of his time to have his students produce a popular newspaper as part of a sociology class (Vincent 1905).

More than a century later, timed to the launch of his wildly anticipated website FiveThirtyEight, political journalist and quantitative modeler Nate Silver released a manifesto in which he decried the ad hoc, evidence-free nature of much political reporting. "The problem [with this reporting] is not the failure to cite quantitative evidence. It's doing so in a way that can be anecdotal and ad hoc, rather than rigorous and empirical, and failing to ask the right questions of the data." And while Silver went on to note that his "methods [were] not meant to replace 'traditional' or conventional journalism," and while he nuanced his data-driven, causality-oriented model in a number of interesting ways, he fundamentally set up a contrast between quantitative and qualitative forms of evidence gathering, and between what he called anecdotal (read: journalistic) and rigorous (read: social scientific) forms of analysis. In short, Silver made a basic argument that journalism—by embracing data, by seeking to determine causality, by showing more openness to quantitative approaches—should be more like social science, not less (Silver 2014).

In the move from a world where a leading sociologist could embrace notions of industrial truth production in the journalistic style to a world where a renegade journalist called on his profession to be more like sociology and political science, much has obviously changed in the fields of both journalism and sociology. One such change has been the emergence of a boundary between journalism and social science, one that we take for granted today, but one whose contours were far less evident at the turn of the twentieth century. In this chapter I want to map the divisions and boundary markers that have driven the knowledge-building occupations of journalism and sociology apart for more than a century but also trace the threads that still link, however tenuously, George Vincent and Nate Silver's very different professional worlds.

As we have already seen, early-twentieth-century social science was barely a discipline at all. Emerging as it did out of the intersection of social service, an impulse toward empirical data collection, a desire for reform, and the understanding that only through journalistic publicity could this reform take root, this heterogeneous mixture was unsustainable in the professionalizing decades of the early twentieth century (Haskell 1977; see also Williams and Delli Carpini 2011). A period of epistemological hybridity and professional uncertainty was thus followed by a disciplinary "sorting out" in which journalism, social work, sociology, and reformist politics were categorized as properly belonging to a particular intellectual field. Sociology, the main subject of this chapter, accomplished this professional task by denigrating its earlier belief in social amelioration and radical reform under the guise of methodological critique and by later denigrating journalism for lacking theory and for "writing too well." Journalism, meanwhile—the elder and for a long time the more intellectually coherent knowledge discipline—was largely unaffected by these developments, at least until the late 1930s, at which point a desire to interpret facts as well as report them began to be voiced by certain thinkers in the news industry. This fact—that journalism was expelled from the sociological tool kit at the very moment (in the late 1930s and 1940s) when it began to grow intellectually more sophisticated—marks one of the major paradoxes of this book, one that that this chapter will begin to address.

In the pages that follow I examine the mechanisms by which sociology intellectually purified itself, shedding first its affinities with journalism, and then its links to a more generalized reformist impulse, and argue that these two processes were inextricably linked, with the uneasy synthesis between publicity, quantitative mapping, visualization, and reform coming undone in the years following World War I. I begin by conducting a discourse analysis of the manner by which the major journals of sociology—the *AJS* and the *American Sociological Review* (*ASR*)—framed journalism and its relationship to sociological thought between 1889 and 2000. In this we can see that from the early 1940s on, journalism was progressively denigrated in the sociological imagination as too popular, too well written, and fundamentally unscientific in its approach to understanding the modern world. I then summarize new research on the history of sociology that chronicles the manner by which the emergent discipline also wrote the social surveyors and reformers (such as Jane Addams and W.E.B. DuBois) out of its canon. While Addams and DuBois were, on the surface, critiqued for their primitive empirical methods and lack of theoretical insight, revisionist scholarship has demonstrated that the underlying reasons for their expulsion from sociology were as much related to gender, race, and a conservative comfort with the political status quo as they were with epistemology or methods per se. I discuss the intellectual relationship between Robert Park and the profession of journalism in light of this new scholarship, especially insofar as it allows us to gain a deeper understanding of the larger structural differences between journalism and social science.

And yet, at exactly the time sociology was distancing itself from journalism, journalism had begun to more explicitly embrace some of the techniques and reporting methods absent in the Progressive Era—more coverage of patterns and causes as opposed to occurrences, the use of data and the visualization of that data, and an embryonic rethinking of traditional objectivity. The second part of the chapter traces this paradox: that the boundary line between journalism and sociology grew more refined and sturdier even as the intellectual standpoints of journalism and sociology moved, in some ways, closer together. It shows how the visualizations embraced by the MRFM embedded themselves within the emerging genre of interpretive reporting, moving from serving as the centerpiece of an odd little journal called the *Survey Graphic* to anchoring the far better known and more influential Henry Luce magazine *Fortune*. I then turn to an overview of the front pages of the *New York Times*, seeking to gain a wider perspective on how information visualization in news changed over the course of the twentieth century. Doesn't this use of visual information, combined with journalism's increasing comfort in adopting an interpretive frame, demonstrate that journalism and sociology were becoming more alike? No, it doesn't, in large part because the "empiricism" of visuals was starting to be denigrated by sociology and social science in general in favor of the use of statistics and variables. Finally, I conduct a second discourse analysis (the mirror image of the analysis that begins the chapter) looking at journalistic "self-talk" regarding social science and empirical techniques more generally. This discussion leads us into the next chapter—and to the heart of our history— with the emergence of precision journalism in the 1960s. But it also begins to shed light on the role played by both journalistic culture *and* varieties of what I call "empirical materiality," an intersection that has much to say about the way different knowledge groups integrate evidentiary objects, their own professional culture, and their integration of evidence into networked chains of expertise that divide the modern world into what might be known and who might know it.

Erecting Walls: The Professional Journals Consider Journalism (1899–1999)

Matthew Carlson has emerged as the foremost scholar of present day journalistic boundary work. In his introduction to *Boundaries of Journalism: Professionalism, Practices, and Participation*, (which he co-edited with Seth Lewis) Carlson invokes Thomas Gieryn's understanding of *rhetoric* as one of the means through which retroactively proper demarcations between different forms of expert knowledge are fixed. "It is through rhetorical means that various groups engage in 'boundary-work' to compete publicly for 'epistemic authority': 'the legitimate power to define, describe, and explain bounded domains of reality'" (Carlson 2015, 1). One of the strategies of boundary work is *expulsion*, in which deviant group members, deviant practices, and deviant values are all publicly cast out and branded as no longer acceptable to the expert group. This chapter draws on Carlson's concepts to explore a process of expulsion through rhetorical "othering"—the changing sociological understanding of journalism (and social work, and publicity, and activism) between 1899 and the present day. As we saw in chapter 2, the distinction between journalistic and sociological techniques and values was far from self-evident in the early years of the twentieth century and building the boundary between them required, among other things, active rhetorical work. In this chapter, I am examining more of a process of historical discourse formulation (Foucault 1980) than I am Gieryn's individuated occupational expulsion, though the two concepts differ more in emphasis and method than they do in their underlying understanding of knowledge practices.

Given their uncertain, entangled origins, how did sociology come to distinguish itself from journalism and vice-versa? I want to answer that question a few different ways. My first approach involves trying to understand how sociologists talked about journalism in their professional journals, specifically the *AJS* and the *ASR*, from 1899 until the present. While certainly not the only important journals in sociology, these two journals stand at the center of the academic field (Lengermann 1979) and are regularly among two of the top three "high-impact" journals (along with *Social Forces*) according to *Journal Citation Reports*. Using a JSTOR search, I downloaded every article in *AJS* and *ASR* containing a major reference to either "journalism" or "newspaper[s]," giving me a total of 564 articles. The analysis in the pages that follow draws on an interpretive/inductive approach to content analysis in which each of the articles was eventually categorized according to a set of themes that themselves only came to light after each piece been read and analyzed several times (see, for example, Hsieh and Shannon 2005). These themes can be understood as representative of different understandings of sociology's relationship to journalism and are detailed below. Once these emergent themes were formalized, I returned to a subset of particularly relevant articles (125 in all) and examined them from a more chronological perspective: Do particular article types or particular clusters of article themes emerge at different moments in time, and if so, when? Can we point to any provisional patterns in the way that different theme clusters emerged at different moments? And if so, what does this say about the way journalism came to be understood from the perspective of social science?

This analysis of the *AJS* and the *ASR* resulted in a differentiation between three article types and four thematic article categories:

Article Types
- Scientific articles
- Book reviews
- Abstracts or bibliographies (Along with the familiar distinction between research and review articles, the first several decades of the *AJS* featured a third article type: bibliographic abstracts of research in progress, along with a "News and Notes" section. By the 1950s, however, these lists would disappear.)

Thematic Categories
- A discussion of journalistic methods or a direct comparison of journalism to social science
- Journalism or "the news "as an object of empirical inquiry

- News content as empirical evidence for analyzing other social phenomena
- Journalism as an object for non-empirical inquiry or moral speculation

The first category, "a discussion of journalistic methods or a direct comparison of journalism to social science," is the key one for our analysis insofar as it represents a moment when *AJS* or *ASR* authors were specifically reflecting on the methodologies of journalistic practice or comparing journalistic methods and values to those embraced by social scientists. This can and does include anything from an offhand remark in a book review on public opinion that "the present volume, wherein a professor of journalism presents 'a guide for newspaper men and newspaper readers' . . . will leave most social scientists annoyed" (Suchman 1953, 218) to more extensive but less self-conscious reflections on the relationship between journalism, social science, and the Pittsburgh Survey in articles by Devine (1909) and Bartlett (1928).

The second category, "journalism or 'the news' as an object of empirical inquiry," represents what we today would consider part of the sociology of news. Some of the most famous articles in journalism studies are part of this category, including Tuchman (1972; 1973), Sigelman (1973), and Molotch and Lester (1975).

The third category, "news content as empirical evidence for analyzing other social phenomena," features news content not as an object of analysis in and of itself but as data for investigating other sociological phenomena, such as ecological institutional evolution (using local newspapers as a case study) (Carroll and Huo 1986). One of the most interesting articles in this category actually reflects upon and tests the reliability and validity of using news coverage of urban unrest as a data source (Danzger 1975).

The final category, "journalism as an object for non-empirical inquiry or moral speculation," might appear to be the most unusual to our modern eyes. Suffice it to say that the *AJS* of 1899 resembles today's scientific journals insofar as it has the same title and little else. While journalism and "the news" are the objects of inquiry in many of these early *AJS* articles, this means they are often "the object" of rambling, moralistic discourses with little in the way of empirical evidence and display titles like the 1909 article "Is an Honest and Sane Newspaper Press Possible?" written by "An Independent Journalist." And this very fact helps point to the value of this kind of discursive genealogy—by studying how sociology understood journalism we are not simply studying the relationship between two professional groups. We are studying how sociology understood itself and how that understanding was transformed over the course of the modern era.

A deeper engagement with a subset of 125 particularly relevant articles highlights the emergence of three key trends in the sociological framing of journalism: a normative concern with the relationship between journalistic and

sociological methods and values between 1899 and 1926; a casual or condescending dismissal of "journalistic scholarship" in the 1940s, 1950s, and 1960s;
and a turn toward journalism and journalistic practice as an object of *empirical*
inquiry in the 1970s. While I discuss these trends chronologically, it is important to keep in mind that there are no hard and fast lines between the clusters of
articles discussed here. There may have been a turn toward the empirical study
of journalism as a subject matter in its own right in the 1970s, but even as early as
1910, Frances Fenton would inquire as to the relationship between news framing and crime and investigate the question "how and to what extent do newspaper presentations of crime . . . influence the growth of crime and other types of
anti-social activity" (Fenton 1910, 342) by using content analysis and adding up
newspaper column inches. Nevertheless, there are some meaningful chronological shifts at play here, and all of them are relevant to understanding the boundary
between journalism and sociology as it emerged over the course of the twentieth
century.[1]

SOCIAL SCIENCE AND THE MORAL COHESION
OF THE PRESS

The most important material from the *AJS* in its early years can be characterized by its persistent attempt to understand what sociology itself was—as an
intellectual practice and moral commitment—running alongside a series of
normative inquiries into the various failings of the press. In addition to the
aforementioned article "Is a Sane and Responsible Newspaper Possible?" other
AJS pieces between 1899 and the mid-1920s complained that "the sociologist
would be justified in hailing the modern press as a wonderful moral factor, were
it not for that curse and pestilential nuisance, the 'yellow' variety of newspapers" (Yarros 1899, 372) and praised "attempts at civic publicity represented by
the municipal journals of Baltimore" (Weeks 1916, 502). These pieces are not
entirely context-free laments, however. Indeed, buried within them, one can see
an emerging understanding of journalism, not as a system of information provi-
sion but rather as a system of social control and cohesion. The spirit of Robert
Park, and through him the influence of John Dewey, is much in evidence here.
"The motive, conscious or unconscious, of the writers and of the [urban news-
paper] press is to reproduce, as far as possible, in the city the conditions of village life. In the village everyone knew everyone else. Everyone called everyone
by his first name. The village was democratic. We are a nation of villagers . . . if
public opinion is to continue to govern as much in the future as it has in the
past, if we propose to maintain a democracy as Jefferson conceived it, the newspaper must continue to tell us about ourselves" (Park 1923, 278). Focusing on
the newspaper as a socio-cultural object that fostered community integration

(or alienation) and directed "public opinion" would lead these early sociologists "who themselves marched within the still larger brigades of the charity organization movement and the social gospel" (Abbott 1999, 81) to consider *what kind* of integration and *what kind* of community the newspaper made possible. It was thus roundly and mercilessly criticized, usually without empirical evidence, for a variety of failings.

There is a connection between this moral trepidation directed toward the social influence of the newspaper and the existence of a number of articles, especially between 1899 and the 1920s, that focused on the relationship between journalistic and sociological methods. This connection is the struggle of a newly professionalizing sociology to define exactly what social science was and what methods it ought to embrace. As we have already noted, sociology in its early years was scarcely distinguishable from the various religious reform and social gospel movements of the late Progressive Era, all of which saw the ills of the industrial era as at least partly attributable to something called "society" rather than to solely individual failings. Given this reform-oriented background, what did it mean to be a sociologist, what were proper sociological methods, and how should college-level instruction in sociology take place? In fact, several articles in the early *AJS* document nothing more than the composition of sociology programs at different universities, as well as the various departments in which "Introductory Sociology" is taught. The question also arose how journalistic instruction and practice might be distinguished from sociological theories and methods. One of the most remarkable articles from these early days by Vincent (future president of the ASA), describing at length how he turned his undergraduate sociology class his class into full-time news bureau has already been discussed.

Several articles before 1926 also discuss the Pittsburgh Survey, that touchstone of early sociological and reform-oriented science, inevitably addressing the relationship between the journalistic and sociological aspects of the survey. In a 1909 article summarizing the survey results, Edward Devine lists the findings and then goes on to lament that as a surveyor and sociologist he is "unable to set [our findings free] through yellow journalism methods . , , because these are not consistent with our traditions" (Devine 1909, 667). Park adds that the various urban surveys and reports sponsored by the Carnegie and Russell Sage foundations "are something more than scientific reports. They are rather a **high form of journalism, dealing with conditions critically, and seeking through the agency of publicity to bring about radical reforms**" (Park 1915, 606). In all these examples, the questions of how to reform the press, what sociology is, how the profession of sociology relates to the aforementioned problems of moral reform, and how sociology differs procedurally from journalism, remain entangled (for more on Park, see Jacobs 2009).

Finally, we should note the links between some of the founding fathers of sociology and the newspaper profession. The key figure here is, of course Robert Park, and historians of sociology such as Rolf Linder have devoted entire volumes to the thesis that it was Park's background as a city reporter that helped shape his sociological habitus and his belief in the academic value of "nosing around" (Linder 2006). These blurred boundaries apply not simply to Park, however; even early sociologists now known for their statistical approaches, such as Franklin Giddings, began their careers as journalists. Over the next few decades, however, the pace of professional separation would accelerate and these crossover sociologists would become increasingly rare. The outlines of this separation can be seen more clearly in the pages of the *ASR* and the *AJS*, a shift that accelerated in the 1930s.

CONDESCENSION AND CRITIQUE

It is quite obvious, even in the *ASJ* articles from the 1910s and early 1920s, that sociologists were groping toward a dividing line between so-called higher forms of journalism (like the social survey and even some kinds of muckraking) and social science; in these early days, however, the division was muddled and the sociological critique of journalism was less methodological and more normative in nature. A distinct change in tone, however, can already be seen as early as the mid-1920s. Following Lannoy (2004), we can see clear signs of this shift in the differences between the original and revised versions of Park's "The City," re-published in 1925. Whereas the first version of "The City" makes reference to the survey movement only briefly, describing it as a form of "high journalism," the revised version injects *both* muckraking journalism *and* the social survey as teleological stopping points along the history of social science, of which sociology is the final and highest stage (Lannoy 2004, 51). "Social interest was first stimulated by polemics against the political and social disorders of urban life [i.e., muckraking journalism] . . . [while] sociology sought a surer basis for the solution of the problems from a study of the facts of city life." In this spirit, government statistics provide citizens with data, community surveys gather masses of information and put them in readable form, and settlement writers like Jane Addams have produced "arresting and sympathetic pictures" (Park and Burgess and McKenzie 1925, 331). But only sociology, Park writes later, "yields generalizations of wide or general validity" (Park 1923).

A later *AJS* article on the Pittsburgh Survey puts this critique in even more sophisticated and methodologically confident terms. The survey movement is not social science, Harriett Bartlett argues in a 1928 article, insofar as its goal is practical action located at a specific time and place rather than general hypothesis testing. In the articles on journalism, this is perhaps the earliest case in which we see alternate empirical practices contrasted with the scientific method per se. "In the minds of many persons the survey is confused with research," Bartlett writes. Both are techniques of investigation but should be carefully distinguished . . . the survey makes comparisons, but, instead of leading to generalizations, they are intended to bring out more clearly the particular problem" (Bartlett 1928, 331). The Pittsburgh Survey, the most famous survey of all, is tainted even in its origins insofar as it "started out as a journalistic project, undertaken by a committee of a charity organization journal" (Bartlett 1928, 343), Bartlett writes dismissively. Bartlett, like Devine in 1909, still draws a connecting line between muckraking journalism and the social survey—but by this time both journalistic and survey techniques are radically differentiated from sociology, rather than being seen as somewhat uneasy contributors to a larger scholarly tradition of which sociology is also a part. Her concluding sentence is pointed: "most particularly [this article] does eliminate some of the confusion which exists as to the nature of the survey and brings it out as an essentially practical, not scientific, technique" (Bartlett 1928, 345).

By the 1940s, barely more than a decade after Bartlett's article and Park's revisions to "The City," the lines are set and references to journalism in the mainstream sociology journals can usually only be found in book reviews. In those, it is as an object of condescension, a way of "othering" particularly well written or methodologically unsound sociology books. Reviewing a book which calls for reporters to be "trained in the social sciences, notably sociology, psychology, and economics, in order to explain and interpret the deeper significance of events and utterances," the *ASR* reviewer exclaims "god forbid!" and sarcastically notes that such a change would lead to the terrible prospect of newsboys tossing PhD theses on the piazza every morning (Shalloo 1940, 664). In a 1942 review of a collected volume of readings on the newspaper and society, an *AJS* reviewer notes that the assembled texts are intended "for use by students in classes of journalism . . . .Selections comprising [Part 1] . . . represent primarily contributions of social scientists, and contrast with those other parts of the book which are primarily the work of journalists" (Johns 1942, 274). For this reason, the book is fairly useless to sociologists as a primer on news but can serve as a primary document for sociologists looking for insights into the journalistic mindset as defined by journalists themselves.

By the 1950s, this review of a book on public opinion has become typical of the tenor of the (now nearly non-existent) journalism-related discourse in the *ASR* and the *AJS*:

> almost all of the books recently published on [the] subject [of public opinion] are very uneven, reflecting the competence of the author in his own field and displaying his lack of knowledge in the related fields.

Such is the case in the present volume, wherein a professor of journalism presents "a guide for newspaper men and newspaper readers" which equates public opinion with any and all social thought and action and which attempts to explain human behavior by a popular treatment of such topics as "The Nature of Man" (Chapter 2), and "The Nature of Society" (Chapter 3). As in the case of most such attempts, the oversimplification of basic concepts results in a volume which will leave most social scientists annoyed and displeased. While the present text may be useful in schools of journalism, it probably will be of limited value to social scientists. Furthermore, in this reviewer's opinion, the student of journalism would benefit more from a basic text in social psychology than from the present popular translation. (Suchman 1953, 218)

By 1967, these reviews have reached a fairly high level of dismissive indifference. A book on a recent development in Boise is called "an extraordinarily commendable work of popular journalism by a professor of that subject at New York University." But "as social science, the book makes only a minute contribution . . . it is, alas, not very coherently written, somewhat hysterical in tone . . . and argues "statistically" from an N of twelve—chosen we know not how—about general awareness of deviance in the community. In other words," the review concludes, "the book falls sufficiently short of professionally acceptable standards of rigor in the accumulation of data, the marshaling of evidence, and its interplay with relevant theory to disqualify it as a tool of higher education" (Polsby 1967, 691).

Data collection, evidence analysis, and the relationship of empirical work to theory—this is the rhetoric of a mature science, one that has become confident enough in its procedures and its apparatus to denigrate "an extraordinary commendable work of journalism" for its lack of rigor. The days when a future president of the ASA would turn his classroom into a working newspaper office and when a founder of the field would ruminate on the similarities and differences between urban sociology and urban reporting are long gone.

JOURNALISM AS AN OBJECT OF SOCIOLOGICAL INQUIRY

From the 1940s until the early 1970s, journalism as an object of sociological inquiry almost entirely vanishes. There was scattered empirical investigation into news reporting in the decades before the 1940s, amid all the moral speculation about the public failings of the press, but after the 1940s we are limited to the occasional piece, such as "Newspaper Circulation from Small Metropolitan Centers" (Kinneman 1946). In part, this can be traced to the general sociological abandonment of mass communication research; in part, it should be attributed to the rise of journalism schools and their affiliated "communications" programs (Pooley and Katz 2008). We should keep in mind, however, that many of the articles on journalism in the early years of the *AJS* would barely be recognized as "sociology" today, even given the relative fondness for the Chicago School in sociology's collective memory. In short, there is virtually no tradition of so-called mainstream journalism research in the sociology journals, up until the 1970s; the maturation of sociology into a "legitimate" social science and the establishment of academic communications programs run together in history.

In the 1960s and 1970s, this would briefly change. As Sarah Stonbely puts it in her historical revisiting of American "newsroom studies": "in the 1960s and 1970s, a number of sociologists ventured into newsrooms in America and England to conduct ethnographies on the production of news" (Stonbely 2013, 1). Of the four key studies identified by Stonbely in her article, only one of them (by Tuchman) was originally published in the *ASR* or *AJS* (Tuchman 1972, 1973). Gans garners a lengthy and praiseworthy review in the *AJS* (Johnstone 1982); Fishman's original piece on the reporting of crime waves is found in *Social Problems* (Fishman 1978); and Epstein appears primarily in monograph form (Epstein 1973). Even outside of the ethnographic work, however, the 1970s and early 1980s would see the publication of several other journalism-oriented articles, including two by Molotch and Lester that utilized content analysis and ethnographic research in combination (1974, 1975).

Stonbely (2013) attributes this (brief) return of a sociology of news to overlapping intellectual and socio-political contexts, including the emergence of organizational theory in sociology, a growing critique of professionalism, the impact of Berger and Luckmann's work on the social construction of reality, a broader critique of institutional authority in general, and a liberal call for greater press pluralism. I agree, by and large, with her analysis, and would only add that even with all these factors working in favor of a sociological embrace of journalism studies the majority of the work in this vein did not appear in the central sociological journals and acted as something of an outlier even when it did. By the mid-1980s, this brief resurgence of interest would taper off. If I had to categorize a fourth and final phase of the sociological understanding of journalism I would probably label it as an embrace of raw journalistic data and journalistic settings to understand *other* social phenomena (but not to understand the news or how the news gets made). But the literature in the 1990s is too scattered to make any broad claims, and perhaps we are too close to that moment to fully map the meta-theoretical discourses that lie beneath the placid surface of the academic journal. Suffice it to say that interest in journalism remains low, and I would echo Pooley and Katz (2008) here attribute this divide as an "unintended consequence of the handoff to journalism schools."

The long-term arc is clear: beginning with a tenuous embrace of journalism and a certain level of journalistic–sociological entanglement, sociology had moved to adopt a dismissive, even hostile, attitude toward the epistemological practices of newswork by the early 1940s.While a certain fascination with journalism as an object of study would emerge in the 1960s and 1970s, and while ethnographers often betrayed a grudging fascination with journalistic practice, it was obvious that two relatively coherent, separate fields of inquiry had settled into place by the mid-1930s. This is a classic case of boundary work and the division of intellectual domains in the sense meant by Carlson and Gieryn in their analysis of professional fields. However, journalism was not the only hybrid occupation purged from sociology as it transformed itself into an empirical, university-based, theoretically driven profession. A variety of sociologists—primarily women and African-Americans but including an entire range of more reform-minded social scientists—were gradually "written out" of the sociological canon over the same period of time. In examining this process, we can see that it was not simply the deployment of rhetorical boundary lines that facilitated the separation between journalism, politics, and sociology but also the *assemblage* of a certain set of material objects whose meaning changed as the borders of the professions themselves shifted. This relates to the changing politics of not only academia but the larger American polity as a whole in the 1920s, 1930s, and 1940s. In the previous chapter we saw how a progressive-era crisis in both the political and epistemological realms fostered an embrace of the empirical, objective impulse in both the sciences and journalism. The 1920s and 1930s, in contrast, would see this impulse mainstreamed, domesticated, and integrated into larger professional and occupational structures. The very *radical* nature of the drive toward objective, certainty-enhancing, public-mobilizing data would be shorn off, forgotten, and assimilated to structures of epistemological power. This occurred both by drawing lines and determining what *objects of evidence* lay on which side of which line. The first casualty of this process would be the social survey and the social reformers clustered around it, but it would not be the last.

"Arresting and Sympathetic Pictures"

We have seen how sociology increasingly wrote journalism out of its self-narrative. This ties into the major professional dynamic in sociology from the 1920s until at least the 1940s: the expulsion of the "social workers, social reformers, social prophets, and social critics who, for want of any other academic refuge, had identified themselves with the adolescent science of sociology" (Wirth 1947, 1). Instead, sociology would become an "objective," "empirical science."

This was a complex process of occupational sorting out, one of central importance to the historiography of sociology, and one that was far from simple, linear, or straightforward. I am primarily concerned here with this moment in sociological history insofar as it is deeply implicated in a secondary break between social science and "reformist journalism" that occurred at the same time. The dynamic I want to propose is this: the overlap between reformist journalism and sociology in the early twentieth century was simultaneously an ontological overlap (the obsession with piled up facts, the graphic visualization of such facts, and a notion that a mass of empirical evidence could lead to "truth") and normative one (a general sympathy toward "social amelioration" as the progressives defined it). The overlap was *not* epistemological, insofar as the sociological reformers were concerned with the context in which reform could occur and the mainstream of journalism was primarily interested with documenting the unfolding of individual incidents (as I showed in the previous chapter). As the occupation of journalism and sociology further professionalized in the post-war era, they both increasingly embraced a form of value-free neutrality instead of reformist principles; what's more, journalism increasingly codified its ontological standards of evidence in a way that distinguished itself from scientific sociology. At the same time, journalism began to shift its epistemological center of gravity, growing increasingly concerned with contexts, patterns, and larger social trends, even as it dropped its normative concerns with what these trends meant and its ontological practices proved themselves unable to live up to the tasks it had set for itself. Paradoxically, as journalism became more like sociology in its concerns with the larger context in which facts were embedded and its embrace of value-free objectivity, it became less like sociology insofar as it incorporated widely different *objects of evidence* into its narrative arsenal.

In other words, while sociology and journalism moved further apart ontologically, they converged around the same value-free understandings of objectivity and epistemological lenses through which they viewed what all this gathering of evidence was for. By expelling the social survey reformers and sociological giants like Jane Addams and W.E.B. Dubois, sociology began to understand itself as scientific and value free. Sociology also dismissed visualization as a valid form of evidentiary display, preferring to rely on statistics and the cold certitude of numbers.

Robert Park did as much as anyone to narrate the history of urban sociology and probe the early relationship between journalism and social science. However, Park's narration of the history of the field was also self-serving and biased toward a particular version of what sociology was and ought to be. For Park, the history of the scientific study of the urban environment possessed a teleological character that culminated in the work of the Chicago School under the guidance of Park himself. The primary transformation of urban sociology,

according to Park, was its shift from practical and reformist research to theoretical, generalizing, scientific research. In this way, sociology could no longer be
like the reformist and descriptive journalism Park himself had once practiced.
Pierre Lannoy succinctly and expertly summarizes the process by which Park
"rewrote the city," and so I want to quote his description at some length:

> It is in his 1929 article "The City as Social Laboratory" that Park gives
> the most complete and explicit version of his story of the development
> of urban research. In it he describes "the first local studies" as having
> a **"practical rather than theoretical character"** (Park 1929, 5). He
> includes among these Addams's *Hull House Maps and Papers*, Wood's
> *The City*, the works of Booth and of Rowntree, the Pittsburgh Survey
> well as the series of articles that appeared between 1910 and 1915
> in the *AJS* under the direction of Breckinridge and Abbott. Having
> emphasized the contributions of these studies in terms of the quantity
> of material gathered, Park (1929, 8) nevertheless points out that "they
> do not yield generalizations of wide or general validity." And he makes
> it clear in the next paragraph, in which the present situation of urban
> research is described, that this **comparative and generalizing concern**
> "has been the central theme of a series of special studies of the Chicago
> Urban Community, some of which have already been published, others
> of which are still in progress" (Park 1929, 9). (Lannoy 2004, 52)

Other historians of sociology frame the problem in similar terms. As Stephen
Turner puts it:

> in the 1920s, when the failures of prohibition were evident, the break
> between "sociology" and "social work" in the older sense became
> final. The Rockefeller philanthropies instead funded what they called
> "realistic" social studies [rather than reformist ones]. The social work-
> ers counterattacked: they complained that this research was a waste
> because it was not turned into publicity . . . . The break was brutal, and
> extended to elite sociology in general. Robert E. Park's denunciation
> of reformers as more a part of the problem than the solution, on the
> grounds of their lack of empathy and understanding of the people they
> claimed to be concerned about, reflected the break. (Turner, personal
> communication)

At the heart of this dispute was the social survey itself—its mechanism for gathering facts, its relatively naïve method of representing these facts graphically, and
its concern that these facts be turned into "publicity," aka, "reformist" journalism.

In the most simplistic jurisdictional (Abbott 1991) terms, the previously unified SSM split into two professional camps, with the social workers taking the ameliorative, case-oriented, settlement-house history into their jurisdiction and the sociologists doubling down on their desire to craft general theoretical laws of social behavior through a more statistically oriented method of survey research. The question of what happened to the impulse for reformist publicity—the "journalistic" wing of the social survey—is in many ways the central problem of this book, and it is a problem closely related to the fate of "reform" in the empirical professions after the 1920s. Reform was a casualty of sociology's professional project, as were the "arresting and sympathetic pictures" sociology had once seen as part of its evidentiary arsenal. While social workers adopted the reformers, the journalists would eventually adopt the visualizations.

Let's first examine the expulsion of the sociological reformers. That the "social prophets, and social critics" were particular targets of the drive for value-free subjectivity in sociology is clear from recent critical scholarship on the careers of Jane Addams (Deegan 1990) and W.E.B. DuBois (Morris 2015). The fact that it is only within the past two decades that we have started to even think of Addams and DuBois as social scientists demonstrates just how well the second generation of sociological thinkers like Park and Wirth drew their professional boundary lines. Once again, Addams and DuBois are emblematic pioneers of social survey research as social science; far more so than reformers like Kellogg or Stelzle, they empirically dragged survey work into the scientific realm by originating some remarkable methodological techniques in the 1910s. Addams, through her work at Hull House and the production of the cooperatively authored *Hull House Maps and Papers* (often seen as one of the earliest representations of the social survey in an academic context), "established the major substantive interests and methodological technique of Chicago Sociology that would define the school for the next forty years" (Deegan 1990, 24). But with "Park's active hostility to the 'label' of social reformer . . . and Burgess' wavering commitment to it, the applied political component of sociology languished, and finally died, at the Chicago School" (Deegan 1990, 25). Until recently, W.E.B. DuBois has fared even worse than Addams in the sociological memory. Not only was *The Philadelphia Negro* chronologically antecedent to any of the American survey works we have discussed in this book thus far, it is also one of the most empirically rigorous. It is "America's first major empirical sociological study . . . [and] it rested on an empirical base: not only extensive interviews with all the families in the ward but also surveys, archival data, and ethnographic data from participant observation. Indeed, DuBois emerged from *The Philadelphia Negro* as the first number crunching, surveying, interviewing, participant-observing and fieldworking sociologist in America" (Morris 49). Not only that, but as Morris persuasively argues, *The Philadelphia Negro* was "a comprehensive sociologically informed community study" in ways that *Hull House Maps and Papers* and other survey work of the time was not. Nevertheless, DuBois and his own urban sociology were systematically erased from the remembered history of sociology for more than a hundred years.

In sum, between the 1920s and 1940s, sociology would definitely expel its previous generation of reform-minded colleagues, literally in the case of Addams and DuBois and symbolically in the case of the SSM and the researchers clustered around the RSF and the *Charities and the Commons*. In part, it would use information visualization as a boundary object around which to wage a war against "cruder" versions of social science. Given the close links between reform movements, publicity, and muckraking journalism this would also definitively impact the relationship between journalism and sociology. Ironically, though, journalism itself was becoming more visual, thematic, sophisticated, and quantitative during the same period. What this did *not* mean, in the new professional context of the 1930s, was that journalism was also becoming more scientific, **because what it meant to be scientific was itself changing**. I argued earlier that the relationship between sociology and reformist journalism had normative, ontological, and epistemological elements. In the era of post-war professionalization, both social science and journalism shifted their normative base in the direction of value-free, professional objectivity. Journalism would also become more epistemologically sophisticated. However, in the new terrain of the social sciences, journalism lacked the methodologies and evidentiary interests that would make it a "legitimate science." How journalism began to embrace a more contextual attitude toward the social world, and how it simultaneously was left behind by the now quantitative, data-oriented social sciences, is the subject of the next section of this chapter.

The Emergence of Contextual and Interpretive Journalism and the Rise and Fall of Journalism as a Science

The 1920s through the early 1960s are a relatively neglected area of journalism history, which usually focuses, in the generic textbook, on technological advances in the distribution and production of news—from newspapers to radio to early television. For the sociologist of knowledge, these decades would seem to be an unpromising time for analysis; the professional optimism of the Progressive Era had been replaced by the materiality and cynicism of the post-World War I era, and the mechanisms of journalistic professionalization had been more or less set into motion. It wouldn't be until the mid-1960s, one version of the story goes, that journalism would take the next step and embrace a critical attitude toward government, business, and society at large.

Below the surface, however, journalism was laying the groundwork for its apparently sudden shift toward a more contextual and critical attitude as early as the 1930s. What's more, a variety of reformist trends that first emerged in the 1960s—precision journalism, new journalism, investigative reporting—can be seen to have their roots in these years as well. A number of journalistic commentators, from Phillip Meyer to Tom Wolfe to Everette Dennis, all point to the publication of *Interpretive Reporting* in 1938 by Curtis MacDougall as an event of signal importance in this shift.[2] As Ronald Seyb writes in an overview of Walter Lippmann's work at the *New York World* in the 1920s:

> Author Curtis MacDougall, for example, explained to his readers in 1938 that he had chosen to change the name of his influential primer for reporters from its original 1932 title of *Reporting for Beginners* to *Interpretative Reporting* because the intervening six years had brought "changing social conditions" that were "causing news gathering and disseminating agencies to change their methods of reporting and interpreting news" such that the trend was now "unmistakably in the direction of combining the functions of the interpreter with that of the reporter, after about a half century during which journalistic ethics called for a strict differentiation between narrator and commentator." (Seyb 2015, 58)

In his taxonomic overview of the rise of interpretation in news, Barnhurst notes that this desire on the part of reporters to go beyond simply stating the facts of a particular scenario (the "what") to the reasons behind and meaning of events (the "why") both generated excitement amongst many journalists and drew skepticism from others, with articles in the trade press arguing that reporters should confine themselves to the facts of an event and little more. For Barnhurst, the 1930s stand as a key moment in this shift, with this statement from the American Society of Newspaper Editors in 1933 appearing indicative of the temper of the times: "Editors should devote a larger amount of attention and space to explanatory and interpretive news," they write, "and to presenting a background of information which will enable the average reader more adequately to understand the movement and significance of events" (Barnhurst 2016).

Part of the argument for more interpretation in news was grounded in technological fears and expectations. With the rise of radio, many forward-thinking journalist and editors feared that newspapers would be perennially scooped and lose their ability to break news. If newspapers were to have a role in the journalism of the broadcast age, these commentators argued, they would have to shift toward explaining why things happened and what these things meant, leaving the narration of events to more immediate forms of media. Politicians of the 1930s, for their part, certainly saw an emerging chasm between radio news and newspaper interpretation. As Bruce Lenthall summarizes:

> [President Franklin Delano] Roosevelt disdained the interpretive journalism he saw on the rise. As national events became more complex, reporters frequently used experts to help them explain events to readers; in Roosevelt's view, this denied citizens the chance to make their own decisions from plain facts . . . but, like many of his listeners, Roosevelt saw broadcasting as a way around this informational bottleneck. Radio, he said "could restore direct communication between the masses and their chosen leaders." (Lenthall 2008, 100)

Whatever fears the specter of radio might have fostered amongst newspaper journalists, though, it was actually the *magazine* genre that did the most to foster the emergence of interpretive journalism in the 1930s. Once again, our old friend Paul Kellogg returns to the story, this time in the form of his national magazine the *Survey Graphic*. A brief recounting of how notions of journalistic context and graphic visualization spread from radical professional publications like the *Survey Graphic* to elite, business-oriented magazines like *Fortune*, can shed light on the rise of a form of quasi-scientific interpretation in the early Depression Era, one grounded in persuasive visual displays that sociologists were starting to leave behind.

THE END OF THE SURVEY MOVEMENT: FROM GRAPHIC EXHIBITS TO THE SURVEY GRAPHIC

After the popular survey mania of the Progressive Era abated, the story of the social survey becomes even more deeply intertwined with journalism—specifically the emerging genre of public-facing magazine journalism. Central to this transformation was the *Survey Graphic*. While the pre-World War I social surveyors devoted a great deal of energy and resources to the exhibition and were relatively ignored by the newspaper press, Paul Kellogg and others like him increasingly began to place their faith in journals, that spoke simultaneously to both an emerging professional audience *and* to the public, rather than mass-audience newspapers. The history of the *Survey Graphic* (1923–1952) is complex. The social work journal the *Charities and the Commons* (itself the product of a merger between the magazines *Charities and the Commons*), under the direction of Paul Kellogg, renamed itself the *Survey* in 1912 following the impact and popular success of the Pittsburgh Survey that Kellogg himself had directed. The new name better reflected the increasingly scientific pretensions of the various American reform movements in a way that *Charities* could not (and also piggy-backed onto the fame of the Pittsburgh Survey).

The most important aspect of the *Survey*, and its spin off the *Survey Graphic*, was that it perched uneasily between the professional concerns of social workers as an occupational class and the concerns of the reform-minded public at large. "On the whole," Cara Finnegan (2005) summarizes in her excellent overview of the history of *Survey Graphic*, "during the teens the *Survey* was still a professional work journal, but one with a long lens." Chambers 1971, 79) The trouble came when, as we have already discussed, popular enthusiasm for reform and liberalism in general began to wane in the 1920s. These were years of "sag," Kellogg declared (Chambers 1971, 79), and what was needed for these times was a journal that would "discover and describe every island of hope; to scout out all the new movements in psychology, art, planning, social service as they bore on welfare, to hold faith, and wait for a better day." The models, in Kellogg's mind, were magazines like *Nation* and *New Republic*, with two crucial and intertwined differences. The first was that, rather than "a journal of opinion" (the subtitle of the *Nation*) the newly christened *Survey Graphic* would be a "journal of action." *Nation* and *New Republic* were extensions of the newspaper editorial page, Kellogg averred. *Survey* would hold fast to the strange fusion of science, citizen action, and progress mapped out (often quite literally) by the social survey movement. It was fusion embodied in the city exhibits of the teens, and ignored by most newspapers in the Progressive Era, which would now be reborn in the pages of a popular journal.

A related difference lies in *Survey's* use of graphical items and the role these items played in appeals to the masses at large rather than just a collection of professional social workers. The *Survey* announced a "spin-off" in 1921, the *Survey Graphic*, "an illustrated magazine" that would "reach out beyond the narrow circles consecutively interested in social work and movements." True to its new name, the *Survey Graphic* would "employ photographs, etchings, drawings, and text of a sort which we hope will get a new hearing for the big human concerns which lie underneath all the technical discussion of social problems" (Chambers 1971, 85). Kellogg said elsewhere that he hoped to "engage the attention of a wide audience by use of graphic and literary arts in partnership with the social science, to catch the eye and heart as well as the intellect" (quoted in Chambers 1971, 105). If all went well, a popular *Survey Graphic* could ultimately subsidize the more professionally and technically oriented *Survey*.

All, it seems, did not go as well as Kellogg had hoped, and the *Survey Graphic* never achieved the kind of popular success obtained by the *Nation* or the *New Republic*. Neither did it ever manage to subsidize the *Survey*. It did, however, last for almost three decades and publish a number of important issues, foremost among them "Harlem, Mecca of the New Negro" in 1925, which introduced the writers of the Harlem Renaissance to a wider audience of white Americans for the first time. Nevertheless, the *Survey Graphic* was in a precarious position by the start of World War II, and its problems could be attributed, in part, to larger changes in the world of journalism. If we go by the timeline I outlined earlier, we can see that in the context of interpretive journalism, the *Survey Graphic* was a pioneer. At the time it was launched, few news organizations, or even newsmagazines, were attempting the kind of contextual, empirically grounded, accessible journalism that Kellogg thought was essential for the Progressive Movement to find its footing in the 1920s and beyond. But by the 1950s, as I will show in the next section, journalism had changed. Notions of "context" and "interpretation" had increasingly become incorporated into more mainstream publications like *Fortune* magazine. On the other hand, the professional audience that the *Survey Graphic* had historically engaged was increasingly finding its voice in scholarly, peer-reviewed publications, making a general-interest social work magazine increasingly superfluous. The *Survey Graphic* was closed by its board of directors, with little fanfare, in 1952. In essence, the middle ground occupied by the *Survey* in the 1930s—between reformism, social work, contextual reporting, graphical elegance, and empirical journalism, was increasingly crowded with new, more politically up-to-date publications and the concerns of the professional class of social workers were increasingly insulated from the general public. These shifts spelled doom for the *Survey Graphic* and for the final embers of the survey movement more generally. What they did not spell doom for, however, was interpretive journalism, which by the 1950s had begun to flower in a variety of different formats.

DATA JOURNALISM COMES TO *FORTUNE*

Fortune was not the most important mainstream, commercially-oriented newsmagazine to bring a more contextual, interpretive take on the news to a mass audience—that distinction probably belongs to other titles in the publication stable of publishing pioneer Henry Luce, such as *Time* and *Life*. As historian Alan Brinkley notes in his magisterial biography of Luce, Luce and his partner Briton Hadden were inspired to launch *Time* in part because of their dissatisfaction with the news media of the time:

> Both men were critical of the daily newspapers of the 1920s . . . Hadden was particularly contemptuous of the Hearst and Pulitzer papers, whose sensationalism, he said, pandered to the ignorance of their working-class readers, whom he disdained as "gum-chewers." But he and Luce were almost equally contemptuous of the "serious" newspapers—what

they considered their leaden formulaic prose, their slavish adherence to the mechanical style of the Associated Press, and their excessive length. Anyone interested in lively or imaginative writing, a professor at the Columbia School of Journalism wrote in 1922, "makes a nuisance of himself in the newspaper." An eye for "objective facts" and "clean copy" were what editors should want. (Brinkley 2010, 217)

Luce and Hadden were also surprisingly scornful of the august *New York Times*, criticizing it for its "sober language, statesmanlike non-partisan conservatism, . . . the vast transcripts of speeches and press conferences, [and] the scrupulous resistance to analysis or overt expressions of opinion" (Brinkley 2010, 220). Or in the more positive formulation of author Isaiah Wilner:

> In order to make the news accessible to a wide audience, Hadden told the news just as he viewed it—as a grand and comic epic spectacle. He hooked readers on the news and sold them on its importance by flavoring the facts with color and detail, and by painting vivid portraits of the people who made headlines. Hadden's entertaining writing style, marked by a reverse-course sentence structure ("To Versailles swarmed empurpled princelings . . ."), proved so popular that it quickly spawned imitators. *As the rest of the media took up Hadden's brand of narrative reporting, journalists transformed themselves from mere recorders into storytellers.* (Wilner 2006)

Multiple historians of journalism have pointed out the connection between the rise of the journalistic style pioneered by Luce and Hadden and the growth of the interpretive journalism of the 1930s that I've already discussed. I am less interested here in the general growth of interpretation in news (Barnhurst 2016; Fink and Schudson 2014) than I am in the way that a few specific, empirical and visual techniques found in that other Luce publication—*Fortune*—came to be retroactively cited by pioneers of data and precision journalism decades later as a model for their work. Everette Dennis, the originator of the term precision journalism, noted in an interview that the *Fortune* of the early 1930s, "could be seen as an early practitioner of so-called 'data journalism.' " Dennis' student Neil Felgenhauer, in a chapter on precision journalism for the *Magic Writing Machine*, contends that while publisher Edward W. Scripps praised the notion of journalism as a "science service" as early as the 1870s, the true birth of "scientific journalism" could be found in the July 1935 issue of *Fortune*. Under the headline "A New Technique in Journalism," *Fortune* announced its publication of the first in what was to be a long-running series of public opinion polls on topics of particular interest to the general *Fortune* reader: "How many Americans smoke cigarettes and what brands? What makes of car do they intend to buy, and when? Which is more popular, the power company or the tax collector? And who favors sharing the wealth?" (quoted in Felgenhauer 1971, 67). More than the results themselves, the truly interesting thing about the launch of the soon-to-be-famous *Fortune* survey is how the exercise was framed. "For the first time," the article brags, "*Fortune* applies to factual journalism the techniques of the commercial survey—a sampling of public opinion by methods long familiar to the industrialist in the sampling of ore and cotton."

Fortune was clearly influenced by its primary literary rival, *Readers Digest*, which ran a series of unscientific but well-received straw polls starting in 1920 (Brinkley 2010). *Fortune*, however, took the matter more seriously and was far more advanced in its technique, utilizing the soon-to-be-famous polling firm of Chevington, Roper, and Wood, and claiming a margin of error (even the term at that time was exotic) of less than 1%. They also scolded their readers for their own lack of knowledge about how scientific polling worked (Felgenhauer 1971, 67). Given *Fortune's* close ties to industrial America, it is not surprising that it was such an early journalistic adopter of public opinion techniques just then making serious inroads into the consumer-oriented business market. But it also adopted information techniques that demonstrate that the magazine's ambitions lay as much in the realm of culture and taste as in pretentions to science. As data visualization pioneer and University of Miami professor Albert Cairo has noted, "It's impossible to talk about the history of news graphics and visualization without mentioning *Fortune*" (Cairo 2014). And while the full-color maps from the March 1938 issue display a level of print detail and sophistication unmatched by anything we have seen so far over the course of this study, the issue also contains charts and graphs that wouldn't have seemed out of place in a social survey publication (or indeed, the *Survey Graphic*) from a few decades earlier.

A number of motivating factors appear to be at work in generating the lush and quantitative visual style of *Fortune*. There was the desire to create a beautiful magazine (in part to cater to a wealthy and sophisticated audience) but also the desire to embrace the latest scientific techniques of information gathering and display to separate out "what happened" in the news of the day from the larger question that obsessed Luce and the other interpretive journalists of the 1930s: *why* was it happening, and *what* did it mean? From a variety of angles, then, we can see that the journalistic assault on incidental and old-style "objective," de-contextualized, "visualization-lite" reporting is well underway by the 1930s.

How, then, do we reconcile the increasingly sharp-edged sociological dismissal of journalism chronicled in the opening section of this chapter with the very clear evidence that journalism—or at least small segments of it—were becoming more explanatory, pattern-oriented, and focused on larger trends?

In part, of course, because "journalism" did and can mean a great many things, but also in part because the visualizing, publicizing, and graphically inclined elements of the survey movement, particularly those that had migrated to magazines were *also* becoming expelled from sociology. In other words, sociology stopped thinking of itself as a visual science. It might be natural to assume that the creative and clever use of visualization in sociological reportage to display quantitative information unfolded in a progressively linear direction within the sociological field and that crude visualization devices were replaced by increasingly sophisticated graphics. We might also assume that the sheer amount of information visualization in sociology increased over time as graphical technology improved. Neither of these assumptions is true, as Michael Friendly (2008) demonstrates in his *Brief History of Data Visualization*. For Friendly, the exact time period under discussion here—the 1890s through the 1950s—is a paradoxical moment in which a so-called Golden Age of data visualization climaxed in the late nineteenth century and was followed by a five-decade-or-so period he calls the "dark ages" of information display. On the one hand, in the early twentieth century, "there were few graphical innovations and by the mid-1930s visualization which had characterized the late 1800s had been supplanted by the rise of quantification and formal, often statistical models in the social sciences. Numbers, parameter estimates, and, especially, those with standard errors were precise. Pictures were, well, just pictures: pretty and evocative perhaps but incapable of stating a "fact" to three or more decimals" (Friendly 2008, 37). Scientists, and social scientists, turned from pictures to numbers.

On the other hand, however, the first half of the twentieth century also saw the *popularization* of information visualization—"in this period, statistical graphics became mainstream" (Friendly 2008, 37). In other words, we see a dual movement. Science became increasingly identified with statistics and numerical precision while, at the same time, earlier visualization techniques seized hold of the popular and professional imagination across a wide variety of fields. We have seen this trend in this chapter and the previous one with the rise of the social survey and the wide variety of exhibits and graphical paraphernalia that went along with it. As social science professionalized and objectivized, it left information visualization behind, free now to be adopted by less sophisticated empirical professions—such as journalism.

In other words: the simultaneous rise of sophisticated statistical techniques and the popularization of information visualization served not to bring the empirical professions closer together, but to drive them further apart. The visual, publicity-oriented social survey, as stated earlier, "started out as a journalistic project, undertaken by a committee of a charity organization journal" (Bartlett 1928, 331). Robert Park denigrates the visual even further in his dismissal of reformist sociology; settlement writers may have produced "*arresting and sympathetic pictures*" (Park, Burgess and McKenzie 1925, 331), but only sociology "yields generalizations of wide or general validity" (Park 1929). The fact that Park was seen by later writers like James Carey as the representative of a more humanistic, visual, and qualitatively inclined social science is as much a comment on the later direction of sociology as it is a historical fact (Carey 1978). Compared to the reporters, reformers, and social surveyors of the previous sociological-cum-journalistic generation, Park was a scientist, and one resolutely opposed to sympathetic pictures.

Through the Looking Glass: Journalism, Social Science, Data, and Databases

I argued in chapter 2 that newspapers failed to capture much of the publicity generated by the social surveyors in general and the MRFM in particular and that this failure stemmed, in part, from a journalistic focus on immediate happenings (MRFM meetings, marches, dinners, and so on) to the detriment of the more contextual focus of the MRFM message. This focus on the incident began to shift in the 1930s with the rise of interpretive journalism, although the implications of this shift would not be fully understood until the 1960s. I've already discussed the evolving ways that sociology understood journalism from the late nineteenth to the late twentieth century, and what this can tell us about how sociology changed during this time period. But what about *journalism*? How did it understand what *social science* was and its own relationship to it? In this final section I travel "through the looking glass" in an attempt to tease out the different ways that journalism thought about sociology, data, maps, and databases in the middle third of the twentieth century.

STATISTICS AND VISUALIZATIONS IN THE NEWS

Even though interpretive journalism was beginning to emerge in magazines as diverse as *Fortune* and *Survey Graphic*, these isolated occurrences do not fully document trends in journalism during the time period under examination here. In order to try to tease out the larger trends at work, I (1) conducted a qualitative discourse analysis of the use of the keyword "statistics" or "data" in the "Chronicling America" newspaper archive at the Library of Congress and (2) examined a week's worth of front pages in the *New York Times*, one decade at a time, from 1885 to 2005.

Both of my methodological techniques here are fairly rudimentary. In the case of the newspaper archive, I was primarily interested in the frequency of word use—was there a pattern to how often the words "statistics" or "data" appeared over time during the Progressive Era? To answer this, I simply counted the number of articles that used those words over the course of every year, from 1865 to 1922. My analysis of the three-year moving average between these years suggests that there is indeed a pattern.

The use of quantitative terminology in the news began to rise steadily in frequency starting around 1895, with a sharp peak during the period 1907–1910. Frequency of use rose from 2 occurrences on average in 1868 to 30 by 1888, reaching 88 occurrences in 1906 and then increasing to 141 in 1907, 173 in 1908, 171 in 1909, and 125 in 1910. Average occurrence then quickly falls until 1914, when it holds steady at its pre-1907 levels of an average of about 60–70 articles per year, until 1922. Obviously, this is quite a small number of occurrences compared, for instance, to today. But we can learn several things from even this cursory analysis. First, the discussion of statistics or data in the news really did begin to rise starting in about 1895—an important year for many sociologists of science and knowledge, as this is about the time when quantification and objectivity began to assume a more important role in American intellectual life (Ross 1992; Schudson 1978). Second, we can also see that the "rise of data in the news" was a gradual rise, followed by a leveling off with a period of "statistics effervescence" between 1907 and 1909. Once again, this simple exercise in counting words reinforces the claim of the social surveyors, discussed in chapter 2, that a "mania for counting and surveying" took hold in the early twentieth century, followed by a graduate cooling of enthusiasm after World War I.

Simply counting words, however, does not really give us all that much insight into how data was used and displayed in news reports, especially when we consider that much of this usage was graphical in nature. To further probe these complexities, I also analyzed the front pages of the *New York Times*, for one week per decade, from 1885 until 2005. In other words, I looked at a week's worth of front-page news in 1885, 1895, 1905, 1915, 1925, and so on, all the way up to 2005. The goal here was not to obtain exact causal knowledge but to get a very general sense of what Barnhurst and Nerone have called the "form of news" (Barnhurst and Nerone 2001) during a certain moment in time. While Barnhurst and Nerone posit a number of insightful and complex social categories to explain the transformation of news since the eighteenth century, my question here is far simpler. How were data and statistics used and displayed on the front pages of the New York Times, and how did this use and display change over time?

Compare the *New York Times* front-pages from May 4, 1885 and October 2, 1895. We might notice, first, the use of line drawings in 1895 and an increasingly sophisticated use of headlines. The paper from 1885 literally presents all news as roughly the same, a miscellaneous list of items with little priority afforded to any one over another. The paper from 1895 displays a slightly more professional sophistication, with both pictures and journalistic judgment about what news "matters" most (Barnhurst and Nerone 2001). However, there are deeper currents at work here, particularly in terms of the journalistic use of data. One of the salient aspects of the 1895 paper is the *prominence of lists, columns of numbers and names, and "ordinal data."* While the use of financial data in this fashion might not be surprising, we also see data lists like these in other papers from 1895, a list of the names of those injured in an accident, and data column accompanying a story on widespread violations of Sunday prohibition in Brooklyn (see Fig. 3.1).

This use of lists is a feature of journalism, moreover, unique to this particular time period. In no other decade to we see this fetishization of stacked-up facts and the general belief in the power of simply presenting unadorned information in list form. While graphical and statistical use would grow in sophistication over the coming decades, never was the power of the single fact presented with such clarity as in the 1890s.

Compare an article about extreme heat-related deaths in 1935 with the earlier discussion of hot weather and urban mortality from a *New York Times* story in 1895. In 1895, the data use was primarily in the form of lists of the names of those killed. In 1935, the data was a running tally of the temperature during the course of a single day. Rather than listing the names of those killed, the decision to focus on the temperature already demonstrates how data in 1935 was more closely tied to the context in which events occurred (i.e., the weather rather than those individuals killed by the weather). Finally, by 2005, we can see the full flowering of informational graphics, the kind we now expect on a regular basis from top-tier news organizations like the *New York Times*. Indeed, these graphics demonstrate that they are now primarily meant as much for the Web than they are for the printed page.

This analysis of *New York Times* front pages demonstrates that the fetishization of individual facts or lists of facts was eventually overtaken by a journalistic contextualism in which informational graphics would eventually play a prominent role. Given the findings in presented here—particularly the rhetoric of the SSM about the importance of data; the overall lack of informational graphics and context in the news reports about the MRFM; and the growth in journalistic use of the terms "data" and "statistics after 1895—this analysis of the *Times* adds further evidence to the argument that US society was obsessed with relatively content-free data in the very early twentieth century, and that contextualization would grow in importance for both journalism and social science as the century progressed. This stress on the readily discernable single fact also helped unite journalism and early sociology under the banner of empiricism,

There were 530 arrests in New-York in the
same period.

The record is as follows:

	Arrests in Brooklyn.	Arrests in New-York.
Sunday, July 7......0		116
Sunday, July 14.....1		138
Sunday, July 21.....1		130
Sunday, July 28.....0		146

There are 4,700 saloons in Brooklyn, and
8,500 in New-York.

There are 1,700 policemen in Brooklyn
and 3,000 in New-York. The proportion of
police to saloons is thus about the same in
the two cities.

"Public decency and order,"—how are
they observed in Brooklyn Sunday under
Mr. Schieren's "side-door" policy? The
records show that drunkenness has increased in Brooklyn under this policy. The
records show a fact of even greater significance, namely, that nearly three-quarters
of all the arrests made by the police in
Brooklyn Sunday are for intoxication.

Take, for instance, the figures of the
police reports for Sunday, July 28:

Sunday "Drunks."

Precinct.	Whole Number of Arrests.	Arrests for Intoxication.
1............................	7	6
2............................	2	2
3............................	3	2
4............................	0	0
5............................	7	5
6............................	1	1
7............................	6	6
8............................	6	2
9............................	3	3
10...........................	6	3
11...........................	11	8
12...........................	3	2
13...........................	8	3
14...........................	8	2
15...........................	7	7
16...........................	6	0
17...........................	4	3
18...........................	2	2
18 (mounted squad).........	1	1
19...........................	1	1
21...........................	5	4
22...........................	4	4
23...........................	1	1
*24 (Coney Island)..........	28	0
25...........................	1	1
25 (sub-precinct)...........	1	1
Central Office Squad.......	Made no arrests.	
Total.......................116		79

* The percentage would have been larger but
for the raiding of a disorderly house on Coney

Figure 3.1 Front page, *New York Times*, August 5, 1895 Source: Front page, *New York Times*,
August 5, 1895, online at https://timesmachine.nytimes.com/browser/

a fusion that, as we have seen, became increasingly frayed as the professions
parted ways. While sociology stressed the kind of analytic context that could
only be discernable via the application of the scientific method, variables, and
statistics, journalism increasingly embraced the interpretive role that sociology
had once seen as its key guiding principle, and buttressed this contextualism
with visual display. This, ironically, served to make it less like science as viewed
by social scientists.

Nevertheless, despite the growing use of contextual information in the *New York Times* and other media outlets, information graphics were still not widely adopted by most news organizations until the 1980s and 1990s. The shifting technological affordances of news production are part of the reason why this is so—changes in technology made it easier to print sophisticated graphics in newspapers at a relatively rapid clip. However, specific journalistic *visions of technology* are also at play here, particularly the way the occupation of journalism understood what computers and databases *could do* for journalism, and the way that this particular vision could bridge the gap between journalistic explanation and more traditionally scientific methods. I close this chapter with an analysis of these "professional visions of technology" that would shape the deployment of so-called objective data. It was the changing understanding of specific technological devices that allowed journalism to adopt some of the trappings of sociology—particularly its methodologically oriented scientism—that it had previously either ignored or dismissed. If journalism and sociology had drifted apart—despite journalism's adoption of more contextual reporting methods and visual displays of information—shifting journalistic understandings of technology would be among the forces that would begin to draw the two fields back together.

Editor and Publisher, Columbia Journalism Review, and Professional Journalistic Discourse Around Technology and Method

To get a more nuanced sense of journalistic discourse around methodology and technology—how journalists understood sociology and data, for instance—we can conduct the mirror opposite of the exercise engaged in for sociology earlier in the chapter. Rather than looking at how sociology journals discussed journalism, we can turn instead to how journalism journals discussed sociology. For this, I analyzed two primary sources of professional "shop-talk": *Editor and Publisher* (*E&P*) (1907–2016) and the *Columbia Journalism Review* (*CJR*) (1961–2016). My analysis of *CJR* was fairly targeted: I searched it for all articles that mentioned "social science" or "sociology" and found thirty-six. I undertook a broader and more wide-ranging approach to *E&P*, searching its extensive database of articles for the terms "sociology" and "social science," but also "database," "data," and "census." "Data" and "database" search results required far more extensive pruning but also brought up some of the most thought provoking and intriguing pieces. The way to understand the journalism–sociology relationship from the journalistic perspective, it turns out, is not to focus so much on the way journalists understand another empirical professional discipline but rather to focus on the way they talk about the objects that make that discipline possible. We need to focus less, in other words, on how journalism journals understood sociology than on how those journals understood statistical analysis, computers, and databases. The first part of this analysis, on *E&P* and focusing on how journalists talked about sociology and social science, is presented here. I turn to the discourse surrounding computers and databases in chapter 5.

There was an almost one-to-one overlap between *E&P* articles with "sociology" and "social science" keywords, which is perhaps not surprising. There were, in general, four types of stories included in this sample, which resulted in thirty-two articles for both categories. The first and least interesting category were articles about developments at journalism schools in which social science or sociology departments were mentioned offhand. Typical of this type of article is "Big Lift for Journalism School" (March 25, 1995), which recounts how the University of Washington decided not to close its journalism school, and in which faculty in sociology are mentioned in an offhand fashion. A second category might be called "the sociology paper piece," which includes stories that summarize scientific studies of the media system of particular relevance to journalists. These actually make up the majority of the articles in my corpus, with pieces ranging from "Consulting Group Says Change Poses Challenge for News People" in 1983 to "Politically Correct Press: Research Shows Reps, Dems Treated Equally In Papers" in 1999.

More interesting are the handful of stories in the third category that discuss exemplary journalists with a social scientific bent, for instance, a profile of Thomas C. Fleming, who stepped down as executive editor of the San Francisco Sun-Reporter in July 1997, after fifty-three years on the job. "Retirement has little altered Fleming's work habits," the article states, "as he continues to produce a regular column for the African-American weekly and to write a syndicated piece, 'Reflections on Black History,' for African-American newspapers throughout America" ("Black Press, Human Race," January 31, 1998). As might be clear from the summary, this piece focuses on a minority newspaper editor, which I actually found to be true for nearly *all* the stories that attributed a sociological or social scientific habitus to individual journalists. Other pieces of this type discussed a "Woman at War" (the profile of Knight-Ridder Baghdad bureau chief Hannah Allam) and how Akron Beacon Journal writer Regina Brett, a breast cancer survivor and sociologically inclined journalist, was moving "from chemotherapy to an organization presidency" (June 13, 1998). While there are too few articles in this survey to make further generalizations about the types of journalists who are seen as "potentially sociological," it is certainly worthy of note that there was tight correlation between non-white, non-male, journalists and the implication that they possessed a certain "social insight" denied to their more, so-called, mainstream colleagues.

The most relevant, for our purposes, is a fourth and final category of journalistic shop-talk: *E&P* pieces that specifically interrogate a type of journalistic–sociological story. There are several positive takes on these forms of journalistic work (for example, the 2007 story "One Paper Shatters Black 'Taboos,'" in which "according to real estate developer and newspaper owner and editor Michael Pittman, the *Capital City Courier* aims to raise issues that African-Americans discuss in private but do not generally talk about in public." Once again, though, the stories of this kind most often cited by *E&P* are those dealing with minority issues (another article is titled "Black Journalists Peer into the Future"). Two articles buck this trend by taking direct aim at "fad words" (and, implicitly, at the jargon of sociology and academia). They are, in effect, the mirror image of the *AJS* articles discussed earlier in this chapter. Rather than sociologists dismissing journalists for writing too well, journalists here dismiss sociologists for writing too badly.

Both articles, interestingly enough, are written by Jack Hart, then working as an editor, reporter, writing coach, and journalism school professor in Portland, OR. The first, "Trend Speak," was published in 1993 and the second, "Fad Words," in 1996. To some degree, Hart is repeating himself, for while the examples in both columns are different, the basic thrust of the articles are the same: trendy, "sociological" jargon is off-putting and elitist, is an example of bad writing, and has no place in journalism. Nevertheless, Hart argues, the profession is being corrupted by the use of these sociological words. The 1993 piece argues that such "trendy" words as "venue," "newsie," and "eatery" migrated from alt-weekly publications, where they were used to cater to an upscale, urban, hip audience, to national newspapers. The primary argument in this first piece is that the primary sin of trendy jargon is that it is *imprecise*; but a second argument is that it is *elitist*. "Not that Trendspeakers care much about real people," Hart writes. "The dialect is naturally elitist. For one thing, it's preoccupied with hot restaurants, art films and the kind of avant-garde literature that seldom sells in supermarkets." Hart then moves into a brief indictment of sociology: trendspeak is "a pastiche of pretentious abstractions, fad words, breezy syntax, overdone alliteration and sophomoric sociology jargon."

The 1996 article moves on somewhat from alternative weeklies and focuses more directly on the jargon of academia and sociology. The first paragraph is telling: "The woman had a Ph.D. in one of those frothy social sciences, the sort that serve as breeding grounds for jargon and gobbledygook. She paced between overhead projector and screen, lecturing on what she called 'learning styles.'" It is all here: the description of "frothy" social science and the implication that the primary contribution of these fields to the English language is that they serve as an incubator for jargon. If the first article took fad words to task for their classist origins, this article damns them—and by extension, "frothy" social science—for fostering *imprecision:*

> Word fads can cripple the language because they operate by a kind of verbal Gresham's Law. Fad words are almost always vague. And vague words drive their more specific alternatives out of our common vocabulary. Every time we adopt a fad word, we lose, by at least some small measure, our ability to discriminate and communicate.

These kinds of boundary-drawing articles were plentiful in the *ASR* and *AJS* corpus I examined earlier. The most relevant data point with regard to the reverse analysis in *E&P* is the fact that there were so few of them. Journalism, it might be clearly assumed, gave little thought to sociology before the emergence of data journalism in the 1990s. The importance of Jack Hart's articles should not be over-estimated—they account for only two of the tens of thousands of articles published by *E&P* over the course of its history. Nevertheless, it is remarkable that *the only* articles to draw boundary lines with sociology at all in *E&P* focused on jargon, elitism, and imprecision. There is no clearer summary of classic journalistic resistance to social science than this simultaneous focus on understandability and precision, and how sociology denudes both.

Moving to the second corpus of occupational self-talk, the thirty-six articles in the *CJR*, we see additional evidence that there are few patterns to those journalism articles that discuss sociology or social science. Journalism, in other words, ignored sociology and social science except as potential reporting leads. A few other articles (again, mostly book reviews) directly took on the relationship between the two empirical domains. And finally, there is a key article by Philip Meyer in 1971 called "The Limits of Intuition," as well as two reviews of Meyer's book *Precision Journalism* in 1973 and 2002.

Some of the most famous names in media sociology occasionally grace the pages of *CJR*. Kurt and Gladys Lang discuss the impact of televised hearings in a piece from 1973 (Lang and Lang 1973). Herbert Gans writes about "multi-perspective news" in 1979 (Gans 1979) and Michael Schudson contributes a "research report" in the 2000s. Vincent Mosco writes an article on the institutional relationship between minority organizing groups and the FCC (Mosco 1980), and there is the occasional letter from Todd Gitlin. There are less well-known, straight academic studies as well, including at least one article adopted from a media sociology doctoral thesis published in *CJR's* early days (Grey 1966).

By and large, however, such articles are rare. Even less common are articles looking directly or obliquely at the journalism–sociology relationship. One of the few can be found in a review, "Journalism and Social Science: Continuities and Discontinuities," by Gerald Grant in a collection of essays honoring David Riesman (*Columbia Journalism Review* 1979). The reviewer notes that Grant attempts to absolve journalism from claims that it is intellectually lightweight, dividing journalism into "Type One" reporting (the beat reporter), "Type Two" (the investigative reporter), and "Type Three" ("the analytical journalist"), this last "the journalism that most nearly approximates social science. Indeed, it is to social scientists like Nathan Glazer, Daniel Bell, James Coleman, and David Riesman that such journalists turn for models" (*Columbia Journalism Review* 1979, 95). The review is not entirely dismissive; nevertheless, it does conclude with the pointed speculation that "Some journalists, however, may wish to question [Grant's] implicit assumption that they represent a lower link in the great chain of informational being," and begins by wryly noting that "Every once in a while someone discovers an analogy between the practice of journalism and some other discipline—an archaeological dig, say, or a psychoanalytic probe" (*Columbia Journalism Review* 1979, 95). While it is hard to say if this remark refers to any "someone" in particular, it is written eight years after Philip Meyer's call, in the pages of *CJR* and elsewhere, regarding the limits of journalistic intuition and the need to fuse journalism and social science techniques more deliberately. It is quite likely about him.

Conclusion

This chapter has recounted how sociology purged itself of its various progressive-era tendencies as part of its professionalization project and its drive to establish itself as a theoretical, empirical, largely quantitative science of society. To that end, sociology increasingly distanced itself from the African-American and female scholars (such as W.E.B. Dubois and Jane Addams) who had formed a key part of its early history and its early successes. These now-marginalized scholars, along with others, had also been active in the social survey movement and its various offshoots. While ameliorative social goals were increasingly claimed by social work, the other half of the survey movement tent—the side concerned with mobilizing the public through the deployment of objective facts and compelling visual displays—was only slowly picked up by professional journalism. By the 1930s, journalists had only just begun to explore a contextualizing, popularizing, visually oriented form of reporting the news. These tendencies were certainly not at the center of journalistic production, and in any case, the changes that once might have made journalism more like social science—a focus on the qualitative understanding of patterns, an increasing attention to visuals, and a concern with *the public* as both an audience and as an object of analysis—now had the opposite effect. They made journalism less scientific instead of more so. According to many sociologists, journalism's use of pictures, its concerns with the public ramifications of larger social trends, and the sheer readability of its prose were enough to render it decidedly *not* science—because the meaning of science itself had been transformed.

At the same time, what it meant to be a reporter was also shifting. By 1991, journalism had changed so much that a freelance writer with *E&P* was able to list a number of institutional resources available to assist journalists who wanted to use computers to do social science journalism. Obviously, something at the fringes of the journalistic epistemological paradigm had begun to change. The key, as it turns out, is the emergence of the journalism reformer Philip Meyer and his notion of what he called precision journalism. Meyer, with his attempt to fuse journalistic and social science methods, straddles the gap between journalism and social science in the second half of the twentieth century, the emergence of which I have chronicled over the course of these pages. How Meyer tried to bridge this gap, and how successful he was in doing so, is the subject of the next two chapters. In them, we will see that one key to understanding the emergence of social-science journalism in the 1960s and 1970s was an increased professional certitude about what it meant to be "objective," alongside a growing confidence that journalists themselves could mobilize and assemble publics through the deployment of unproblematic factual data.

4

Context, Social Science, and the Birth of Precision Journalism

Introduction

By early evening of Sunday, July 23, 1967, the 12th Street neighborhood in Detroit was on fire.

What later became known as the 1967 Detroit Riots (known to many at the time as the 12th Street Riots) were only the most dramatic in a series of events shaking US cities in the late 1960s. By now the images of American unrest from the 1960s and early 1970s are well known almost to the point of becoming clichés—the assassinations of John F. Kennedy, Malcolm X., Martin Luther King Jr., and Bobby Kennedy; the protests outside the 1968 Democratic National Convention in Chicago; urban unrest in dozens of US cities, from Newark to Watts; the 1972 presidential election and the eventual resignation of President Richard M. Nixon in 1974; the summer of love; and more. In general, historians and scholars of the press have documented two responses by journalists to this turmoil. On the one hand they became more expressive, literary, and even "alternative," with shifts in journalistic voice running from the New Journalism experiments of Tom Wolfe, Hunter S. Thompson, Joan Didion, and Truman Capote to underground newspapers and radical magazines. On the other hand, even more traditional journalists began to operate as a more distinct center of political "counterpower" in the 1960s, increasingly skeptical of government claims and less willing to defer to officials in power in their construction of daily news routines (Schudson 1978).

In this chapter I argue that there was a third cluster of journalistic responses to the crisis of political authority that emerged in the 1960s, one that linked this political upheaval to a developing epistemological crisis in the nature of professional knowledge. This response involved a doubling down on journalistic objectivity and journalistic certitude, in part by re-establishing the links between journalism and social science that were severed (as we have seen in chapters 1–3) four decades earlier. The pioneer of this particular response was the founder of precision journalism Phillip Meyer: Knight Ridder reporter, editor, and University of North Carolina professor. Meyer—far from being the lone inventor of a particular genre of news—formulated his thoughts on precision journalism, however, against a larger socio-technical backdrop, one which not only saw rapid technological change in newsrooms but also a foundation-sponsored move to further embed quantitative social science within different professional institutions. The emergence of precision journalism, and the tentative reconciliation between elements of journalism and sociology, can thus only be understood as part of this larger societal crisis and the wider framework for re-thinking journalistic objectivity that was proposed to address it.

In chapter 3, we saw how journalism's movement toward a more contextual, data-oriented, visual style of reporting did little to mark it as more scientific in the decades following World War I. In part, this is due to that fact that social science itself had changed in that time. Sociology and political science dismissed visualization techniques in favor of the rigor of statistics and variables; moreover, they embraced a new understanding of what it might mean to assemble a public, an understanding that specifically denigrated the reformist impulses of earlier decades. In the 1950s and 1960s, sociology and political science embedded themselves more firmly within the governmental policy-making apparatus, seeking to influence the direction of society through expert advice and access to decision makers, rather than through the public mobilization of reformers. Journalism marks a key inflection point in this transformation insofar as it was the institutional entity standing between social science, government, and the public. It was increasingly tasked with explaining the ramifications of social developments on behalf of a sociology that no longer cared to do so. For some, like grant makers in the RSF, this obligated social scientists and journalists to forge a better working relationship. For others, like Phillip Meyer, it meant that journalists themselves should take on some of the expert tasks of the sociologist. In that vein, I want to begin this chapter by discussing the cultural status of social science in the post-war years. I will be spending a fair amount of time discussing both the vision of mainstream sociology that existed within popular culture during this time, as well as the work of the RSF's "Social Science in the Professions" project, which tried to unite social science methods with professional practices in the law, social work, and eventually, journalism. I then turn to one of the key outputs of that project, the first edition of Phillip Meyer's *Precision Journalism*. While Meyer has now told the story about the writing of *Precision Journalism* multiple times in interviews, speeches, and his memoir *Paper Route: Finding My Way to Precision Journalism*, I want to focus on his time at the RSF and, in particular, on the early reviews and responses to his book from the journalistic community. The archives at the Rockefeller Foundation in Tarrytown, NY, contain the complete record of Meyer's year at the RSF, including multiple rejection letters from publishers he approached with his book manuscript. Given the subsequent impact that *Precision Journalism* would have on the larger journalistic field, the original perspectives on his project from mainstream members of the journalism and social science communities are telling. The chapter concludes by turning, once again, to the status of the journalism–social science border as it stood when Meyer finally published *Precision Journalism* in 1973.

I should note that the pages that follow present something of a heroic narrative when it comes to Meyer's work in founding and popularizing precision journalism, though I have tried to contextualize his work as much as possible. I have also tried to grapple with a very real difficulty—the fact that Meyer's story is worth telling on its own as well as the fact that he clearly did not "act alone" in founding what eventually became known as data journalism—by dividing this part of the story in two. This chapter focuses on Philip Meyer the individual, and his path to writing *Precision Journalism*. Chapter 5 then goes back to look at the web of institutions, networks, and individuals who made the ideas Meyer initially formulated something that actually existed in the world. The heroic narrative of this chapter is flipped on its head in Chapter 5.

Social Science and Journalism in the Cold War Imagination

The natural sciences—particularly physics, which had in the minds of many Americans won the war against Japan through the Manhattan project—entered the post-World War II era flush with enhanced prestige and an unprecedented level of government funding. In part, this reflected far more fundamental changes in the structure of the American state by mid-century in the aftermath of the Great Depression and World War II. It also reflected a society grappling with the threat posed by Communism, one that sought to leaven the obviously enhanced powers of the state by focusing on the cultivation of patriotism and the American "national character" (Turner 2015), in part by fostering an approach to the hard sciences that was distinctly democratic and American. The establishment of the National Science Foundation (NSF) by an act of Congress in 1950 (National Science Foundation 1994) reflected both the enhanced power and the increased state centralization of "basic" science research in the United States.

The situation of the social sciences and journalism in the Cold War era was just as complex and fraught with internal tensions as that of the natural sciences. The sociology of the 1950s was barely recognizable as belonging to the same discipline of the sociology of the 1920s, as I have discussed in earlier chapters. Institutionally, sociologists had moved into various governmental agencies during the Great Depression and World War II, particularly the US Department of Agriculture and the Research Branch of the War Department. The ASA was five times the size it had been in 1940, and sociology departments had spread across the US university system (Abbott and Sparrow 2008), with important outposts at Columbia and Harvard University joining the University of Chicago as leaders in the field. Social science had also moved closer to embracing a dominant intellectual paradigm by the second half of the twentieth century, one that combined a new scientific and sampling-based survey methodology with Parsonian systems theory and an overarching positivist orientation (Abbott and Sparrow 2008, 285). On the other hand, the social sciences were well aware of their subordinate position in the new centralized research order. They were inferior to the natural sciences in terms of rigor, utility, and research funding. Journalism, for its part, had begun to grapple with the tensions between its own surface-level professional certitude, the growing power and secrecy of the national security state, and the challenge interpretive journalism posed to traditional notions of objectivity.

The contrast between methodological certitude and a barely acknowledged intellectual inferiority is instructive for understanding the state of journalism and sociology at this particular moment in their development. The era between the Great Depression and the mid-1960s would see both sociology and journalism come as close to establishing a "normal science" paradigm as they ever had before. George Steinmetz refers to the emerging sociological philosophy after World War II as one of *positivism*, by which he means a search for regular probabilistic laws of society, an empiricist ontology that links observation to the ability to make scientific statements, and a belief that the social sciences should model themselves on the natural sciences (Steinmetz 2008, 316). Methodologically, sociology expanded its use of surveys, but these were surveys of a radically different character than those discussed in chapter 1. They were usually national, large-scale project surveys that made use of the latest sampling methods and statistical techniques. For intellectual inspiration they drew on the famous Gallup presidential surveys of the 1930s and 1940s and were represented as a paradigm case in sociology by Samuel Stouffer's *American Soldier*. Talcott Parsons, finally, provided a theoretical ballast, often indecipherable, for the mainstream elements of the discipline, one that gained in stature through its invocation of the sociological "founding fathers" (primarily Emile Durkheim and Max Weber) all of whom were prestigiously European and conveniently dead.

Talcott Parsons' struggles with the NSF and the Social Science Research Council (SSRC) in the mid-1940s over the status of social science, however, demonstrate that this intellectual hegemony was both relative and relational. As the debate raged over whether the newly formed NSF ought to fund social science alongside the natural sciences (Solovey and Pooley 2011), Parsons was tasked by the SSRC with producing a position paper which could make the case that social science ought to receive equal treatment and equal funding from the NSF. As Klausner and Lidz suggest, Parsons did this by arguing that the "sciences," social or natural, could be said to represent a unified system and that indeed there was thus no "choice," per-se, to be made with regard to funding insofar as sociology and physics were really unified at an appropriately high level of abstraction. Even more provocatively, Parsons argued, social science actually required *more* funding than the natural sciences because the nature of its problems were so much more complex. While members of the SSRC reacted poorly to Parsons' draft proposal—seeing it as unnecessarily scientistic or inscrutable or both—the attempt to yoke social to natural science from a position of professional weakness would characterize most attempts to secure government funding for sociological, anthropological, political, and psychological research. Despite the interventions of Parsons and like-minded scholars, the 1950 bill establishing the NSF referred only to "other sciences," which "could be read to include the social sciences entrance but gave them second-rate status compared to the mathematical, physical, biological, medical, and engineering sciences that were specifically mentioned in the statute" (National Science Foundation 1994). By 1958 the situation was slightly clearer; the NSF established an official office of social science to manage this type of research. Nevertheless, "even though they had to meet rigorous standards of 'objectivity, verifiability, and generality,'" a great many scientists opposed including the social sciences in the NSF scheme. One board member commented in 1958: ". . . we have to face up to the fact that the social sciences—except for a few extremely limited areas—are a source of trouble beyond anything released by Pandora" (National Science Foundation 1994).

And so on the one hand, we can see the relatively weak position of the social sciences here, especially in relation to the natural sciences. The social sciences in the late 1940s and 1950s were looked at skeptically by the increasingly assertive community of natural scientists (Bush 1945). Many government policy makers, especially Republicans, also saw them as politically tainted due to the involvement of social scientists in the administration of Franklin D. Roosevelt, in the implementation of the New Deal, and in the association of "sociology" with reformism and even "socialism" in the 1900s and 1910s. Social scientists responded to these challenges by internalizing their subordinate position in relation to the natural sciences and adopting a scientistic attitude that aped the phenomenology and methodology of the natural sciences. From this angle, it is hard to argue that sociology (along with psychology, anthropology, and political science) had attained any type of intellectually commanding position in the post-war era. However, the situation looks different if seen from a more historical perspective (Solovey, M & Jefferson Pooley 2011). Compare, after all, the sort of sociology we discussed in chapter 1 with the pretensions of the social science community by 1950. What had once been a disparate, epistemologically fractured collection of social-gospel preachers and reform-minded scientists had coalesced into a far more professionally secure and centralized discipline. Like their counterparts in physics and the other natural sciences, sociologists and anthropologists had been active at various levels and in various departments during the war. This, combined with growing institutional cohesion and a few remarkable public successes (Gallup's correct prediction of the 1936 presidential election, the best-selling status of *Middletown*, the powerful methodological statements that lay behind *The American Soldier*) created an intellectual universe in which sociology was considered by many to at least be *a* science, if not quite the "queen" (or even the prince) of the sciences.

The situation also looks different if we step back a bit from formal policy battles and official statements of intellectual purpose and consider the wider national context of the United States in the 1950s and early 1960s. Take the realm of popular fiction, for example. Two books in particular—the *Foundation Trilogy* by Isaac Asimov and *The 480* by Eugene Burdick—capture the mood of the time, and one of them (*The 480*) would be name-checked by Philip Meyer in his public discussion of the influences on *Precision Journalism*. Through this more expansive lens of popular culture, it is possible to argue that social science (and sociology in particular) had gained a level of prominence in the popular consciousness that far outstripped anything it had experienced since the glory days of the SSM prior to World War I.

In the *Foundation Trilogy* (first published as a series of short stories in *Astounding Magazine* between 1942 and 1950 and then collected in three volumes in 1951, 1952, and 1953) Isaac Asimov retells the story of the decline and fall of the Roman Empire with a "Galactic Empire" standing in for Rome and with the added twist that the empire's collapse is foreseeable by the "psychohistorian" Hari Seldon. For Seldon, the future path of the Galactic Empire can be predicted with a high degree of certainty by statistical modeling of the enormous imperial population. The essence of psychohistory is summarized in *Foundation* (the first volume in the trilogy) by the "Three Theorems of Psychohistorical Quantitivity:"

> The population under scrutiny is oblivious to the existence of the science of Psychohistory.
> The time periods dealt with are in the region of 3 generations.
> The population must be in the billions (±75 billions) for a statistical probability to have a psychohistorical validity." (Asimov 1951)

In other words, given a large enough number of people (and with the caveat that these people cannot be aware of the method through which their behavior is being analyzed), large-scale social trends can be modeled, predicted, and controlled. Seldon, armed with the knowledge that the Galactic Empire is inevitably doomed, comes to understand that the period of barbarism between the first and second empires (read: the European "dark ages") can be shortened by the establishment of a Foundation to preserve the knowledge and initiative of humankind. Most of the first volume of the *Foundation Trilogy* consists of the fledgling Foundation facing a series of tests, which it then overcomes—not necessarily because of any particular action taken on the part of the main characters but through the general working out of sociological trends. To cap individual chapters of the first volume, a hologram of the long-dead Hari Seldon appears to explain how psychohistory predicted the resolution of the crisis.

The nominal hero of *Foundation*, despite the fact that he is alive only in the first chapter of the book, is Hari Seldon, the great psychohistorian (read: social scientist). Most of the dramatic tension in the story lies in the counter-intuitive nature of the resolution of the sociological crises faced by the Foundation—the manner by which psychohistorical laws trump individual initiative or the best laid plans of the actual protagonists. The success of a novel in which the results are foreordained is itself a remarkable accomplishment (indeed, the standard crisis/resolution framework could only carry the first volume of the trilogy; with the appearance of the mutant known as The Mule the dramatic action grows more complex). To some degree, *Foundation* is a working out of what C. Wright Mills famously called the sociological imagination, the structure and the drift of society that emerges out of the nexus of human agency and social structure, with readers in awe of the manner by which structure triumphs nearly every time. Does this say anything about the social sciences in the post-war era? I think it does. Only in a world in which sociology was conceivable as a predictive, quantitative science would a series of books like the *Foundation Trilogy* make any sense, much less appeal to large numbers of readers and ultimately make science fiction history by winning a Hugo Award for the "greatest science fiction series" in 1966.

If *Foundation* fictionalized the power of social science and took place in the long-distant future, *The 480*, by University of California political scientist Eugene Burdick, fictionalized the predictive power of computers in the present day (1964). Gaining its title from the classification of the US electorate into "480 demographic groups" by political operatives and social scientists, *The 480* tells the story of a stealth presidential candidate, John Thatch, who is plucked out of obscurity by these operatives and pre-packaged as the most scientifically sensible political candidate as determined by psychologists, sociologists, and computers. Most of the interesting plot points of the novel revolve around the conflicts generated between old-school ward-heelers and cigar-smoking party bosses and the benign political operatives using quantitative political science techniques to advance their candidate. Inspired by the real-life Simulatics

Corporation headed by MIT political science professor Ithiel De Sola Pool and Columbia's William McPhee and credited by newspapers in 1960 as John F. Kennedy's "secret weapon" in his presidential victory, the "innocent and well intentioned" new political mandarins

> Work with slide rules and calculating machines and computers which can retain an almost infinite number of bits of information as well as sort, categorize, and reproduce this information at the press of a button. Most of these people are highly educated, many of them are PhDs, and none I have met have malignant designs on the American public. They may, however, radically reconstruct the American political system, build a new politics, and even modify revered and venerable American institutions—facts of which they are blissfully innocent. They are technicians and artists; all of them want, desperately, to be scientists. (Burdick 1964, vii)

The world of the dystopian 480, Burdick predicts, is not that far away; indeed, it may have already arrived. "The Simulatics Corporation is a real company," he writes. "It formulated the concept of the 480 and was employed by and gave advice to the people who directed Senator Kennedy's Presidential campaign in 1960" (ix). Between the writing of the *Foundation* in the early 1950s and *The 480* in 1964, the major change in the fictional potential of social science appears to be the emergence of computers. Hari Seldon's primary technological tool in *Foundation* is a slide rule, but as the cover of *The 480* makes, clear, the image of *the computer* now dominates the intellectual landscape of analysis and prediction.

Unlike Burdick's previous books *The Ugly American* and *Fail Safe* (the latter made into a 1964 film by Sidney Lumet with Harry Fonda in the lead role), *The 480* disappeared without leaving a much of a mark on the popular imagination. In her discussion of the emerging science of political "big data," Jill Lepore calls *The 480* "vintage Cold War: the Strangelovian fear of the machine" (Lepore 2015) and notes accurately that the politics of data were something of a dead letter in the Democratic Party until the rise of Howard Dean and Barack Obama in the early 2000s (see also Kreiss 2012; 2016). One attentive reader of *The 480*, however, was Philip Meyer. Indeed, the book occupies a central position in Meyer's narrative description of how he first became interested in the relationship between computers, social science, and journalism:

> The basis for my application to the Nieman Foundation was that politicians are using computers to study public opinion and to make predictions about voting behavior and tailoring their campaigns to fit what those models told them. I found out about that from reading a work

of dystopian fiction by Eugene Burdick who was a political scientist who wrote novels. It was called *The 480* and it was based on a real story because a political scientist named Ithiel De Sola Pool used such a model, used a public opinion model, for advising John F. Kennedy on his campaign in 1960 . . . . And so I thought it was really important that a newspaper reporter understand this because I covered politics.

In the years to come, Phillip Meyer would often be identified as the "inventor" of a social-science-inflected journalism and the grandfather of CAR, a story that begins with Meyer's acceptance into the Neiman Fellowship Program at Harvard University. The designation of Meyer as CAR's "inventor" is not untrue, but it is important to remember that Meyer's work occurred within the larger context we have just described—a world in which sociology was both coming into its own and resentful of its subordinate status vis a vis the natural sciences, a world in which a future-predicting, big-data psychohistorian could be the hero of a best-selling science fiction series and the specter of a data-crunching computer could serve as the dystopian genesis for a political thriller. Meyer sought to increase journalistic claims to factual certainty, and reduce the uncertainty of social life, by mobilizing the techniques of social science on journalism's behalf.

Sociology, Political Science, and the Professions in the 1960s

I have already discussed the pioneering role played by the RSF in funding the social survey—as an empirical evidence-gathering technique and a media event—in the later decades of the Progressive Era (chapter 2). In chronicling the origins of data journalism, we now encounter the RSF again, this time in the context of its work to increase the visibility and role of the social sciences in formulating public policy responses to social problems. In a shift away from its earlier concerns with directly solving problems like poverty, medical care, and prison conditions, the post-war foundation devoted more energy to fostering the social sciences *themselves*, seeing a better a social science as one of the keys to addressing urban problems in a more general sense. To this end, the RSF developed what it called the "Social Sciences in the Professions" program whose goal was to increase the understanding and use of behavioral science in professional domains such as medicine, social work, and the law. Medical policy workers, for example, would be well served if they were more familiar with the latest behavioral science techniques and research strategies surrounding issues of health, wellness, and poverty, as would lawyers and social workers.

On May 23, 1965, an internal RSF memo was drafted in response to an earlier proposal from the Columbia University Graduate School of Journalism titled "Proposal for a Training and Research Program in Social Science and the Mass Media." The RSF would be well served by developing a meaningful program in social science and the mass media to accompany their existing professional program work in law, medicine, and social work, the internal memo began. It could begin to develop such a program by working more closely with journalism programs at schools such as Columbia and the University of Wisconsin-Madison (UW-Madison) along the lines suggested by an earlier Columbia grant proposal. The goal of this social science and mass media program would be to better communicate social science ideas and findings in journalistic news reports. If partnerships with such schools were to make sense, the memo notes, any such program should have several components: one talented journalism school faculty member who could dedicate themselves full-time to the program, two social scientists with a similar level of commitment, RSF fellowships for students participating in the program, and research funds to study the program's success and failures. Most importantly for our story here is the final plank of the proposed program: "the preparation of manuscripts for Russell Sage Foundation publication that deal with the problem of communicating social science materials in the mass media" (Sociology in the Professions Project, March 23, 1965). As we will see, it is this aspect of the program that led directly to the writing of *Precision Journalism*.

In their comprehensive history of the RSF up through the 1970s, David Hammack and Stanton Wheeler summarize the difficulties encountered by the Social Science and the Mass Media program. "Journalism and the mass media proved more difficult to infiltrate and influence than had been the case for medicine, social work, and the law, and the Foundation was never confident it had made a really significant impact in the form of improved use of social science findings by the media" (Hammack and Wheeler 1994, 121). But, they add "it was certainly not for want to trying." Indeed, my own archival research bears out this conclusion: in reviewing program documents I encountered a number of disparate efforts on the part of the foundation to influence journalism and improve its understanding of social and behavioral science as part of larger sociology in the professions initiatives. The majority of these efforts were based in and around the journalism schools at Columbia and UW-Madison, following an earlier logic applied to law and medicine that the easiest leverage point for professional change lay in schools of professional training. As a starting point, both UW-Madison and Columbia received RSF funds in order to launch mid-career student programs designed explicitly to train students in understanding and reporting on the social sciences.

Comparing the relationship between journalists and social scientists to the state of mutual incomprehension that existed between humanists and natural scientists (and referencing the seminal work of Charles Snow in his *Two Cultures*), UW-Madison argued for the development of "specialist reporters trained in the substance of the social sciences and techniques of the skilled communicator . . . . Essentially, the work of the social scientist must be understood and communicated so that it can be used in day-to-day decisions by leaders in society as well as by the general public" (University of Wisconsin School of Journalism to Russell Sage Foundation). Pointing to similar areas of mutual incomprehension, Columbia University put together a successful grant proposal that called for "(1) fellowships for mid-career training in the social sciences for superior journalists; (2) research and field-work in social science reporting; (3) a seminar on concept formation and research methods in public communication; and (4) a joint Foundation-School conference on behavioral sciences and mass media" (Columbia University Graduate School of Journalism to the Russell Sage Foundation).

On April 1–3 1966, the Arlen House in upstate New York hosted the RSF/Columbia conference on journalism and behavioral science; in attendance were such scholars as Leo Bogart and journalists as Ben Bagdikian, as well as a host of figures whose names are less familiar to journalism scholars, including the key figure W. Philips Davison, who had been working at the journalism school as the social science expert guiding the RSF program. Topics included "Public and Mass Media Uses of the Behavioral Sciences," "Journalists and Behavioral Scientists," and "Prospects: Training Journalists in the Behavioral Sciences." In the 1980s, Davison would go on to coin the key communications term "third person affect," a social-psychological theory that argued that people tend to think the mass media has a greater impact on others than themselves. But in the mid-1960s, his was a joint appointment at the Columbia schools of sociology and journalism where he worked hard to corral an unwieldy mix of mutually suspicious social scientists and journalists into a productive working team.

Key to the Columbia and UW-Madison grants, but also emblematic of the larger difficulties in the social sciences and media program, were the student fellowships for "mid-career journalists of talent with an interest in the social sciences." Although the UW-Madison program lasted longer and was buttressed by the journalism school's placement in the social science division of the university, both Columbia and the RSF had trouble finding the proper mix of journalism students who possessed an interest and ability in social science. One major problem was simply an inability to find enough interested applicants; Columbia was unable to fill its class ranks in the first targeted year of 1965–1966, though administrators chalked that failure up to the newness of the program. A second difficulty lay in the fact that the many of the fellows who had been accepted were unable to find appropriate publication venues for their social-science-oriented work. Perhaps the third and most severe difficulty lay in the inability of many students to grasp the quantitative methods that working sociologists like Davison considered essential for any true immersion in social science practice. As the relatively upbeat interim report on the fellowship program for the 1966–1967 fellowship year admitted:

> A third problem area involved the use of statistics and computers in the social sciences. It became apparent in the Spring term of 1967 that none of the Fellows felt comfortable when confronted by quantitative data, and that too little attention had been given the use of quantitative methods. We do not feel that Fellows should be required to take courses in statistics or computer methods—although these will always be open to the interested—but we will increase the attention given to quantitative data with the aim of insuring that Fellows are at least able to read and criticize tables and that they are aware of the principal ways in which social scientists use statistics and computers. (Report on the Russell Sage Program in Journalism)

As opposed to statistics and quantitative methodologies, the fellows *did* display a great deal of interest in "social theory . . . and during some periods they gave almost exclusive attention to reading in this field. Indeed, the Program Coordinator became concerned that they might be devoting undue time to their course work" (Report on the Russell Sage Program in Journalism). In other words, even the students who displayed the most natural interest and aptitude for social science work preferred a humanities-oriented course of study ("social theory" and "reading") to a sociological or behavioralist one (statistics and computers).

We don't have direct written evidence as to *why* the fellows program was terminated at Columbia after only three years; what we do know is that there was obvious dissatisfaction at both Columbia and UW-Madison over the status of these mid-career fellowships. At Columbia, a much smaller grant in 1967, of $30,000, attempted to carry forward the larger goals of the program, but without the fellowships. Given that *every* journalist should be aware of the social sciences, Columbia rationalized, it made more sense to spread a general understanding of these issues and techniques throughout the school. At both UW-Madison and Columbia, later investments were made in journalistic organizations outside of the university, in the form of grants to write articles that highlighted behavioralist research (in 1968), sponsoring a Nieman Fellow in the social sciences (in 1970), and fostering a newspaper internship program (in 1971). The direct relationship between the RSF and the two universities ended in the early 1970s, at least in part because of arrival of a new dean at Wisconsin, but clearly also due to a general dissatisfaction with the results the program had achieved.

One additional aspect of the RSF Social Science and the Media initiative is worthy of brief comment due to the additional light it sheds on the attitudes of journalists and social scientists toward each other in the mid-1960s. A major piece of research emerged from joint Columbia-RSF, "Communication of Social Science Information Through Mass Media," consisting of a multi-method analysis of the ways in which social science research and findings were reported by newspapers. Almost entirely forgotten today, this report actually anticipates a good deal of the journalism research conducted by sociologists in the late 1960s and early 1970s, research I have discussed in chapter 3. For my purposes here, the findings of the study are less important than the reaction of several RSF program officers to an early draft of one section of the report, which was forwarded by W. Phillips Davidson of Columbia University to foundation president Orville Brim. Davidson is enthusiastic about what amounts to a three-week content analysis of social science reporting in the *New York Times*. "The reason I thought you might like to see this paper," he wrote, "is that it suggests advantages in combining journalistic and social scientific approaches to the study of newspaper content. A social scientist would have approached the problem quite differently, and would probably have done a number of things that didn't occur to Grace [the student researcher and co-author]. On the other hand, I doubt whether a social scientist would have . . . [for instance] included relationships to domestic and international news among his categories of analysis" (W. Phillips Davidson to Orville Brim May 15, 1967).

Others, however, were less than impressed. Magazine editor and outside reviewer John Lear admits that while "I don't yet understand Foundation operations well enough to be sure just what may be meaningful criticism [of the mass media program] . . . the need for a strong approach to mass media is being underestimated in several aspects of the Russell Sage procedure . . . I don't think Phil should have passed along Grace Bennett's 'study' of the *New York Times*. He should have instead turned it back to her and told her to tighten it up : . . as a journalist she has just as much responsibility to be precise as does a scientist. We are never going to establish a really effective relationship between the press and social scientists until the equality of the responsibility of the two sides is accepted." Note the rather condescending use of quotes ("study") as well as the reference to Bennett as a journalist who must take responsibility for journalism's inability to understand behavioral research accurately. Other comments similar to this are scattered throughout the RSF archives in memos that consider the success and impact of the project.

These tensions—whether journalists ought to take the "social science point of view" in considering the role of the media in modern society; the degree to which journalists ought themselves be able to master basic social science concepts (especially quantitative research) in order to better understand what research meant; and the question of whether there could ever be a publishing home for journalistic reporting that tackled larger social-scientific issues—would dog the RSF Mass Media and Social Science program over the course of its existence. What was rarely, if ever, questioned, however, was that the goal of the initiative was to foster better reporting on social and behavioral science issues by the members of the press. If the press better understood what social science was and how it worked, the theory went, then the press would have a better understanding of how important it was and would convey more of its perspective in a more positive manner. In some ways, this attitude is similar to the one adopted by the social surveyors in the Progressive Era; the line between empirical accuracy and good public relations is blurred. However, there was little expectation that journalists *themselves* would become social scientists. Even for the members of the experimental group of Columbia University journalism fellows, the idea was always that they would work primarily as traditional journalists, with an undergirding of sociological and political understanding that could be called upon when needed. The failure of that program certainly did not convince the RSF that it ought to expect *more* of reporters. It is this very question—the degree to which journalists ought to re-embrace social scientific processes that had largely left them behind since the earliest days of the sociological profession—that would animate Philip Meyer's time at the RSF. And it is a dissenting perspective that would—while initially creating difficulties in finding a publisher for *Precision Journalism*—eventually push the relationship between journalism and quantitative evidence into unexplored professional territory.

Phillip Meyer, *Precision Journalism*, and Rethinking Objectivity

FROM KANSAS TO HARVARD[1]

Phillip Meyer occupies an outsized role in our account of the history of quantitative news, and has frequently written about himself (his memoir, *Paper Route*, was published in 2012) and the origins of precision journalism. For that reason, a brief introductory sketch of his life may be helpful in orienting the reader. Born in 1930 in Deshler, Nebraska, Meyer began his journalism career with a neighborhood paper route and then worked for both his high school newspaper and yearbook. Drawn to the journalism school at the University of Missouri, the expense of out-of-state tuition led him to Kansas State University, which he entered as a freshman in 1948. His first formal newspaper job was at the *Topeka Daily Capital*, while still in college; he worked there again following some quasi-journalistic work with the US Navy during the Korean War. A crucial juncture in his career came when he enrolled as a masters student of political science at the University of North Carolina-Chapel Hill (UNC) in 1956, writing his master's thesis on the controversy over the building of the Tuttle Creek Dam with data drawn from his reporting while an editor at the *Daily Capital*. A job at the *Miami Herald* followed graduation, this reporting stint interrupted by a second return to academia, as a Nieman Fellow in 1966–1967. It was as a Nieman Fellow that the formal outline of a program to combine social-science methods with news reporting took shape, inspired, as I have already noted, by the growing use of computer technologies in national politics. Meyer first applied the lessons of the precision journalism technique in Detroit following the urban riots of 1968, in a series of stories that won the paper a Pulitzer Prize and led directly to the offer of a RSF fellowship in 1969–1970, during which *Precision Journalism* was written. Published by Indiana University in 1973, this book has gone through four editions and is widely considered as having jump-started the CAR and data journalism movements in the United States and around the world.

Recounted as a capsule summary, the story of Phillip Meyer's career follows the standard "inventor" life arc: a combination of personal experience and a flash of insight fuels an innovative idea that is demonstrated to have succeeded in practice. Despite this, or perhaps because of it, the original innovation—sitting so far outside the box—is initially rejected by all but the hardy few. This rejection, however, is eventually followed a larger-scale triumph as society catches up to the initial idea. Each of the bullet points in the history just described, however, contains a welter of contradictions and ironies. The invention and adoption of precision journalism was far from pre-ordained, and a closer examination of the tangled and complex processes at work over the course of its history can reveal a great deal about quantitative journalism writ large.

A key moment in Meyer's life history, and one that seems relevant to the development of precision journalism writ large, was his decision to obtain a master's degree in political science from UNC in 1956. Such a decision, while increasingly common among journalists today, was still unusual in the 1950s. By 1978, only one third of the news correspondents working in Washington, DC, had advanced degrees (Hess 1981), and we should assume that Meyer was part of the earliest wave of this advancing professionalization if not an outright leader. Interestingly, Meyer's political science experience at UNC also taught him the value of behavioralist research *as seen through the eyes of an embattled intellectual minority*. The political science professors there were primarily institutional historians, concerned with understanding US politics by charting the history of the major governmental branches and bureaucracies; the notion of political science as a predictive, statistical science concerned with articulating general patterns of political behavior (such as voting) had not yet taken root (Meyer, January

16, 2016 interview). "The number crunching political scientists were a rag-tag minority on the faculty as well as among the graduate students," Meyer writes. "Some of [these graduate students] called attempts to measure political behavior 'the new scholasticism.'" Indeed, Meyer did not really begin to see the value of statistical work in graduate school, noting that he found it easier to dismiss quantitative research than master it. "I figured a qualitative understanding of political institutions would serve me well in an election year" (Meyer 2012a, 168–169).

The fact that behavioral research was disrespected within the broader field of political science in the 1950s helped foster an attitude of innovative insurgency among its early practitioners. We are used to seeing the field of political science (and social science more broadly) through the lens of its current behaviorist, experimental, and statistical paradigm, and we often forget that an entirely different consensus about what research into politics should consist of held methodological sway in a previous era (Karpf et al. 2015). In short, Meyer came of intellectual age at a time when behavioralists and statisticians were an insurgent minority—a vanguard that was at the bottom of the political science pecking order but was clearly on its way up. Such attitudes would also color his view of CAR in his profession of journalism.

In Meyer's discussion of his own career, certain news stories stand in for what philosopher of science Thomas Kuhn might recognize as paradigmatic reporting projects, with the 1967 Detroit Riots story occupying a central position. Certain other stories, including the Miami school insurance story that won an American Political Science Association (APSA) public affairs reporting award in 1959, also shed light on the development of precision journalism, particularly its focus on "pattern recognition" and a predilection toward "documentary evidence"—two qualities that Meyer regards as essential to conducting meaningful investigative reporting. The Miami story was about the awarding of building fire and hurricane insurance contracts in the Miami School District, a process that seemed irregular to both Meyer and Louise Blanchard, the education reporter for the rival *Miami News*. It seemed clear that the contracts were being awarded on a no-bid basis, but beyond this basic fact, malfeasance was hard to prove. Whereas Blanchard attempted to find a human source to tell her that the insurance system was rigged, "of course, no one who was involved would do that," Meyer recalls. "The puzzle had to be assembled one piece at a time *and the story would be in the pattern, not the pieces*" (Meyer 2012a, 194). As Meyer investigated this story, he relied primarily on data he gathered about other insurance costs and competitive bid systems in Miami (the "control group") and records of campaign contributions to school board members obtained through Florida's open records laws. To compare campaign donations and insurance contracts, Meyer created index cards with details on individual insurance officers and agents, which he sorted, by hand, to show correlations between insurance companies and board officials. As Meyer notes, such sorting and tabulation are key functions of a modern computer, and if he had been writing the story ten years later he would have used one.

The Miami school district insurance story demonstrates certain attitudes toward evidence and "what counts" as a news story, attitudes that precede the development of computers and even precede the application of social science methodologies to journalistic problems. In seeking to construct an investigative news report based on patterns rather than pieces, Meyer avoids interview-based evidence gathering up until the moment his story is almost complete, drawing instead on public records and documents—that is, paper forms of evidence. Rather than an unambiguous, direct revelation of malfeasance through verbal means, Meyer adopts a social science mindset, looking for patterns in documents, control groups, and institutional behavior (i.e., campaign contributions) that can be documented by correlating data in records and files. Part of this focus on the materiality of patterned evidence may indeed be common to investigative reporting as a whole, whether it calls itself precision journalism or something else.

A news story based primarily on documents and social patterns need not be data or precision journalism, then, although there are important resonances between the two forms of journalistic work that I will explore more in chapter 5. But the APSA public service journalism award also facilitated a week-long seminar with other winners at which Meyer began to lose his fear of hard-edged quantitative social science. Warren Miller from the Survey Research Center at the University of Michigan gave a memorable talk that forever clarified the notion of a probability sample, and Howard Penniman of Georgetown University encouraged Meyer to apply for a Congressional fellowship designed for hybrid journalist-scholars. Also at the seminar was Neal Copple, who mounted a technological and ecosystemic argument that newspapers—under pressure from the immediacy provided by radio and especially television—should embrace a new, "more sophisticated" form of news reporting. Because they could never scoop television, Copple argued, newspapers should focus on providing analysis that illuminated social and political patterns and trends (Meyer 2012b, 204–206).

In recounting Meyer's career, it becomes clear that much of his path was shaped by the personal connections he established while pursuing a range of academic interests that were broader than those of your average post-war newspaper reporter. John W. Reynolds, one of Meyer's earliest professors at Kansas State, assured him that he could get him a teaching assistantship at UNC to fund his master's degree in political science. Old and new connections were further solidified during the APSA seminar. It is not that members of his network "made" Meyer's career or "created" his interest in social science journalism; rather, an already-established interest in the more scientific aspects of journalistic work must have obviously seemed compelling to other, more established scholars working at the boundary between sociology, political science, journalism, and public policy. This interplay between personal interests and personal connections holds true for Meyer's application for the 1966–1967 Harvard Nieman Fellowship. A former supervisor of Meyer's in Washington, DC, Ed Lahey, had been one of the inaugural Nieman fellows in 1938–1939. Meyer had himself temporarily been correspondent for the District of Columbia Knight Ridder newspaper, also on Nieman Fellowship leave in 1961–1962. It is clear that a bridgehead between Harvard and the small Knight Ridder Washington, DC, office had already been established, perhaps in part because Lahey was a graduate of Harvard.

If Meyer's general interests resembled those of other journalist-scholars, though, his application to the Nieman Fellowship program was utterly unique. Established in 1938 following a $1.4 million bequest from Agnes Wahl Nieman, widow of Lucius W. Nieman, the foundation's goal was to "promote and elevate the standards of journalism in the United States and educate persons deemed specially qualified for journalism" through fellowships for a select group of working journalists that would allow them to spend a year at Harvard to expand their intellectual interests in any way they saw fit—formulating projects, attending the full range of Harvard classes, and bonding with current and former fellows. In the introduction to this chapter I described how Meyer framed his Harvard research interests in relationship to the computers described in popular culture (*The 480*). Political behavior was increasingly subject to statistical analysis and predictive decision-making, and these techniques were mediated by computers and used by politicians hoping to gain electoral advantage. In trying to cover these advances, Meyer acutely felt the "educational gaps" in his own experience and alludes to them in his application:

> My limited information [on the subject of data and computers] comes mostly from half-remembered conversations at Chapel Hill a decade ago. At that time, I didn't think it was important. Now, however, I think it is necessary for a reporter who covers national government and politics to understand what is happening in this developing branch of political science.
>
> There are two basic reasons for this view. One is the obvious need to understand and keep up with the substantive findings now being made in the area of voting behavior . . . I don't suggest that reporters should necessarily imitate social scientists, but I do think they should know what they are doing and be able to interpret their findings for the public. We should also know something about their methodology. Total reliance on intuitive analysis in political reporting was adequate

when politicians operated the same way. But increasingly they do not. Therein lies the second reason for studying this field. There is a big and mostly unreported story—because nobody understands it—in the use of behavioral science methods by political candidates and political parties. (Meyer, Personal Archive)

Meyer learned much at Harvard, both in terms of his basic quantitative science skills and the personal connections he made. On Friday evenings there were dinners with guests from outside Harvard, including academic communicatrions researchers James Bryant Conant and Leo Bogart. It quickly became clear to Meyer that he was unprepared for a graduate-level course in quantitative methods and so he enrolled instead in an undergraduate methods course. In addition to providing an overview of social science methods, the course also provided an introduction to DATA-TEXT, a machine-language computer programming code designed for the IBM 7090. It was through working with this computer that a number of fundamental quantitative social science concepts became clear to Meyer, leading to this fundamental insight: "Journalists and scientists, I realized, were basically in the same business, discovering and imparting the truth. Now I saw how statistical tools could dredge meaning from large bodies of data, and I grew confident that I could learn to collect and organize such bodies of data on my own . . . Harvard's DATA-TEXT software instantly made computers accessible to people like me" (Meyer 2012b, 246). It was through learning how a simple computer could simplify the calculation of social scientific information that paradoxically led Myer to take on the challenge of learning chi-square processes by hand. If the drudgery were eliminated, he concluded, then the intellectual effort of the work itself was no great challenge.

The Harvard experience, and his exposure to computers there, led to an important and fundamental shift in Meyer's thinking. No longer should journalists simply be aware of behavioralist research in order to better report on sociological and political research, or to understand how politicians were using these techniques for their own gain. Rather, journalists themselves—some of them anyway—could report the news as if they were social scientists themselves.. This would bridge the gap that had opened between journalism and sociology discussed in chapter 3, but on social science's own terms. And it would bring journalism closer to understanding the truth. The very real professional radicalism of this position is only apparent when we turn to a discussion of Meyer's time at the RSF a few years later. Here we will see that not everyone thought the gap between journalism and science could be closed so easily—or that it even ought to be. A great many reporters and editors doubted that journalism could ever claim to possess certain knowledge about the social world—they worked too quickly, were too ignorant, and were too in the thrall with their sources to be factual in the manner of the social scientist. It was this view that Meyer wanted to challenge on behalf of a newly emboldened profession of journalism.

MEYER, RSF, AND THE TRAVAILS OF *PRECISION JOURNALISM*

After pioneering the use of social science techniques in his reporting on the 1967 Detroit Riots, and after coordinating a series in the *Miami Herald* looking at how African-American attitudes were changing the aftermath of the assassination of Martin Luther King Jr., Meyer was solicited for a number of engagements that would draw him closer to academia. The American Association of Public Opinion Research (AAPOR) invited him to a plenary panel with Burns Roper and Leo Bogart to discuss polling and new reporting, and the RSF, headed at the time by Orville Brim, approached Meyer to sound out areas of common interest. As Meyer had already decided to write a book detailing the different ways social science techniques could be applied to news reporting, the possibility of a writing fellowship at RSF in 1969–1970 seemed fortuitous. A stipend and office would be provided to writing fellows, and RSF would have the right of first refusal on any manuscript that emerged at the end of the year-long fellowship. "The book," Meyer wrote in his application to RSF, "would be addressed to the working journalist. It would attempt to show him [*sic*] how existing social science research methods can be applied to correct for some of the shortcomings of traditional newspaper reporting methods. It would also enhance the reporter's ability to appreciate and report on the application of social sciences to public policy" (Philip Meyer to Russell Sage Foundation). Given the foundation's interests in drawing the professions and the social sciences more closely together, and given the work they had already initiated in the Mass Media and Social Science program, the match seemed like a good one. Meyer began his New York fellowship in July 1969, commuting there from Washington, DC, several days a week and completing his writing in the summer of 1970.

It is interesting to observe the changes between the initial draft proposed by Meyer in 1969 and the book that eventually became *Precision Journalism* as published in 1973. All of Part II of the original manuscript, "The Use of Social Science by Policy Makers," seems to have more or less been excised by the time we get to the published version, with more practical analyses of government behavioral science research ("Measuring the War on Poverty," "Finding What Works in Education," "Manipulating the Voter") dropped from the final draft. Part III, "Adapting Social Science Methods to Journalism," ended up being the heart of the 1973 edition, with practical examples and guidelines for how working journalists might put the book to use. Most interestingly, perhaps, the manuscript devotes far more space to the programmatic exploration of the philosophical overlaps between the journalistic and social scientific methods, with two early chapters entitled "The Journalistic Tradition," and "The Scientific Tradition." The published version of *Precision Journalism* opens with a long justification of its utility in a chapter titled "The Need for New Tools." Although I will turn to a more detailed analysis of this first chapter and its metamorphosis in the next chapter of this book, I do think that we can see the aggressive justification for the book's practical utility as a direct response to external reviews of the RSF manuscript in 1971 and 1972. To put it bluntly, these reviews were not positive. Some were downright hostile.

The opening blow came from RSF itself, which solicited Paul Lancaster, the front-page editor of the *Wall Street Journal*, to review the book. While admitting that "flashes of enlightenment are scattered throughout the book," his four-page review is quite negative. The insights the book does contain, Lancaster argues, are interspersed with highly technical sections that could have been relegated to an appendix or left out altogether. The book simply contains too much detail to be useful to either the working journalist or the editor who will be the one who "makes the decisions about how to use money and people" (Paul Lancaster to the Russell Sage Foundation; see also Meyer 2012b). In a telling passage Lancaster notes, "for some reason, the discussion of counter-sorters bothered me in particular.[2] Surely, most of the people who would read this book would hire people to run their counter-sorters" (Meyer 2012b). Lancaster makes similar criticisms throughout his review, wondering how the division of labor implied in the manuscript will play out in real life, complaining about too much detail on technical operations that most people will find boring, and suggesting that few newsroom reporters would care about these techniques.

Most fundamentally, Lancaster seems uncertain about who the book's audience is and argues that this failing is the fault of the manuscript itself. His review opens with this question: "you ask if I think the book on computer research merits publication. My principal response is a question: for whom are you writing it?" There is, in essence, no audience for the book. Social scientists will find the techniques described in it to be laughably simple; as for reporters themselves, "I strongly doubt that a reporter or editor would feel competent to handle any of the procedures described even after the closest of readings" (2). In his cover letter, Lancaster is even blunter, writing that "journalists are notoriously unscientific—and maybe lazy too—and there's still a lot of resistance to the painstaking methods Phil advocates" (1). If social scientists would find the book too basic, and reporters will find it overwhelming and incomprehensible, then the only remaining audience is that of newsroom managers—the ones who spend the money, as we noted before. But for this audience, the book is also too technical and, quite frankly, boring; it contains too much about dull methods and does not make a persuasive case that a more social scientific journalism is necessary.

Precision Journalism is fundamentally a solution in search of a problem—and a dull solution at that.

Brim's reply to Lancaster is succinct and implies that he found similar problems with the manuscript: "too technical for some and too thin for others," as he puts it. The review process—which began in October 1970—dragged on until late April 1971, at which point Brim notified Meyer that RSF was going to pass on publication. Meyer must have known something was amiss as the review time period went on, and he began to cast about for other publishers. The reply from Praeger (in June) is interesting insofar as the reporter solicited to comment on the book echoed many of Lancaster's earlier comments. "He is addressing an insider audience of journalists and social scientists," journalist Bill Wetherby writes, and "like many former reporters he is overly impressed with the academic world, and seems to be sold on the idea that reporters should become poor men's social scientists." The Praeger review proceeds to mount a general case against the notion of academic journalism, contending that good journalism requires an "experience of many levels of life—a healthy sophistication and cynicism— . . . and is not provided merely by some college training." Harvard University Press also doubted there was much of an audience for the book. "Despite your best efforts, the book is hard going in places; it needs to be studied, I think, not just read rapidly through for enjoyment." And "how many newspapermen would buy it?" they wonder, echoing earlier concerns. "I can't summon much optimism about that."

Meyer sums up his efforts to find a publisher in an October 1971 letter to Hugh Cline of RSF. He lists the number of publishers who have declined the manuscript because of their concerns about market viability and whether enough journalists would be interested in (or even capable of) learning the lessons promised by the volume. Meyer does note, parenthetically, that Indiana University Press had expressed some interest, but concludes with the thought that "it seems clearly non-viable if I stick to the original intent of a handbook for journalists. Any suggestions will be appreciated" (Philip Meyer to Hugh Cline).

The Limits of Data-Driven Journalism in the Early 1970s

Obviously, selling *Precision Journalism* was hard going, though it is not unusual for a book to get multiple rejection letters before it finds a publishing home. It seems clear that RSF itself would have been the ideal publishing choice—the book was written with a specialized audience in mind from the perch of a foundation working to interject a better understanding of the social sciences into the professions writ large. Why, then, did RSF ultimately pass, and why did attempts to sell book to other publishers encounter such a forbidding climate?

It is hard to avoid the conclusion that Meyer fundamentally misunderstood the larger goals of the RSF Social Science and the Media program, particularly after the discontinuation of the journalism school fellowship program. The RSF's goals for journalism always had a dual character, as I noted in the opening sections of this chapter. One the one hand, they wanted journalists to better understand social science practices so they could better report on social science findings. On the other, they simply wanted social science to be better represented in media debates over public policy. This tension—between good public relations and the accurate conveyance of objective facts—is not a new one; indeed, we saw something like it play out in the activity of the MRFM in the 1910s. Better coverage of social science findings does *not* inherently require, however, journalists who conduct reporting as if they themselves are social scientists. Indeed, the limited success of the fellowship positions at Columbia and the UW-Madison drove this point home clearly. The number of journalists who could carry out this type of work would seem to be rare. The fact that nearly all the reviews of *Precision Journalism* emphasized this point, and tied it to the limited market that existed for the book, must have convinced Brim that the plan to shift gears at the RSF was the right decision. Lancaster's point in his review about the incompatibility of the journalist and social science methods summarizes the general take well: "journalists are notoriously unscientific—and maybe lazy too—and there's still a lot of resistance to the painstaking methods Phil advocates." This was a rather damning indictment of the entire premise of precision journalism, and in part a playing out of the professional boundary work that had guided journalism and social science since the late 1920s (see chapter 3).

We can see the that the boundary between journalism and social science remained as contested as ever when we examine some of the reviews and post-mortems that accompanied the winding down of the RSF program, post-mortems which shed further light on the difficulties encountered by Meyer in finding a publisher for *Precision Journalism*. Like many foundations, both in the 1970s and today, RSF was looking to capture some final, broader wisdom about the successes and failures of its series of grants in order to guide future decision making. The most interesting analysis of this kind is the overview entitled "Scribes, Scholars, and Scientists" written in the early 1970s by Steven E. Chaffee.[3] In reviewing the RSF Social Science Reporting Program, Chaffee does acknowledge that "there are many reasons why the journalist *should* feel at home with social science." Prime among these is the fact that many journalists majored in political science and sociology and that, moreover, a "reporter frequently employs the techniques of the social scientist. The interview, that indispensable tool of journalism, has been refined mostly by social survey researchers. Data from public opinion polls, are reported as news, and some large publications have their own scientific pollsters" (Steven E. Chafee to the Russell Sage Foundation). Despite all this, however, the borders and boundaries between journalism and social science are wide and difficult to cross. It is hard to avoid the condescension toward journalism that literally drips from the Chaffee letter. Journalism may (may!) be a profession, but if it is one, it is a newer one and one without a proper home in the academy. Unlike other new or quasi-professions (business, social work), journalism does not always even value a "sheepskin" diploma. For about fifty years, most journalism research was carried out after the fashion of the humanities, with legal scholars discussing the limits of libel law and historians composing (usually hagiographic) accounts of the great newspaper owners of the past. Journalism, in short, has much about it that is commendable, but it is not particularly well known for its academic rigor.

By the mid twentieth century, to the degree there is an "academic" component to journalism education at all, it usually consists of social science research being conducted in schools of mass communication by so-called communicologists. Most of this research is carried out independently of the news industry, and to the degree that its findings have a bearing on journalism at all (such as the two-step flow), journalism often does not pay attention. Chaffee argues that there are three primary reasons why attempts to fuse journalism and social science have not been very successful. The first has to do with different attitudes toward "theory." "The social scientist is guided primarily by theory rather than concrete fact . . . thus, the scientist may spend more time thinking up theories rather than checking them out, and he is less likely to be able to explain what he thinks he knows than how he hopes to know it" (Steven E. Chafee to the Russell Sage Foundation).

The second difference lies in what Chafee calls a difference between "extensive" and "intensive . . . attempts to tease out the complex causes of a particular event," or differences in what we might recognize as a difference between a concern with "events" and with "patterns." A journalist might be interested in why a particular newspaper closed (particularly if he worked for that paper himself); a social scientist would care more to discover the causes of why newspapers close *in general* and would indeed *ignore* the closing of individual newspapers if they were outliers to the general pattern. This relative disinterest in the individual (event or cause) is particular unappealing to journalists Chafee argues.

The third and final disconnect between journalists and social scientists, Chafee argues, can be found in their different attitudes toward "basic" and "applied" research. Given the choice, the scientist would almost always prefer to be working on basic research. What's more, generating the kind of research that is "practically useful" to individual newspapers is the kind of work for which the scientist would almost certainly insist on being paid. "The scientist recalls that such aids to medicine as penicillin or X-Rays were not discovered by 'applied' medical research but people in other, basic scientific fields." The journalist, on the other hand, is consumed with immediate and practical problems. To the degree he or she cares about knowledge at all it is usually knowledge of the practical kind, the kind that will allow a reporter to complete a story or gain insight into a particular and concrete situation.

> The newspaper, one of the largest manufacturing industries in the nation, spends little on journalism education and next to nothing on basic research. In spite of this failure of those who would call the tune to pay the piper, a fair amount of research is contributed gratis by journalism professors. No other profession is so fortunate, but the research effort is spasmodic and fragmented because it is conducted in spare time. The results have been less than revolutionary. (Chafee to the Russell Sage Foundation)

James Byrne, a RSF fellow from 1967–1968, was solicited to respond to Chafee's critique and takes an interesting approach. He admits that there has been little intersection, to date, between journalism schools, journalists, social scientists, and communication researchers. But he sees little reason why journalists should adopt an ideological opposition to social science in general. Research can only assist the journalist in becoming a better reporter, and if the findings of social science contradict certain standard journalistic practices and processes, then there is no harm in changing them. Moreover, Byrne does not see that the gap between social scientists and journalists is as wide as Chafee suspects. "A reporter is in deep sympathy with the social science researcher," he writes, almost plaintively. "Both want to understand man in society and communicate their findings to a receptive audience. It is an unimaginative reporter, indeed, who chases fire trucks and does not wonder if fire protection in general can be improved" (James Byrne to the Russell Sage Foundation). This attitude—that a concern with the incident of the dramatic fire does not mean the reporter has no time to think about fire policy—is far closer to Meyer's idea of the relationship between social science and journalism than Chafee's more pessimistic outlook. For Meyer's vision of the relationship between journalists, documents, data, incidents, and patterns to have a chance of succeeding, there would have to be a lot more reporters who thought like Byrne and far fewer social scientists who were as defensive and dismissive as Chafee.

Conclusion

This chapter has discussed the various social, political, and intellectual crises that dominated the American intellectual. landscape as the 1950s faded into the

1960s and 1970s and has chronicled the different ways in which social science and journalism sought to come to terms with an era characterized by deep social and intellectual tumult. We have seen that the sociology of the 1950s was a much different animal than the sociology discussed in previous chapters. In the 1950s, sociology saw itself as a true science, equal in rigor and capability to the natural sciences (and, according to some interested observers like Talcott Parsons, surpassing them). The shifts in scientific funding after World War II, new techniques pioneered by sociologists and behaviorists (including the mass survey), formalized programs of study in universities, and a move away from a consideration of more practical public problems toward generating abstract social scientific knowledge all helped push social science in the direction of *science*. The cultural image of sociology and social science, too, had never been better, with books like Isaac Asimov's *Foundation* and Eugene Burdick's *The 480* fictionalizing a world in which quantitative behavioralists were either benevolently powerful (Asimov) or simply powerful (Burdick). When it came to explaining the importance of social science to the public however, or to demonstrating how sociological findings actually mattered in people's everyday lives, or to demonstrating the relationship between government policy and social changes, the responsibility for such activity fell increasingly on journalism. Journalism—several decades into its interpretive, explanatory turn and increasingly comfortable with using visual data to capture elements of social reality—needed to become the key interlocutor between a science of society and the understanding of ordinary people. It was a daunting task. Journalism would need to speak to the public through its deployment of certitude and its invocation of objective fact.

Against this backdrop, the RSF launched its Mass Media and the Social Sciences grant program, attempting to better integrate these new sciences with journalism. The RSF wanted better coverage of social scientific issues in the press, it wanted journalists to make better use of sociological "experts," and it wanted journalists to have a better basic understanding of how these sciences worked. The RSF provided Philip Meyer with funding and office space to write a book grappling with these issues. Perhaps to the surprise of RSF, however, Meyer pushed the argument one step further, contending that journalists could not only understand and propagandize sociology but could even make use of its techniques to improve the profession. But the foundation ultimately rejected the book it had commissioned from Meyer following a series of negative reviews that found the book's focus on journalists acting as publicly minded social scientists to be misguided or impossible to achieve, or both.

This brings me to the three brief points with which I want to conclude this chapter. First, we can see that once again important segments of journalism and social science responded to a crisis in the social and political world by *doubling down on scientific objectivity*, much as they both did in the 1910s and 1920s.

While other elements of journalism embraced an interpretive turn that empha-sized subjectivity and artistic narrative (as we will see in chapter 5), journalism did not as a whole react to crisis by abandoning objectivity. Indeed, journalists attempted to raise the stakes by which objectivity could be pursued. In an age of complex problems and dispute over the causes and consequences of social action, empiricists argued that the knowledge professions could not retreat into a zone of subjective assessment or chastened, more modest claims to knowledge. Rather, by employing new forms of evidence, new research techniques, and new technology, they could become even more objective. Faced with the political cri-sis of how late-nineteenth- and early-twentieth-century society ought to be gov-erned and how knowledge professionals ought to obtain information about that society, researchers turned to the social survey, primitive statistical assessment, infographics, survey exhibitions, and eventually, professional social science and journalism. Faced with the tumult of the 1960s and early 1970s, sociologists and political scientists turned to the variable, the large-scale statistical survey, the computer, and the regression equation. Some journalists also turned to these techniques as they attempted to respond to the tumult of the 1960s.

Second: it is interesting that in the exact moment in which sociology and political science attempted to leave their public policy concerns behind and adopt the mantle of truly independent scientific experts, countervailing trends from within journalism and small parts of the foundation world were pushing the other way. After World War I, and especially after World War II, sociology attempted to leave its public concerns behind and embrace a more scientific out-look. In the 1960s and 1970s there was pushback from both inside and outside the profession; there were moves, in other words, to reintegrate more practical, programmatic political issues into the mandate of social science. A world more like the one we have already discussed in earlier chapters—in which sociology and journalism were fused in particular ways—would of course not have *needed* to argue that journalists ought to make better use of social scientific findings. The grounds upon which this re-integration was proposed, however had changed radically. If sociology teachers in the early twentieth century could have plau-sibly argued in print that they ought to teach their students how to run a news-paper in order to be better sociologists, fringe journalists in the 1960s were now arguing that they ought to adopt more of the techniques, evidentiary practices, and research methods of psychologists, "communicologists," political scientists, and sociologists.

And the final point, or rather, a question: was a reintegration even possible on the terms demanded by mid-century social science? Obviously, this was a matter of great dispute, as witnessed by the hostility faced by Phillip Meyer in his attempts to publish *Precision Journalism*. Throughout the early 1970s, Meyer had to deal with extraordinary skepticism from a number of journalists and not a small number of social scientists that doubted that journalists were capable of or interested in mastering the basic tenets of behavioral and sociological research. Such journalism, they feared, would be neither journalism *nor* sociology; it would be too simple for the sociologists and too complicated for the journalists.

Obviously, *Precision Journalism* **was** published—and was not only published but has now gone through four editions. It is the book that made Meyer's career. It is also widely acknowledged as the founding text of the CAR and data journalism movements. Data journalism itself has gone on to be a widely practiced reportorial form, complete with its own awards, conferences, and newsroom teams. How did this change occur? What does this transformation in the meaning of precision journalism tell us about the new roles played by documents, data, and other quantitative objects in the practice of reporting the news? It is important to remember that Meyer himself did not always focus on the ability of journalists to act like social scientists. His application to the Nieman program at Harvard emphasized the importance of journalism in acting as a watchdog of the increasingly quantitative and behaviorally-minded political establishment, not necessarily the need to shrink the boundary line dividing journalism and science. It appears that the change in perspective was a gradual one and occurred sometime around the reporting of the Detroit Riots and Meyer's introduction to the power of computing techniques. The role played by the idea of computation, the abstract notion of the computer's capabilities, and what the computer would bring to the practice of journalism, will be the subject of the next chapter, for it is this **image of the computer**—or perhaps more accurately, the image of the computer as a database—that did much to transform notions of what journalism was capable of in the late twentieth and early twenty-first century. By drawing on the procedural speed that that computational practices made possible, journalism could raise its professional standards and more confidently deploy its own claims to certitude and factual knowledge.

5

Precision Becomes Data

Introduction

For Phillip Meyer, Indiana University Press was the publisher that came through. After the series of rejections chronicled in the previous chapter, *Precision Journalism: A Reporter's Introduction to Social Science Methods* was published in 1973, with the first two chapters based on previously published work in *Playboy* (1969)[1] and the *Columbia Journalism Review* (1971). The book has now gone through four editions, with the second edition (1979) largely identical to the first and with the greatest change in editions occurring between the second and third. The third edition was a major update (in parts almost an entire reconceptualization) and carried the title *The New Precision Journalism* (1991). The fourth and likely last edition was simply called, once again, *Precision Journalism* (2002); it restored an excised chapter on game theory, added two major chapters on what Meyer called "lurking variables," and incorporated extensive new information on databases.

As I have argued throughout this book, a close analysis of particular moments in the institutional relationship between data, quantification, documents, and "truth" can shed light on larger political, social, economic, and technological currents in US history in the twentieth and early twenty-first centuries. In this chapter I treat *Precision Journalism* as a canonic text, applying hermeneutic analysis to its various editions and the differences between them in order to explore how the controversial and largely ignored ideas of Phil Meyer and other quantitatively inclined journalists of the 1960s and 1970s had become mainstream by the 1990s. I want to argue that there were four driving forces at work in this transformation: institutional (the rise of NICAR and the relationship between NICAR and data journalism), cultural (a vision of technology, mainly of computers and databases, that allowed social science methods to be "smuggled into" newsrooms), occupational (the increasing number of PhD-holding professors at journalism schools) and finally, political (a period of relative intellectual and political stability in US "knowledge professions" that allowed previously marginal perspectives to be integrated into journalistic work). The dynamic displayed here resembles the one I discussed in chapter 3, in which a period of intellectual professionalization that ran from the 1920s to the late 1950s enabled the "sorting out" of previously insurgent intellectual methods, standards of evidence, and occupational relationships. But whereas the 1920s saw the carving up of the knowledge professions into discrete occupational domains, the 1980s and 1990s would see attempts at their re-integration.

This chapter begins by returning to the discussion of Phillip Meyer and *Precision Journalism*, analyzing how the book evolved over its forty-year career and four editions. This overview, in turn, raises four important issues: first, the conflict between standpoint, narrative, and method raised by the embrace of social science by journalists; second, the role played by the database in facilitating a certain notion of journalistic professionalism; third, the new institutions which helped ground these quantitative journalistic practices; fourth and finally, the larger social and political contexts in which these shifts were grounded. Each of these developments helped precision journalism not only survive its uneasy beginnings in the 1970s but thrive well on into the 1980s, 1990s, and beyond.

Varieties of *Precision Journalism*

The major intellectual accomplishment of *Precision Journalism*, as we will see, is that it formalized and codified the interpretative and explanatory turn that had been percolating through journalism since at least the 1930s. While not alone in doing so, it unapologetically argued that journalism, as a profession dedicated to the formulation of public knowledge, could not simply content itself with the chronicling of individual events or public utterances without any regard for what those utterances and events meant or how they fit into a larger schema of social facts. Moreover, it contended that journalists could not simply be stenographers, collecting scattered data without consciously analyzing whether or not that data was meaningful and true. To do this, however, journalists needed to adopt the standpoint, and the methods, of social scientists. Journalism was incapable of achieving contextual relevance through good explanations, or through narrative skill, or even through good pictures of data. It needed to adopt the methods, judgment, and objectivity of the social scientist.

The opening pages of the first edition of *Precision Journalism* begin with an overview of some major journalistic mistakes of the previous decade, perhaps responding to reviews (discussed in the previous chapter) arguing that Meyer needed to make a stronger case for how precision journalism could help reporters and editors avoid embarrassing errors. The book discusses reporting about African-American militancy in the wake of the assassination of Martin Luther King Jr., speculation about the causes of the Detroit riots, and news stories about the role played by the anti-war movement in American political life. The central thesis of the volume is then stated succinctly: "journalists would be wrong less often if we adapted to our own use some of the research tools of the social scientist" (Meyer 1973, 3).

At the heart of the opening chapter is a devastating evisceration of a particular concept of journalistic objectivity, one that we today might call a "value free" or "all sides could be right" notion of reportage. For too long, Meyer argues, reporters have ignored questions of journalistic method (how ought journalists gain knowledge?) in favor of arguments about journalistic stance (should journalists have an opinion?) In short, arguments about the news have primarily been conducted over how journalists ought to be "objective." But the debate over objectivity is a facile one, Meyer contends, if it is approached in a simplistic manner—the easiest and oldest conception of objectivity is one in which the reporter is simply a stenographer who transmits "all sides" of an issue and gives them equal weight. Adopting a historical and teleological framework for his discussion, Meyer argues that this form of journalism as neutrality has been rendered out of date by multiple intersecting developments: more intelligent and educated readers who demand more from their news; the growth of television, which is able to convey simple facts and events more quickly and compellingly than newspapers ever will; and an overall increase in the general complexity of the world which renders simple journalistic stenography inadequate (Meyer 1973, 7). What is needed now, he argues, is "interpretive reporting"—a journalism that provides context to events, weighs the validity of truth claims, and provides a more holistic sense of the causes and consequences of public decisions. A journalist having an opinion about truth, Meyer contends, is not the same thing as a journalist having an opinion more generally. For interpretive journalism to succeed, however, it needs an anchor point. "Old-fashioned objective reporting needed no anchor; it merely bobbed along the surface of the news like a Ping-Pong ball floating down a mountain stream. Interpretation requires a reference point. One must begin with a pre-judgment, a position of some kind" (Meyer 1973, 8).

What follows then is a remarkable and compact analysis of the four different ways a journalist can obtain these "anchor points." New journalists like Tom Wolfe and Gay Talese obtain it "within their own heads" (ibid.), from their own interior, Romantic, and individual perspective, and in so doing push journalism closer to art. Other reporters (and Meyer does not specify who he means here, but it seems he is alluding to a variety of political or radical journalists operating in the 1960s and early 1970s) obtain it through a conscious ideology, an articulated framework of how the world operates in general. The major-ity of reporters also adopt an ideology in order to anchor their interpretation of the world, but it is an ideology that does not acknowledge itself as such. It can be understood, rather, as "conventional wisdom" (Meyer 1973, 9; see also Gans 1979). "As reporters . . . we tend to have our heads geared to reinforce the conventional wisdom. The effect is multiplied because we tend to imitate and reinforce each other" (Meyer 1973, 11). And it is at this moment that Meyer introduces the idea of a final and superior anchor point: social science. Being up on the latest social science research—which often challenges conventional wisdom—can help temporarily jolt us out of our own ideology. Perhaps more importantly, the techniques of precision journalism are based on intensive, systematic fact-finding efforts. Precision journalism—grounded in behavioral science—helps reporters not simply regurgitate different opinions while taking each one at face value but, in Meyer's words, helps "determine what compet-ing viewpoints are worth." Perhaps drawing on his own experience at Harvard's Nieman program and his own introduction to mainframe computing, Meyer admits that while the work of social science might have once seemed to involve too much drudgery for the average reporter, computers now do the drudgery for the journalist. Given this combination of social need and technological capacity. Meyer concludes, journalism must and can become "social science in a hurry."

By the third edition in 1991, this remarkable analysis of objectivity and inter-pretive journalism had all but disappeared. There are several reasons why this might be the case. Perhaps Meyer felt that the battle was won—as scholars like Schudson and Fink (2014) and Barnhurst and Mutz (1997) have shown, "event centered" reporting declined from the 1960s on, replaced by varied degrees of contextual and analytic reporting. In any case, it seems clear that the other vari-eties of interpretive journalistic forms Meyer discusses in the 1973 edition—"new" journalism and ideologically oriented news—had ceased to be live issues by the 1990s. Meyer mentions cases in which narrative journalists had been caught lying or fudging facts and does not even bother to critique the radical journalism of the 1960s and 1970s, which had declined in quantity and impor-tance in a more sedate post-Vietnam War era. Whatever the explanation, the third and fourth editions of *Precision Journalism* dispense with much of the more intellectual rumination about objectivity and dive right in to the more practical question of method and technique.

The third edition of *Precision Journalism* (*The* New *Precision Journalism*) is more explicit than the first and second in its contention that journalism and sci-ence (note that I say science here, not *social science*) share a common lineage and common goals. Meyer quotes physicist Lawrence Cranberg, who argued in 1989 that "journalism is itself a science" and that a properly qualified journalist could be considered a scientist. He goes on to make the scientific comparison more strongly a few pages further into the book, writing that

> The new precision journalism is scientific journalism. . . . It means treating journalism as if it were a science, adapting scientific methods, scientific objectivity, and scientific ideals to the entire process of mass communication. If that sounds absurdly pretentious, remember that science itself is restrained about its achievements and its possibilities and has its own sanctions against pretension. (Meyer 1991, x)

This new rhetorical emphasis on "science" in the opening chapter of *The New Precision Journalism* led cultural studies scholar Stephen Lamble to argue that Meyer had abandoned the rhetoric of social science for that of pure science (Lamble 2001). This is a serious overstatement. Not only is the bulk of the third edition similar to the first two, its emphasis on the techniques of the social and behavioral sciences (the remaining nine chapters are primarily devoted to the basic sociology and political science concepts discussed in the earlier books), but Lamble's purpose on emphasizing this distinction between "social science" and "science" is unclear. Meyer himself has taken issue with Lamble's claim, responding that

> Anyone who thinks that *Precision Journalism* shifted from subjective to objective data or from qualitative to quantitative methods across its four editions hasn't read it very carefully . . . . In the first edition, striving to make its ideas acceptable to traditionalists, I argued that precision journalism was still journalism—using more powerful tools but with the same goals. By the third edition, I stressed that continuity less and added more methodological detail because I had learned more by then. (Meyer 2009)

All that said, I think it is clear—and I think Meyer would agree—that the third edition of *Precision Journalism* was a more confident book, better able mount to a strong argument against more traditional journalists who would ground their knowledge in the words of their sources or other forms of entirely verbal evidence. To some degree, this confidence manifests itself in a stronger claim to the status of journalism as science. But it also manifests itself in a stronger emphasis on the *theories* journalists employ and the relationship between reportorial method and reportorial theory. Meyer's discussion of the four "hooks" of objectivity in the first and second editions, in other words, has been replaced by a more abstract discussion of theory. Moving from a discussion of perceptual schemas to the importance of tacit or explicit theories for understanding the world in a scientific fashion, Meyer argues that a good theory allows the scientist the opportunity to invalidate that theory by testing it against empirical reality. In this sense, science is an open process. The problem with journalism, however, is that

> Instead of testing reality directly with their own observations, deductions, and experiments, [journalists] are normally content to do their cross-checking by consulting different authorities with different viewpoints and different interests. The flaw in this methodology is that the journalists may not have any good basis for evaluating conflicting sources and may be forced into q traditional, objectivist stance, one that demands the unlikely assumption that all voices have an equal claim to the truth. *The journalist who adopts the tools of the scientific method to his or her own trade can be in a position to make useful evaluations with the more positive objectivity of science.* (Meyer 1991, 13)

More than any change in the methods discussed or the "scientific" pretensions of *The New Precision Journalism*, the replacement of the discussion of the hooks of objectivity with a more abstract conversation about "theories" is the biggest shift between the second and third editions of Meyer's book, and one that does indicate a more formalist notion of journalism than that first proposed in the 1970s. However, I also think this shift remains firmly grounded in the methods and mindset of social science, and there is no move from a squishy sociology to a more objective science on display here. For Meyer, social science is (or at least can be) as objective as the natural sciences. In that regard, he remains true to his intellectual roots during the post-war high-water mark of the social sciences.

By the time we get to the fourth edition (now again renamed, simply, *Precision Journalism*) we are clearly in the consolidation and valedictory phase of this particular text. Helpfully, the changes in this edition are specifically outlined in its opening pages. First, in the preface, there is a discussion of the uncertain status of "truth" in the aftermath of the post-modern revolution in the academy and in the West at large. Meyer has also added two more chapters, on "lurking variables," or "hidden causal effects," in effect increasing the rigor of the analytical methods deployed. Finally, his chapter on game theory is back after being absent in the third edition ("at the insistence of my students") (Meyer 2002, xi).

There are also several more differences between the fourth and earlier editions of *Precision Journalism* not detailed in the introduction. Meyer adds a fourth item to his earliest discussion of what a journalist needs to know (Meyer 2002, 2)— how *much* empirical precision a journalist must use to solve a particular problem or write a particular story. He also inserts a bit more detail on how journalistic theories emerge, drawing on the origins of some of the important CAR articles of the last several decades to consider the emergence of reportorial frameworks. Meyer also extends an olive branch to the New Journalists and the proponents of a more "artistic" or "Romantic" journalism. Finally, there is significantly more detail in the fourth edition on the relationship between journalists and databases. Indeed, it is possible to track a through-line of technological development in *Precision Journalism* by discussing the different ways Meyer interrogates the database as an object. The material factors that allow journalists to think of themselves as information synthesizers as well as information originators not only included the computer but also the database—a development I already briefly alluded to in chapter 3. The database is as important as the computer in facilitating the intellectual and occupational transition from precision journalism to data journalism that took place in the 1980s and 1990s. I will turn to this analysis of the journalistic understanding of the database at the conclusion of this chapter.

Narrative, Art, and Accepted Methodologies

Having chronicled some of the changes in the different versions of *Precision Journalism*, I want to pause briefly before I turn to a more formal discussion of some of the factors that led the precision journalism of the 1970s to become the data journalism of the early twenty-first century, including the key conceptual reinterpretation of the notion of the database. In the history of empirical research we have recounted up until this point, the growth of social science and the knowledge professions in general has been facilitated by the sharp separation between individual perspective on the one hand and detached fact on the other. As these notions of science have solidified, however, we can also see how certain methodologies have become institutionalized in ways that problematize this neat dichotomy between the "social" and "scientific" standpoint. In *Precision Journalism* Meyer leans strongly on this dichotomy—between the "romantic" and "scientific" anchor points, in other words—to build a case for the superiority of his form of interpretive journalism to others.

I am contending, in other words, that the under-acknowledged professional "enemy" in the early editions of *Precision Journalism* is the New Journalism of Tom Wolfe, Gay Talese, Truman Capote, Hunter S. Thompson, Joan Didion, and other journalists who sought to fuse fictional and non-fictional techniques. In part, Meyer acknowledged the importance of narrative journalism retroactively, highlighting the oppositional role it played in his thinking once he declared that the time had come to make peace with it. Recall the four original interpretive anchor points outlined in the first and second editions of *Precision Journalism*—the romantic anchor point of the new journalists, the open ideological anchor point of partisan or movement journalists, the conventional ideological ("common sense") anchor point of most journalists, and the scientific anchor point provided by precision journalism. What is acknowledged here is that some sort of standpoint is unavoidable in any modern journalism worthy of the name; the difference between forms of news reporting lies in the methods different journalists choose to anchor their standpoints. In an October 2012 speech to the Austrian Academy of Sciences, Meyer described the methodologies at work in narrative journalism as including: "fiction-like techniques [which] include internal monologue—what a newsworthy person was thinking—and detailed character development and scene building . . . . Narrative journalism, like precision journalism, is a lot of work. To give reporting the rich, creative structure of fiction, the writer must first assemble a very large body of facts, and then choose those that can fit a narrative structure" (Meyer 2012b), 13. In this speech Meyer acknowledges, "for decades, as a precision journalist I considered narrative journalists my natural enemies" and adds that "it didn't help that the early practitioners sometimes got caught making things up." He follows this assertion with a rather lengthy recounting of some of the more tawdry new journalism scandals of the 1970s, 1980s, and 1990s (ibid). In a gesture of accommodation, however, the speech concludes that

> Both genres, narrative journalism and precision journalism, are special forms requiring special skills. If we were to blend the two, what should we call it? I like the term "evidence-based narrative." It implies good storytelling based on verifiable evidence. Yes, that would be an esoteric specialty. But I believe that a market for it is developing. The information marketplace is moving us inexorably toward greater and greater specialization. (Meyer 2012b, 35)

Nevertheless, it seems clear that the underlying *methodological grounding* of this "evidence-based journalism," as opposed to its narrative form, would be the precision journalism techniques of Meyer and others, thus leaving social science as the ultimate basis for this new fusion of journalistic skill. **In the end, the *methods* of the narrative journalism of Wolfe, Talese, Breslin, and others are inadequate for Meyer because they remain grounded in reportorial forms of the type conducted by good reporters for decades**—a point emphasized by Wolfe in his path-breaking article on the rise of new journalism in *New Yorker* magazine. "With a little reworking," Wolfe writes in describing his initial encounter with "Joe Louis: The King as a Middle-Aged Man," in the pages of *Esquire* by Gay Talese,

> the whole article could have read like a short story. The passages in between the scenes, the expository passages, were conventional

1950s-style magazine journalism, but they could have been easily recast. The piece could have been turned into a non-fiction short story with very little effort. The really unique thing about it, however, was the reporting. This I frankly couldn't comprehend at first. I really didn't understand how anyone could manage to do reporting on things like the personal by-play between a man and his fourth wife at an airport and then follow it up with that amazing cakewalk down Memory Lane in his second wife's living room. My instinctive, defensive reaction was that the man had piped it, as the saying went . . . winged it, made up the dialogue. Really stylish reporting was something no one knew how to deal with, since no one was used to thinking of reporting as having an *aesthetic* dimension. (Wolfe 1972, 35)

Wolfe likewise describes the revolutionary impact of Jimmy Breslin's style of column writing for the *New York Herald,* one that also hangs on reporting as a central methodology. Breslin "made a revolutionary discovery. He made the discovery that it was feasible for a columnist to leave the building, go outside and do reporting on his own, actual legwork. Breslin would go up to the city editor and ask what stories and assignments were coming up, choose one, go out, leave the building, cover the story as a reporter, and write about it in his column." (Wolfe 1972, 35). Once again, we see a more fluid narrative and interpretive journalistic form grounded in traditional news reporting as it has been practiced for decades.

Precision journalism was different, Meyer argues and represents a step beyond interpretive journalism in its pretensions to epistemological rigor. It claimed, in essence, the mantle of science—it would adopt transparent processes drawn from the social science canon, would posit testable hypotheses, and would step forward bravely as a falsifiable mode of public communication. It would not simply interpret in the way that a variety of other reporters adopting tried and true journalistic methods had up until this point. And it would fulfill the progressive dream—first encountered in chapter 1—and become a scientifically grounded, professionally assertive commentator on political and social life.

This hermeneutic analysis of the varieties of *Precision Journalism* has demonstrated that there is, in essence, a single thread guiding the development of Meyer's ideas over the course of his long career, an idea that marked a genuine and important moment of transformation in the professional epistemology of the modern journalist. It comes in his opening pages of the first edition—the argument that journalists need to abandon their obsession with standpoint and turn more fruitfully to questions of method. With the growth of contextual journalism in the decades that followed, Meyer turned from the explicit analysis of arguments about objectivity to a more granular consideration of the fusion between journalistic and social science methods, particularly insofar as they challenged traditional journalistic practices and self-conceptions. The key dichotomy was thus the difference between old and new methodologies of reporting. The actual manner in which precision journalism developed—how it adapted and mutated in the digital age, and the ways in which it partially succeeded and partially failed to fulfill these scientific ideals—are the subjects of the remaining sections of this chapter. Tracing out these institutional developments will take us up to the present day and will show how so much of what we think is "new" about data journalism really has its intellectual origins in the 1970s and 1980s.

From Precision Journalism to CAR to Data Journalism

Our story now proceeds along several tangled paths. My main goal is to trace how Philip Meyer's precision journalism became the data journalism of the early twenty-first century. Data journalism, of course, is one of the most discussed, written about, and commented upon aspects of journalism in the early twenty-first century, in both professional and academic discourse about the news, and it would be impossible to do justice here to the extensive scholarly literature about it. It has grown to encompass many of the techniques and methods discussed already: data visualization, graphs, social science, the use of databases, interactive news, and so on. Nevertheless, I want to reflect first upon what we *do* know about data journalism today by providing a rough outline of its history from the 1970s to the present through some of its exemplary cases. I then want to step back into *Precision Journalism* one last time, linking the evolving ways that Meyer writes about the "database" to larger shifts in the transition from precision journalism, to CAR, to investigative journalism, to data journalism more broadly. The adoption of the database, with its promise that it could aid reporters in their journalistic work, marks it as a key boundary object helping smooth the way for the integration of sociology with news reporting.

EXEMPLARY CASES

In his brilliant taxonomy of the different types of quantitative journalism in the twenty-first century, Mark Coddington distinguishes CAR from data journalism, which is in turn different from "computational reporting" (Coddington 2014).

In the remainder of this book I will lean heavily on these distinctions, with the proviso that the longer historical lens of this book can help us understand that there are deeper genealogies to all of these quantitative journalistic forms, and that a focus on history can help us understand more clearly how attempts to use data, visualizations, and quantitative forms of journalistic evidence intersected with larger American political and social currents. To that end, let's now turn to the question of how the *ideas* of precision journalism, outlined in the last two chapters, intersected with the larger institutions of mid-century news making in the United States. We've looked at how Meyer's ideas changed, but simply understanding these ideas is not enough; we must examine the organizations in which these ideas were embedded in order to understand how data journalism came to exist in a recognizable way.

One way to start is with some exemplary *examples* of data journalism, stories that have lodged themselves in the journalistic collective memory. Journalists remember certain stories as being particularly meaningful for the profession, particularly stories that codified emergent professional behaviors, values, or norms (Schudson 1992; Zelizer 1992). Quite often, these are stories that have won prizes. Four data stories that are regularly referenced in journalistic memoirs, online histories, and data journalism training manuals as particularly important are "Crime and Injustice" by Donald Barlett and James Steele (*Philadelphia Enquirer*, 1973); a story looking at variations in assessed property values in Miami-Dade country by Rich Morin and Fred Tasker (*Miami Herald*, 1978); "The Color of Money" by Bill Dedman (*Atlanta Journal-Constitution*, 1988), and "America: What Went Wrong?" also by Barlett and Steele (*Philadelphia Enquirer*, 1991). Each of the first three stories made increasingly sophisticated use of computer databases: "Crime and Injustice," which probed inequalities in the Philadelphia criminal justice system, required the reporters to obtain a sample of paper records from the District Attorney's office, hire clerks to transcribe them into coding forms that could then be analyzed computationally, and load the forms into a specially designed IBM-7090 coding program designed by Meyer. Morin and Tasker's piece on Florida property assessments had the advantage of using public records that had already been compiled and computerized by a government agency. The reporters, having obtained a computer tape of assessment values, loaded it onto the *Miami-Herald* mainframe and analyzed it using The Statistical Package for the Social Sciences (SPSS). "The Color of Money"—a four-day package of more than two-dozen articles looking at mortgage redlining in Atlanta that won the 1989 Pulitzer Prize—required compiling data from multiple sources and made use of both census figures and federally mandated disclosure data on mortgage lending practices.

"America: What Went Wrong?" was somewhat different. Drawing on a wide variety of statistical, shoe leather, and secondary forms of journalistic evidence, this study of the "decline of middle class America" resembled a high-protein non-fiction book when it was published by the *Enquirer* in 1991. In these articles, Barlett and Steele did not focus on a particular data set (or even data *sets*) in order to answer a particular question or address a specific issue—unless we see "specific issue" as encompassing the entire breadth of socio-demographic and economic changes in the United States in the post-World War II era. "America: What Went Wrong?" is an important inflection point in this chronicle of social-science-influenced journalism. Sociological methods and findings (often research carried out by scholars or government) were both seamlessly integrated into the professional journalistic narrative, but at the same time, they were not accompanied by a great deal of hand-waving about their scientific imaginations. "America: What Went Wrong?" marked a full flowering of the sociological-journalistic dreams harbored by the MRFM, the RSF, Paul Kellogg, and others, but did so in an entirely un-self-conscious fashion. High-level, data-driven, non-fiction journalism had most certainly arrived, but, as we will see shortly, the very question of "what type" of journalism "America: What Went Wrong?" was would trouble some of the profession's central arbiters in some important ways. Regardless of these intra-professional conversations, however, it is fair to say that by 1991, a form of data-rich sociological journalism had been normalized within the profession.

In explaining the gradual emergence of contextual and analytic journalism, scholars (Fink and Schudson 2014; Barnhurst and Mutz 1997) have pointed to the rising educational level, in the United States in general and of journalists in particular, as an important factor behind this improvement in journalistic quality. A more educated citizenry—or at least a substantial minority of it—increasingly demanded a more substantive journalism, and an increasingly well-educated cohort of journalists was prepared to provide it. I think these arguments are both likely and plausible; however, they also shift the explanatory narrative to a high level of abstraction at just the moment that we need more direct answers about *why* journalism has grown more scientific, more contextual, or more analytic. Over the course of my interviews for this book, a number of journalism educators offered a related, but oblique, explanation for the rise of social scientific techniques among segments of the journalistic workforce (Meyer interview January 13, 2016; Ross interview August 22, 2016; Waite interview January 7, 2016). Not only were more and more journalists going to school from the 1970s on, they noted, but journalism schools were increasingly hiring instructors with PhDs and universities were expecting these formerly profession-focused departments to produce academic research (Carey 1978). A relatively straightforward way to bring social science into a journalism school curriculum was to teach precision journalism techniques, techniques that could then be used to develop a new type of reporting as well as a form of research that would satisfy increasingly academically oriented administrators of the larger university system. The fact that this form of quantitative journalism had already been professionally legitimated in the form of Meyer's book *Precision Journalism,* and that stories using it had won journalism prizes, made precision journalism the perfect boundary object (Star and Bowker 2000) to meet these internal university expectations. In other words, if we want to explain the general rise of contextual reporting from the 1950s onward, we can add intra-institutional dynamics in the field of higher education to more social and cultural explanations about overall upward trends in US education levels.

I noted that precision journalism was increasingly being called CAR in the decade following the publication of Meyer's book. This was not an entirely meaningless terminological shift. The emergence of NICAR and its eventual merger with Investigative Reporters and Editors (IRE) is part of the story here, as were the visions of the computer and the database that increasingly dominated journalistic thinking about technology. Another part of the story is the changing meaning of precision journalism for ordinary journalists, in a highly technical sense. In essence, precision journalism was becoming understood as basic survey research carried out for journalistic purposes for both editorial and business (back office) reasons. If you were to ask your average journalist or journalism educator in the 1990s what precision journalism was, they would have most likely told you that it was "polling." In part, the explanation for this can be found in developments in Meyer's own career, particularly his move to the business side of Knight-Ridder in 1978 as the director of news and circulation research. In part, it was Meyer's facility with the social science techniques of quantitative public opinion measurement that helped facilitate this move into the executive suite, but it was also a move that started to pigeonhole precision journalism as survey research.

In a number of speeches and public writings from this era, Meyer himself laments the fact that precision journalism was often seen as shorthand for the newsroom-based public opinion poll, when in fact it ought to be seen more generally and methodologically as the application of a wide variety of social science techniques to journalistic work. There are, indeed, a wide number of quantitative sociological methods discussed in all four editions of *Precision Journalism;* nevertheless, it is also clear that surveys and opinion polls dominate the practice of precision journalism in both theory and practice. Along with Meyer's increasingly high-profile role on the marketing side of the news business, the origins of precision journalism in the social science milieu of the early 1960s also play a more subtle role. Meyer was not simply influenced by social science as he developed his notions of precision journalism—he was influenced by a particular social science embedded within a particular historical time and with particular methodological assumptions. As Andrew Abbott and James T. Sparrow write regarding mainstream sociology in the decades after World War II:

> Over three-quarters of the ASA membership in 1955 came from the post-1945 graduate school cohort; the discipline became extremely young. Moreover, tertiary education's continuing expansion through the 1950s and 1960s meant boundless job prospects not only for this cohort but for several generations of its students. As a result, whatever was the sociological orthodoxy of the moment during the postwar generation's training years would be spread without interruption for decades. To the extent there was such an orthodoxy, *it happened to be Parsonianism and survey analysis,* and so it is not surprising that these dominated sociology until 1970 and, in the case of survey analysis even beyond. (Abbott and Sparrow 2008, 293, emphasis added)

In the case of precision journalism, we can see how these orthodoxies affected not only sociology itself but made their mark on epistemological innovations undertaken by thinkers in aligned fields influenced by these social sciences. Meyer regularly mentions the importance of the sociologist Samuel Stouffer in his discussions of how journalists can incorporate scientific surveys into their arsenal of reportorial techniques. Surveys like the ones Stouffer pioneered in *The American Soldier* (Stouffer 1949) moved sociology from being an armchair discipline to an empirical, scientific one, Meyer argues in the first chapter of *Precision Journalism,* and journalists should take a page from the sociologist's book in this regard. But while he praises empirical sociology in general, what Meyer is practically endorsing in terms of techniques is the scientific survey. Being strongly influenced by 1960s mainstream social science, in other words, it is no surprise that precision journalism would import some of the orthodoxies of that science into its original DNA. Precision journalism was more than scientific surveys, but scientific surveys were the most obvious, accessible, and empirically defensible sociological technique for journalists and editors to understand. They also dominated sociology itself for many decades.

Data-oriented contextual journalism was, in short, on the rise in the 1970s and 1980s, in part due to changes in journalism school education, but also in part because of larger social, cultural, and educational shifts in the American polity. While precision journalism (both the book and the larger movement) could serve as a rallying point and boundary object for quantitatively minded journalists and editors, CAR eventually became the go-to term during the heyday of this form of journalistic reportage. In other words: pure precision journalism became increasingly defined as survey research and public opinion polling, even as it inspired journalists on a normative and cultural level. CAR, though, was the offshoot of precision journalism that would have the biggest impact going forward. The explanation for this is, once again, a field-level one, and is tied in to the establishment of IRE and NICAR at the University of Missouri.

IRE AND NICAR: QUANTITATIVE JOURNALISM FINDS AN INSTITUTIONAL HOME

Even as it became a "normal" part of everyday journalistic work, quantitative contextual journalism did not find its central institutional home in the news-rooms of the United States. Rather, it created its own umbrella institutions in the form of the Missouri Institute for Computer Assisted Reporting (MICAR, later re-named NICAR) and IRE. Elliott Jaspin founded MICAR in 1989, following a stint as a Gannett Center Fellow in New York City (Dennis interview August 7, 2016). Its first office was in the basement of the world renowned Missouri Journalism School, which it shared with IRE, founded in 1978. In 1992, Brant Houston was named director of MICAR, and in 1993, IRE and the newly renamed NICAR functionally merged, supported by a large grant from the Gannett Center, with Houston as president of both organizations. The Gannett Center—a think tank at the Columbia Graduate School of Journalism in the 1980s and early 1990s—played a major role in the mainstreaming of CAR. Both Jaspin and Phil Meyer were there in its early years, and it was directed by Everett Dennis, who coined the term precision journalism. "Being in New York City in 1985 [as part of the first Gannett Center class of fellows] allowed precision journalism and Phil Meyer to get attention from the press and the New York City journalism elite in a way he would not have in North Carolina," Dennis told me (Dennis interview August 7, 2016)). Jaspin, whose primary focus was on the relationship between digital government records and the potential to use these records for investigative purposes, thus forms a crucial link between the precision journalism of the 1970s and the CAR of the 1990s.

Arguably, the association of CAR with investigative journalism also helped shape the type of news stories that were associated with "computer work" and the manner through which CAR techniques diffused across newsrooms. CAR became, in effect, the preserve of elite journalists doing high-level news work. Early edu-cators in the quantitative journalism field, some of them less well-remembered than pioneers such as Meyer, Dennis, and Houston, also provide insights into the process through which CAR became identified with elite journalistic practices. Some of those educators have contended that there were other ways in which journalism might have become more open to computational techniques, one that integrated it more firmly into daily forms of news work and not just into investiga-tive journalism. Steve Ross—a data journalism professor at Columbia University in the 1980s and 1990s and for a long time one of the only Columbia Journalism

School students with a bachelor's degree in a hard science—tried to advocate for this more entry-level perspective. Ross became interested in journalism thanks to his work with I.F. Stone on underground nuclear testing in the 1970s; Stone needed an expert opinion on how the shock waves generated by a nuclear explosion would travel underground and sought out the rabble-rousing, former student activist Ross. But despite his scientific background, Ross always thought that a facility with data, government records, and basic quantitative skills should be a part of the toolbox of *every* journalist, not simply those working on investigative news stories. "What we were aiming at was not just getting information out of big bureaucracies for purposes of uncovering some major bit of malfeasance, but the little story you could also build on it. Budget stories. We should get the budget stories. This was also a required class for everyone at Columbia, not just people doing investigative work." In other words, Ross argued that the purpose of his data class was to instill a quantitative sensibility in *all* journalists, from the beat reporter to the sports reporter to the high-level investigator of corruption. "You can write a smarter day-of beat story if you have a facility with numbers and government records rattling around in the back of your head, and if you're able to treat numbers and databases as just another source for regular reporting projects, just like you would any government official." But it was a tough slog in a largely literary field, and Ross remembers his students as being almost entirely mathematically illiterate: "First of all, journalists don't know math," he told me. "A quarter of my students [when I was teaching how to use data in news in the 1980s and 90s], that's about 25%, somewhere around 1 in 4, could not calculate a percent. That's why I put those tips [about math] on the bottom of the page in my syllabus. These are Ivy League students. If Columbia students couldn't do it, well, that's a sad commentary" (Ross interview August 17, 2016). Rather than data skills becoming widely diffused across local, regional, and national newsrooms, a combination of industry complacency, journalistic professional interest, and the excitement generated by the IRE-NICAR merger in the 1980s would move to link data practices with elite investigative reporting.

We should also keep in mind that the links between IRE and NICAR were not foreordained. As recounted in the online history of IRE:

> In the late '60s and early '70s, reporters in different cities had been scrutinizing illegality and corruption. IRE was the brainchild of a group of journalists that gathered in Indianapolis. "There was a lot of ferment going on at the time, a lot of people becoming aware of investigative reporting," said Jim Steele, an IRE member since the beginning. "A lot of people pin it to Watergate, but the impetus really came from the Vietnam War and the critical journalism that came up in the coverage of the war." (IRE: A History)

IRE was founded, in other words, to give an institutional imprimatur to investigative reporting, itself fueled by the turmoil of the 1960s and the emerging genre
of "journalistic outrage" (Glasser and Ettema, 1984). But the IRE of the early
1970s was radical, fringe, deeply embedded in the 1970s counterculture, and
interested in specific examples of outright government malfeasance. How did it
come to make database-driven, quantitative news reporting part of its investigative and institutional arsenal? The work of Barlett and Steele marks something of
a transitional moment here as well. Uncovering governmental malfeasance and
using databases that the government itself supplied to document larger social
trends are not the same thing; "Watergate" and "The Color of Money" are, on
the surface, very different stories. As the IRE history notes, there was a specific
moment when the shift occurred, and a specific controversy that preceded it:

> [In the early 1980s] a debate was brewing among members of IRE
> and the journalism community at large about the definition of inves-
> tigative reporting. At IRE's conception, many assumed that the craft
> was limited to probing illegal activities. But [executive director] Steve
> Weinberg was among those who insisted that investigative journalism
> could be much more than that. "It didn't have to just look into illegal-
> ity," Weinberg said. "Quality investigative reporting could be in-depth,
> explanatory reporting." He and others argued that the work of veteran
> investigative reporters and longtime IRE members Don Barlett and
> Jim Steele should be considered for the IRE awards, even though their
> reporting on the failures of the American Dream had little to do with
> investigations into illegal undertakings. In essence, during the 1980s,
> IRE played a role in the evolving definition of investigative reporting.
> (IRE: A History.)

CAR could thus find a home in this new, larger, and more contextual vision
of investigative reporting. "Databases and journalism go hand in hand," Brant
Houston states in the IRE online history. "Once you blend these things together,
investigative reporting can have a much greater impact." It is worth highlighting the irony here: a journalistic format primarily concerned with uncovering
governmental abuse found it suddenly possible to integrate highly sociological
work on large-scale political and social trends into its epistemological and methodological mindset, using data provided by the government bureaucracy itself.
There is no reason why this would necessarily be true, but true it is, and true to
such a degree that it now passes for journalistic common sense.

However, for computers and databases to be seen as legitimate sources of
journalistic evidence in investigative news pieces, computers and databases
would have to evolve—both in terms of their technological capacity and in

terms of the way that journalists themselves understood what these computers and databases could do. It is to these more material considerations of technology that I now turn.

SHIFTING CULTURAL UNDERSTANDINGS: WHAT IS DATA, WHAT ARE COMPUTERS?

Let's first go back to Phil Meyer's work, which was talking about databases from the start. How did the discussion of computers and databases evolve through the different editions of *Precision Journalism*, and how did this evolution relate to and refract larger conversations about technology in the news? For those journalists working at the nexus of data and investigative reporting in the 1970s, 1980s, and 1990s, both computers and databases would grow to assume increasing prominence, not just in terms of their actual material affordances but also in the way they were understood by reporters and incorporated into various professional work practices. I want to argue here that one of the key shifts in this broader conversation was the symbolic migration of computers from the "back" of the journalistic office (as elements of the production process) to the "front" of the office (as key aspects in the more valorized work of reporting the news). This, then, helped make it possible for journalists as a professional class to begin to understand "computers," "data," and "databases" as news tools. So far I have poked at this question from a number of angles, primarily in chapters 2 and 3. I've looked at how journalists interfaced with a social movement that specifically attempted to use data and data visualization as a publicity tool as well as a "scientific" description of the social world (chapter 2). I've analyzed the content of a large corpus of daily newspapers between 1865 and 1922 to see how often they used the term "data" or "statistics," and in what fashion (chapter 3). Finally, I've undertaken a survey of the *New York Times'* front pages to see both how it visualized information (in the form of graphical representation) and represented and displayed data more generally (in the form of a list) (chapter 3). None of these methods can directly answer the question of how journalists understood quantitative objects of evidence prior to the 1950s. Still, when we add this analysis to the others in this and the earlier chapters, certain general trends start to become clear. Recall that in chapter 3 I analyzed two primary sites of professional discourse: *E&P* (1907–2016) and *CJR* (1961–2016). While my analysis of *CJR* was minimal and related directly to journalistic understandings of sociology, I undertook a broader and more wide-ranging approach to *E&P*, searching its extensive database of articles for the terms "sociology" and "social science," as well as the terms "database," "data," and "census." The "data" and "database" search results required far more extensive pruning but also surfaced some of the most thought provoking and intriguing pieces.

A key piece of scholarship addressing all of these issues is an article on "technologically specific work" by Matthew Powers (2011). Also based on a content analysis of the trade press (including E&P) from the years 1975 through 2011, the basic argument is two-fold. First, over the course of these 30 years Powers demonstrates that journalists discussed technology in one of three ways, as providing: continuity for, negative disruption of, or positive reinvention of already existing journalistic practices. He also alludes to the manner by which "technologically specific work" discursively migrated from the "back of shop" (in the bowels of production) to the "front of the shop" (in the realm of editing and reporting). In other words, technology increasingly began to be seen as part of the central work of journalism, rather than something mostly done by the technical staff (Powers 2011, see also Bockzkowski 2004). I see a fundamentally similar pattern in my analysis of E&P's discussion of "data," "the database," or "the census" (which came to include 573 separate pieces, all told). The primary discursive shift in journalistic professional talk about data is a shift from seeing it as primarily related to newspaper marketing or consumer relationships (the business side) to seeing it as a useful object for journalistic production itself. The emergence of videotext (Bockzkowski 2004) is a key moment in this transformation, with articles about this technology taking up substantial space in E&P. Most of these articles serve a dual function: they are concerned with how audience data derived from videotext would integrate with subscription databases in order to create greater customer retention efficiencies but then shade into discussions of the reportorial aspects of this data technology as well. Even this change from a "business" to a "journalistic" understanding of data doesn't tell the entire story, however. Once data began to be seen as a possible object of journalistic production, a distinction still remained as to whether this data simply enabled new forms of journalistic *production* (by which I mean visuals, photographs, pagination and layout, on-screen display, and so on) or whether it helped facilitate a new form of journalistic *reportage*. It was the rhetorical framing of "data" as providing a new type of journalistic *evidence*, and thus enabling new forms of *reporting*, that allowed the long-delayed reunification of journalism and social science, at least at the margins of the field.

Prior to the 1980s, most journalistic discourse in E&P concerned the numerous ways data and databases could be used to better market newspapers, understand reader spending habits, and better organize the increasingly large amounts of consumer data being generated by the US advertising industry. Headlines include: "Home Delivered Reader Survey Gives Income Data" (June 1955): "Audit Bureau of Circulation Brought Us Era of Factual Data" (October 1954); "Nielsen Data Underscore Strength of Daytime TV" (November 1956); "Used Car Ad Contest Develops Useful Data (November 1956); "Survey Data on Newspaper Jobs Offered" (July 1957); and so on. It is important to keep in mind that even as other forms of rhetorical framing began to impact *E&P*'s use of "data" and "database," this notion of data as a news-business asset remained dominant. Well into the 1990s and the emergence of videotext, the majority of articles discussing journalistic use of data were framed in terms of newspaper marketing and audience research.

Nevertheless, with the emergence of videotext in the mid-to-late 1970s, the framing of technology begins to shift. Bockzkowski has done much demonstrate the importance of this videotext in facilitating the transformation of journalism in the pre-internet era (Bockzkowski 2004 It was, in essence, an end-user information system in which content was delivered to a so-called dumb terminal (i.e., a television screen) for consumption at home or at work. By 1982, *E&P* was running regular articles on the new technology—"Videotext Offers New Job Market for Print Journalists" (May 1982); "Affiliated and Knight-Ridder Agree on Possible Viewtron System" (January 1982) and so on. However, in all of these *E&P* pieces, there was never a clear distinction between videotext as a consumer device, as a marketing and database tool, or even as a new way to produce journalism and news. It actually affected all aspects of the news business, from marketing to production to distribution and was seen as having multiple applications to all aspects of news work. In that sense it also served as the perfect rhetorical gateway for an industry about to witness a profound shift in its relationship with "technologically specific work."

By the 1980s, in other words, data and databases were starting to be seen as contributors to news production processes as well as to the business/management side of the industry. By production, however, most writers at *E&P* referred to advances in visual display, new ways of shooting and processing photographs, changes in information graphics, and so on. This intersects with earlier evidence that visualization—abandoned by social science—was one of the first aspects of 1920s sociology to migrate into the newsroom. Visuals were acceptable as a way of smuggling context into news reports. In an article on news coverage during the 1991 Gulf War, for instance, Mark Fitzgerald (1991) noted: "wire and supplemental news services strained to satisfy a nearly insatiable demand for graphics related to the war. . . . United Press International doubled its average output of graphics after the crisis began. At some supplemental services, the output of war graphics is choking computer storage space." Clearly, this framing of data does indeed relate to the (re)emergence of information visualization, but for our purposes here I want to argue that its focus is primarily on the *display* of news rather than the epistemological foundations of reporting itself. A more straightforward example of what I mean by the "production" frame is an earlier article, "The Visual Enhancement of Photos," which discusses the different (and controversial) ways computer imaging and data processing could be used to enhance and edit news photographs in 1989. In all of these pieces data techniques are discussed primarily insofar as they help journalists produce a better consumer product, one that will be more attention-grabbing and better serve the visual needs of news readers.

A final category of stories frames data, databases, and the census as tools that fundamentally alter the manner by which journalists engage in the basic act of reporting the news. This is the quarry we have been hunting since the beginning of this book, and there are some scattered references to it in E&P as early as the 1950s. It forms the key to Phil Meyer's critique, not only of traditional journalism, but of visually oriented journalism, political journalism, and narrative journalism. The most concentrated professional conversations about the use of data as an object of reportorial evidence first emerged in the late 1980s. "Database Journalism Grows in Importance" (July 1989), by Dorothy Brand, is indicative of this trend. Unlike stories dealing with newspaper use of videotext, the focus here is entirely on the way that databases and the data within them can enable new (and in many cases, better) forms of journalistic work. The story begins by recounting how reporters Elliot Jaspin and Maria Miro Johnson noticed a trend of school bus accidents in Rhode Island. This hunch—that something was going on with school buses and their drivers—led them to conduct a more formal investigation into ticketing patterns for school buses in Rhode Island. They "turned to computer tapes to help fish out the story. They analyzed tapes that listed every traffic ticket over a three-year period and every criminal court case over nine years. The *Providence Journal-Bulletin* reporters found bus drivers who were drug dealers and others with horrendous driving records. Without a computer, that story would have been impossible,' Jaspin [said]." The story notes how Jaspin, after a stint at the Gannett Center in Columbia, was moving to the University of Missouri to set up a training center for database reporting (that would become MICAR and then NICAR). The centerpiece of the story is the discussion of a computer program, created by Jaspin and a research assistant, that facilitated the transfer of government data tapes to journalists' personal computers. The key development here is in *evidence gathering*, the ability of journalists to simply transfer already existing government data for their own personal journalistic use. This way of thinking about what journalism could be and the methods it could use to get at important truths, pioneered by Phil Meyer in the late 1960s, had now merged with the data transfer techniques invented by Jaspin in the 1980s to create a powerful discourse about new forms of journalistic accountability. It was this discourse of accountability that would dominate our understanding of data journalism in the late twentieth and early twenty-first century.

The conversation became more focused in November 1991 with the publication of a special report: "Computers and Newspapers." Retrospectively, this issue of E&P can be seen as a landmark moment in the history of the social science–journalism relationship. As the lead article by Mary Ann Chick Whiteside puts it:

It is clear that journalists must learn to use computers to do their work well. Journalists can use computers to sort through databases— collections of records that are gathered on computers by federal, state, or local governments—and to quickly check what other newspapers and magazines have written on nearly every subject. In addition, they can use online services offered by governments and private companies to do research for articles. Computers also provide access to thousands of trade publications and research resources.

A second piece by the same author discussed possible resources for journalists wanting to explore this brave new world of computers:

> Journalists seeking help in starting or executing a computer assisted project can find it from private firms, from universities with formal pro- grams, or other community resources such as economic development agencies. Books, newsletters, and seminars also provide more gen- eral help in learning about this reporting tool. Three graduates of the University of Missouri who have worked with the Missouri Institute for Computer-Assisted Reporting (MICAR) are selling their computer skills through Electronic Public Information Consultants. Their firm, MICAR, is made up of the National Institute for Advanced Reporting at Indiana University in Indianapolis, the Program in Precision Journalism at the University of North Carolina at Chapel Hill, and the Transactional Records Access Clearinghouse at Syracuse University.

When I first began to examine the *E&P* and *CJR* archives, I had a guiding hunch about how computers would be framed within journalistic discourse. My specu- lation was that computers would be seen as enhancing journalistic objectivity, with impersonal techniques of data management bolstering journalists' claims to be able to report the truth without fear of favor. However, this turned out not to be the case. What the examination of the archival evidence demonstrates is not that computers were useful to journalists because they were mechanisti- cally objective but rather because they increased *access* to already existing forms of data (usually provided by government) and because they were *fast*, allow- ing journalists to do their work more quickly. What computers facilitated was the ability to access databases. And the ability to access databases *bolstered* an already existing form of professional activity in which journalists, as working professionals, utilized their own training and judgment to uncover and report on public malfeasance. In others words: journalists valued computers as tools that allowed them to enhance their already existing professional practices and professional authority and to more confidently claim the ability to determine what was certain truth and what was less so. They did not look to computers as a technology providing new types of objectivity; rather, they looked to computers as tools that allowed them to do what they already did faster and using more material. In other words, while data journalists and computer-assisted reporters may have enhanced their expectations of what journalism was capable of, journalists believed those capacities largely resided within the profession itself and could grow without the need to radically reinvent what objectivity was or how it might be obtained.

This, of course, begs the question as to whether journalistic visions of technology, professional objectivity, and journalistic work have evolved further in the more than twenty years that have elapsed since the founding of NICAR. While I tackle this question in more detail in the next chapter, readers may have noticed that we are now nearly more than five chapters into a book on data and digital technology and have yet to spend much time discussing "the internet." There are practical, but also theoretical and empirical, reasons for this. Practically speaking, many of the most important developments relating to the development of digital journalism have been chronicled in recent books, most extensively in Nikki Usher's *Interactive Journalism: Hackers, Data, and Code* (2016). Theoretically, however, my research for this book convinced me that when it comes to major shifts in journalistic knowledge, the most important changes in journalism occurred in the 1960s and 1970s, *not in the internet age*, at least so far. The developments we usually discuss under the umbrella term "data journalism" are largely extensions and refinements of concepts and technologies developed in the post-World War II era: increased digitization of databases, especially government data; the speed afforded to journalism by computers; the increasing prestige of investigative journalism; a focus on the importance of patterns rather than incidents; and articulations that journalism needed to go beyond "he said-she said" objectivity. This does not mean that developments in the 1990s and in the digital age were not important for the profession or the professional work of journalism. Far from it. The primary change has been *organizational*, the diffusion of data-oriented tasks and skills out among a wider number of reporters. But it does mean that, in terms of technology and epistemology, the main story lies elsewhere.

For now, it may be useful to summarize the main points of Usher's book on hackers, data, and code in order to take the reader up to the present day. First, while it is important to remember that Usher focuses on interactive journalism *and not* data journalism, her third chapter does a particularly excellent job parsing the different ways in which journalists understand the differences between "hacker," "interactive," and "CAR" journalists. Drawing on the way these journalists define themselves, Usher points out two major dividing lines between the interactive journalists she studied for her book and the related group of data journalists who have historically worked in newsrooms. The first difference is the *forward facing* nature of interactive journalists' work. While both "data" and "interactive" journalists work with technology and numbers, interactive journalists are primarily defined by the fact that their digital products are audience facing and may even contain elements of the story that can be manipulated by readers. Data journalists, especially those coming out of the CAR tradition, are more concerned with constructing traditional stories and digital narratives for audiences and may not be concerned with interactivity at all. A few other journalists Usher spoke to talked about differences in terms of distinctions between using Microsoft Excel and more sophisticated programming languages or information storage systems. A second difference, in the minds of many technologically oriented journalists, stems from the degree to which the raw material of the journalistic investigation—the datasets, databases, and so forth—are made available to the news consumer in raw form, allowing them to be interacted with and manipulated by users. This notion of interactive journalism makes the raw data itself the object of digital intervention, and it is a key link with more structured forms of journalistic production that I want to discuss in the next chapter.

Usher makes it clear, then, that her book is about interactive journalism, not data journalism per se. However, her second chapter contains a helpful chronological overview of data journalism that takes us roughly from the mid-1990s to the early twenty-first century. According to Usher there are four major moments in the development of interactive journalism after the emergence of CAR. Central to her story is a moment of rapid-fire innovation at the *Lawrence Journal-World*, particularly during the years during which its online division was being run by Rob Curley. *Journal-World*

> projects included a tracker for the state legislature, a database for professors' salaries at KU, a database of every statistic in every box score for every KU football game since the 1890s, a statistical database for every high school player in Kansas, automatically updated weather maps, bar/beer/restaurant specials and guides, interactive and searchable music listings, and beyond. (Usher 2016, 73)

Curley himself was influenced by the writings of Adrian Holovaty, a computer programmer and sometime journalist who developed the Chicago Crime Map in 2005, which dropped crime statistics over a map of the Chicago area. Holovaty, both in his mapping work and through his blog, would come to wield an enormous influence on the world of interactive and data-oriented news, primarily as a symbol of the potential of the new data-driven digital environment. His legend was bolstered by his rather mercurial nature and by the fact that he soon abandoned journalism completely in order to develop musical software. Nothing helps create a legend like leaving an emerging scene before either it (or you) gets too old.

The founding of the Knight Foundation Data Journalism Scholarship Program at Northwestern University is a third key moment in Usher's history of the development of interactive news. Richard Gordon, who founded this program, is a key figure in the linkages between the older world of CAR and the new world of data-oriented interactive news. Gordon, himself a CAR journalist, immediately saw the connections between the emerging forms of journalism on the web and the work that some CAR reporters had already been doing for many years. More importantly, he helped provide institutional ballast to the interactive journalism transition by founding this program at Northwestern, seeded with Knight Foundation money, which aimed to train the next generation of "hacker journalists." Once again Adrian Holovaty was invoked as a model for the perfect Northwestern student; as Usher notes, the many graduates of the Northwestern program went on to play an outsized role in the development of digital news in general. Finally, Usher notes—entirely correctly in my view—that journalism often operates according to a model in which particularly successful stories wield an outsized influence over journalistic collective memory and the development of new skills and reporting forms. We saw this in our discussion of key CAR projects in the 1980s and 1990s, and Zelizer (1992) has theorized it more broadly across various journalistic formats and frames. Pioneering projects such as Snowfall, Faces of the Fallen, the collapse of the I-35 bridge, Nate Silver's coverage of the 2008 presidential election, and the New York Times "dialect quiz" have all entered the collective memory of the journalism profession in a way that would strongly influence future developments in the field.

While developments in journalism since the mid-1990s have been key in shaping the directions and "horizons of the possible" for the industry, the key epistemological work and the key technologies of data journalism were developed in an earlier era. Digital technology has been important for the day-to-day practices of journalism, but less important for the overall epistemology and culture of news. Journalism has indeed entered a golden age of interactive visualization, but the essentials of the evidentiary work and reporting practices of data journalism were primarily codified decades earlier.

Conclusion: The Consolidation of Data Journalism

Data journalism, in short, had become a homogenous, relatively stable field by the early twenty-first century, one with its own internal hierarchies and subdivisions

(Fink and Anderson 2015; Lewis 2015; Usher 2016). It is a field that draws primarily on core ideologies and terms forged in the 1970s, with the addition of a variety of technologies and tools unique to the digital age. Visualization and interactive forms of news (Usher 2016) tap into the visual urge that began to spread across the knowledge professions in the early twentieth century. The use of open data (Baack 2015; Lewis and Usher 2013) and documents (Royal 2010 extend journalistic use of databases into new digital domains, while the "Nate Silver phenomenon" of election prediction (Toff 2015) can be traced back to the desire of *Fortune* and other elite publications to quantitatively map the American mood (Herbst 1993; Igo 2008). The varieties of CAR, particularly those focusing on investigative reporting and the analysis of social trends, mark perhaps the most direct extension of mid-century data techniques into today's newsrooms.

At the same time, sociology itself has become more public, and not only programmatically (Burawoy 2005; Gans 2015); the internet and various forms of social media have extended the ability of scholars to communicate directly with citizens across a variety of platforms. Looked at one way, the dream of such scholars and activists as Jane Addams, W.E.B. DuBois, Philip Meyer, Charles Stelzle, and Paul Kellogg and of foundations, such as RSF, has finally come true: journalists use databases and computers to communicate social context to their audiences, often drawing on social science techniques to do so. Social scientists, for their part, increasingly adopt the techniques of the journalist to communicate with a public that rarely attends conference talks or reads expensive and jargon-laden academic journals. The best of all possible intellectual worlds would seem to have arrived. Journalism can now deploy professional certainty and mobilize the public for democratic purposes by drawing on the evidentiary standards of social science.

And yet, the United States, and the modern West in general, seems to have embraced the emotional, the irrational, the evidence-lite, and the fact-free to a degree not seen since the political upheavals of the 1930s. How can this be? Is data simply a delusion, its effectiveness a myth? Is it nothing but the conceit of the elitist, fact-based community? And if it is, or even if it might be, how are journalism and the social sciences responding to this new epistemological crisis? The final pages of this book pursue these new lines of inquiry. In this pursuit, we can see the value of a historical perspective, for as I tried to show in the opening chapters, the social-science-journalism-variable-data-objectivity paradigm was itself an invention of the early twentieth century. If it could be invented, it can be replaced. I now turn to an empirical and ethnographic analysis of these attempts to forge a new journalistic path.

6

Databases, Stories, Databases

Narrative, Semantics, and Computational Journalism

Structured Journalism and Computational Thinking

Recent political upheavals did not lead journalists to suddenly embrace new paradigms of reporting in any causal fashion, and anyone looking for such a connection in this chapter is bound to be disappointed. What I hope the previous pages of this book have shown, rather, is the following: the social world is wracked by uncertainty. For a multitude of reasons, when confronted by that uncertainty, journalists in the twentieth century have opted to "double down" on their professional claims to objectivity, whether this was embracing styles of contextual, explanatory journalism in the 1930s, precision journalism in the 1960s, or data journalism in later decades. Journalism has grown professionally more robust and might even be considered, in certain instances, to be a science. For this final chapter, there are a number of forms of reporting I could have picked to study: the opinion-laden, blog-style reporting of many digital media outlets (such as Buzzfeed), narrative writing in a more long-form style, the embrace of social media to tell the news in a more granular way, and so on. However, what many have called "computational" or "structured" journalism is the most appropriate choice of subject for this final empirical chapter, for one reason in particular. When we look back on the early twenty-first century, at least since 2003 or so, we will see it as the "age of facts," particularly in the news media. Discussions of alternative facts, the post-truth society, fake news, and so on, are everywhere present in our conversations about the media—and the most prevalent professional journalistic response to this crisis has been to aggressively embrace the importance of data, truth, facts, evidence, and empirical analysis. Structured journalism attempts to create a semantic database of linked facts, and thus further eliminate uncertainty by making its point of reference the database rather than the so-called world outside. Certainty is grounded in the database.

This chapter contends that structured journalism currently represents the furthest extension of *computational thinking* (Wing 2006) into the field of journalistic practice. Insofar as computerization has emerged as one of the dominant trends of twenty-first century social and political life,[1] and insofar as structured journalism is a carrier of this form of thinking into the realm of news production and media work, then it is an important development. It also marks a fundamentally different way of understanding the context in which news events occur, and of the relationship between these events and the larger societal patterns in which these events are embedded. The structured storytellers I examine in the pages to follow are themselves quite conscious of this; indeed, as we shall see, the notion of *the event,* and how the event builds situational context, is fundamental to the underlying philosophical vision of structured stories.

I want to begin this chapter by briefly outlining what I mean by "computational thinking," before turning to Mark Coddington's argument, alluded to in the previous chapter, that we can distinguish between two types of digital journalism that on first glance seem identical: data journalism and computational journalism. Coddington himself has contributed to empirical research in this vein, and I next examine his own work on structured journalism along with that of Lucas Graves. There is also a broader network of computational journalists and project leaders, and I discuss this network in the third section. The fourth section of the chapter turns to my case study: the computational journalism project Structured Stories, the evidence I gathered about its operations, ideologies, and institutional routines, and a discussion of the underlying computational cultures that seem to intersect with larger belief patterns more common to those of traditional journalism. I conclude by examining some of the ways that the evidence gathered here on journalistic work might help us understand general trends, tensions, and critical junctures common to the digital age.

From Data Journalism to Computational Journalism

In chapter 5, I summarized the vast amount of work being done on the deployment of data journalism in modern digital newsrooms. But less work has been done on "computational journalism," as I call it here, following the lead of journalism researcher Mark Coddington (Coddington 2014), or less work, at least on journalism specifically identified as such. I have already alluded to a foundational article on the changing institutional background and cultural meaning of what Powers calls "technologically specific work," in which communications scholar Matthew Powers argues that discussions of technology have always played a role in journalistic self-talk. A primary shift over the past fifty years has been for the definitional location of technology to migrate from the "back of the shop" to the "front of the shop," from the printing plant and spaces of mechanistic production to the newsroom itself and the everyday routines of reporters and editors. We have also seen this play out on the pages of *E&P* when it comes to videotext and databases as well. Scholarship on this shift from the back to the front of office has tended to focus on the generic presence of "computers," "data," "data journalists," "databases," "infographics," and "news interactives" and the ways that these technologies and workers are changing the production and distribution of news. The previous chapters in this book—focusing as they do on varieties of journalistic evidence and the shifting notions of context in news work over time—hopefully broaden our definition of journalistic "data" and allow us to see the broader flow of arguments about journalistic empiricism and objectivity over a longer historical time period. In this context, the distinction I want to make in this chapter between "data journalism" and "computational journalism" should be more intuitively apparent. Moreover, Coddington and journalism scholar Lucas Graves have both made important strides in drawing sharper distinctions between data and computation in the context of journalism. The rise of these computational visions is deeply intertwined with shifting notions of how journalists ought to obtain accurate, objective truth in an age of vast computational powers and the explosion of semantic and other types of databases.

The background for the distinction between data and computation can be glimpsed in the pioneering work of Jeanette Wing and her idea of *computational thinking* (Wing 2008). For Wing, computational thinking—the ability to intuitively think like a computer scientist—can be defined as the *automation of abstractions*, and particularly, the ability to operate along several levels of abstraction at once and understand how shifts in abstraction levels can occur in a recursive, automated fashion in a way that helps human beings solve particular problems. All thinking, of course, involves abstraction. What is different about computational abstraction is that it is more often than not the understanding of the abstraction of symbolic language and how that language relates to both the supposedly more fundamental level of binary code as well as to the level of the actual machinic processes triggered or enacted by that code. In another sense, it can involve thinking in database-relational terms, and the way that various specific entitles, actions, or objects can be contained or nested within broader, more universal structures. Automation, finally, is defined as "the mechanizing of our abstractions, abstraction layers, and their relationships . . . there is some computer, virtual or physical, 'below' " the process itself, one that is in the business of carrying on this manipulation of abstraction without regular human inter-vention. Wing argues that computational thinking will be a core competency of twenty-first century work, as common as reading, writing, and arithmetic are today. In this vein, the notion of computational thinking has been specifically applied to journalism by a variety of scholar-practitioners, including Greg Linch (Linch 2010a) and Jonathan Stray (Stray 2010). For Linch, computational thinking "is about taking the concepts, ideas, practices, etc. from different areas of thinking—including computation—and applying them to do better journal-ism" (Linch 2010b). Stray defines computational journalism as "the application of computer science to the problems of public information, knowledge, and belief, by practitioners who see their mission as outside of both commerce and government" (Stray 2010).

As noted earlier, Mark Coddington has argued that scholars need to do a bet-ter job distinguishing this computational journalism from other quantitative journalistic forms, including those of CAR and data journalism. These three practices," he argues

> are distinct quantitatively oriented journalistic forms: CAR is rooted in social science methods and the deliberate style and public-affairs orien-tation of investigative journalism, data journalism is characterized by its participatory openness and cross-field hybridism, and computational journalism is focused on the application of the processes of abstraction and automation to information. (Coddington 2014, 337)

Many of Coddington's insights in this area stem from the fact that he and Graves are among the few communication scholars to specifically study computational journalism as a set of practices distinct from CAR, data journalism, or other forms of quantitative journalism, even though neither identifies their area of research in these specific terms (though see Graves and Anderson 2017). Coddington, as part of a larger research project on journalistic aggregation, spent a week with the now defunct news organization Circa, an institution widely cited as a pio-neer in structured journalism (a journalistic form deeply indebted to compu-tational thinking, as we will see). Graves studied the journalistic fact-checking movement, and specifically the news organization Politifact, which can be fairly called the grandfather of the structured journalism movement.

In his dissertation, *Gathering Evidence of Evidence: News Aggregation and the Production of Journalistic Knowledge,* Coddington (2015) studied several cases of news aggregation practices, including Circa, a now defunct news app that prom-ised to break down the narrative form of news and establish discrete facts and incidents as the new "atomic unit of journalism." Circa was primarily focused on distributing news through mobile devices and specialized in producing a series of breaking news updates whose individual fragments were tied into a larger series of news topics. Coddington did not originally intend to study computational or structured journalism per se, but his thoughts with regard to Circa are highly relevant for my longer discussion of computational journalism, presented in this chapter. Speaking directly about Circa and its claims to rethink the narrative nature of news stories, Coddington concludes:

> I find that aggregation is not freed from narrative as a device for making sense of and communicating the social world, but is instead bound up in it, though in a different way from traditional journalism. **Aggregation shifts the primary narrative level on which journalism is produced (at least consciously) from the micro level to the meso level, focusing on news stories primarily as the relationship between news events over time and in juxtaposition to other issues and topics, rather than as textual conventions and forms.** In practice, then, the idea of the atomic unit of news is not so much about dismantling textual forms of news as it is about broadening news' sense of narrative by seeing each discrete news event as a part of a larger narrative structure. (Coddington 2015, 116)

As we will see later in this chapter, the notion of story structure as a computable outcome of discrete events is also tremendously important to the Structured Stories paradigm. Coddington's analysis of Circa, despite being conducted with different objectives than my own, can thus shed light on the phenomenon of structured journalism more broadly.

Graves (like Coddington) also did not study computational journalism directly; rather, he studied the growing community of political fact checkers. He analyzed, in his words, the journalistic reform movement that "investigate[s] claims that are already in the news, and publish[es] the results as a new story. The fact-checking movement asks political reporters to do something that can be quite uncomfortable for them: to challenge public figures by publicizing their mistakes, exaggerations, and deceptions" (Graves 2016). One of the fact-checking organizations studied by Graves was Politifact, which is connected to the present study by the presence of Bill Adair, the founder of that organization and the editorial leader of Structured Stories. There is a deeper technological and philosophical relationship between Politifact and Structured Stories as well. Politfact's underlying reportorial goal was to create a living set of relevant news facts, news events, and political statements labeled as either "true" or "not true," and keep those facts and events in a permanent database. Rather than generating a database from already published documents and narratives, in other words, Politifact *first* created a database of political statements which could then be used to generate stories, graphics, interactive digital displays, and other varieties of journalistic output. As we will see, this order of journalistic production—*first* the database, *then* the narrative—is deeply related to Structured Stories.

Networks of Computational Journalists

In chapter 1, I noted that notions of structured journalism had been considered as early as 2008 by my *Philadelphia Daily News* informant who tossed around the idea of combining newspaper archives with geolocational data in order to produce a continuing scroll of past and present news that could be delivered to a smart phone. The origins of this line of thinking, I would argue, can be found in a seminal piece by Adrian Holovaty, the developer of the 2005 Chicago Crime Map. His piece, "A Fundamental Way Newspaper Sites Need to Change" (Holovaty 2005), might be considered the founding document of structured journalism, as Meyer's *Precision Journalism* is for data journalism. If Meyer used a critique of journalistic notions of objectivity as a way to launch his call for empirical reform, Holovaty criticized something perhaps even more fundamental, the very idea of the narrative story as the primary journalistic form. "Newspapers need to stop the story-centric worldview," he wrote. "The problem here is that, for many types of news and information, newspaper stories don't cut it anymore." Holovaty used the term *structured information*, which was commonly used in computer science, but which had not been used in conversations about journalism before this moment. "So much of what local journalists collect day-to-day is *structured information*," he wrote [emphasis in original].

> the type of information that can be sliced-and-diced, in an automated fashion, by computers. Yet the information gets distilled into a big blob of text—a newspaper story—that has no chance of being repurposed. Repurposing and aggregating information is a different story [from putting it in a different display or narrative form], and it requires the information to be stored atomically—and in machine-readable format. For example, say a newspaper has written a story about a local fire. Being able to read that story on a cell phone is fine and dandy. Hooray, technology! But what I really want to be able to do is explore the raw facts of that story, one by one, with layers of attribution, and an infrastructure for comparing the details of the fire—date, time, place, victims, fire station number, distance from fire department, names and years' experience of firemen on the scene, time it took for firemen to arrive—with

the details of previous fires. And subsequent fires, whenever they hap-
pen. (Holovaty 2005)

As we can see, the fundamental criteria discussed above—the ability to disaggre-
gate facts, to reuse them in new ways, to store them permanently, to break them
down into the fundamental components of information outside the container of
a narrative—map clearly onto the strategies used by groups like Politifact, and
Circa. What is structured data? It is "information with attributes that are consistent across a domain." Holovaty then proposes a vast array of examples of how
structured data can be drawn from news events—"An obituary is about a person,
involves dates and funeral homes. A wedding announcement is about a couple,
with a wedding date, engagement date, bride hometown, groom hometown, and
various other happy, flowery pieces of information . . . . A political advertisement has a candidate, a state, a political party, multiple issues, characters, cues,
music and more." With the right mindset, the possibilities for drawing pieces of
structured data out of news events would appear to be endless. "See the theme
here?" Holovaty writes. "A lot of the information that newspaper organizations
collect is relentlessly structured. It just takes somebody to realize the structure
(the easy part), and it just takes somebody to start storing it in a structured format (the hard part)." The essay, like many written in 2006 and since then, goes
on to lambaste news organizations for their inability to change, their arrogance,
and their tendency to dismiss proposals like the above as "not journalism." The
essay discusses how content management systems (CMSs), which are resolutely
story centric, are perhaps the biggest barriers to innovations of this kind (see
Anderson and Kreiss 2013 for a further elaboration of this point). And in a telling update, dated "several years later," Holovaty adds "this essay inspired the creation of the fantastic Politifact, which won the Pulitzer Prize in 2009 and is a
great example of treating news data with respect" (Holovaty 2005).

I quoted from the Holovaty essay at length, because I think it is a foundational document—one that inspired not only Politifact but an entire network of
structured journalists. Developing in a manner that has been widely chronicled
by theorists of organizational change and networked development (for a just a
few examples see Anderson 2013a; Kreiss 2016; Lewis and Usher 2013; Turner
2006), a web of technologies, symposia, conferences, websites, and experiments
emerged to foster the growth of structured journalism. Among the important
players in the evolving structured journalism network were:

Individuals: Chris Amico, Laura Amico, Reg Chua, Bill Adair, David
Caswell, Tristan Ferne, Jaqui Maher, Paul Rissmandel, David Cohn,
David Smyrda.

Organizations: Homicide Watch DC, Structured Stories NY, Politifact, BBC R&D, Factcheck.org, Circa, The Curious City, Mean Streets, The Next to Die (https://docs.google.com/spreadsheets/ d/1z-eaFkrtrDDa51td1gnHY_1myJMRKk9NLoP0otqLO5M/ edit#gid=0)

Websites: (Re)Structuring Journalism, The Duke Reporters Lab, Structured Stories

Conferences and Meetings: Two yearly meetings of the structured stories network (in Cambridge, MA, and New York City); a 2015 presentation at the International Festival of Journalism in Perugia, and others.

When chronicling the development of structured journalism, there are three trends worthy of note (and keep in mind that the concept itself is barely a few years old). The first is that there has been a re-appreciation of the story format after an initial burst of excitement that the story could be demoted in journalistic importance. Structured journalism advocates, of course, would deny that they ever dismissed the story, but it is certainly the case that there has been a greater embrace of the story and other audience-friendly outputs as experiments with structured journalism have evolved. A second trend—perhaps the main one—is the emphasis on structured journalism as an avenue for reader engagement. In an earlier era, perhaps, the entire focus of structured journalism might have been on the producer side, but today there is an equally wide-ranging argument that structured reporting, by breaking down the one-size-fits-all story model, can encourage reader creativity and the freedom to explore issues at multiple levels of interest and expertise. A third and final area of emphasis is on the manner by which structured journalism is distributed—that is, the manner in which it travels across a larger news ecosystem. I turn to each of these issues at the conclusion of the chapter.

The Structured Stories Experiment and a Methodological Overview

Neither of the research projects I've discussed here, however, analyzed journalistic work as a specific subset of computational journalism, though both touched on computational and database-oriented practices as part of their analysis of other forms of journalistic production, primarily aggregation and fact-checking. Thus, when I saw that Politifact founder Bill Adair had partnered with computer scientist David Caswell to conduct a two-month experiment in computational journalism, called Structured Stories, in New York in summer of 2015, I jumped at the chance to observe firsthand how a computational journalism project actually worked on a daily basis. The announcement of the launch of Structured Stories, posted on the Duke Reporters Lab website, read in part:

> The Reporters' Lab has been awarded an Online News Association Challenge Grant [an award which attempts to foster innovation in news] for a project that will develop new forms of journalism to cover local government in New York City. Structured Stories NYC will use a structured journalism approach to cover major stories in New York this summer. It will be a new form of storytelling, a networked account of local news that accumulates over time and enables the local community to quickly access, query, and contribute to sprawling and complex local government stories.

On April 26, I emailed Adair, expressing my interest and asking to spend some time over the summer with him and his group, and he quickly replied in the affirmative. After an initial meeting with Adair and Caswell, I was more or less given free rein to spend as much time with the small, three-person Structured Stories team as I wanted and had complete ethnographic access (with one major exception that I will discuss briefly later). The team was made up of three Duke undergraduates—Ishan T, Nathasha L, and Rachel N—who were paid for their summer of work in New York and rented dorm rooms from the New York University Law School. I was able to hang out in the Structured Stories "newsroom" and watch the production process; more importantly, I was able to attend the three days of training in early June, where I was "baptized" into the Structured Stories mindset, and all of the daily, morning editorial meetings at which the student participants and editors reflected on the events of the day and discussed some of the philosophical and ideological issues they were encountering during the project. I was also able to conduct formal or semi-formal interviews with the students working on Structured Stories at any time I wished, and pepper them with questions as they worked.

In total, I observed the Structured Stories team for twenty-one days during the eight-week project, with a major gap between June 15 and 24, when I was traveling for other work. In the early weeks I was spending the entire day in the Structured Stories newsroom, and by the end of the experiment I was usually there for the morning editorial meeting and a few additional hours. I conducted three formal meetings with the staff (one with each team member), each interview lasting between forty-five minutes and an hour. I also obtained full access to the Structured Stories database and the shared Google Docs through which various editing and operational work was conducted and was able to watch this work take place in real time. By the end of my time at the project, I had filled three small notebooks with observations and taken more than four-dozen digital photos.

A few additional methodological notes: It will soon become clear that the Structured Stories project was an *experiment* and that the participants were analyzing themselves as much as I was studying them. The participants were journalism and public affairs students at Duke University and in no sense "real" employees of the organization, which itself was "real" only in a rather insulated and abstracted sense. Structured Stories NYC had an official beginning and ending date and was under no pressure to make money or even to make its journalism available to the larger public. David Caswell was explicit in arguing that Structured Stories was an academic project; he, Adair, and a University of Missouri PhD student submitted an academic paper about the work to the Columbia University Computation + Journalism Project—they will likely produce more academic work. So, I was observing a laboratory experiment in journalistic production as much as I was observing an actually operational journalism organization of the kind I spent so much time with in Philadelphia. All that said, the experimental nature of Structured Stories often didn't matter much in the heat of its day-to-day operations; the students who ran it worked seven to nine hours a day, like regular workers, for almost two months. Perhaps even more importantly, the experimental nature of the project led to a remarkably extensive series of meta-reflections and cultural self-examinations on the part of the workers. Whereas most newsroom workers have little if any time to think hard about or even articulate what they are up to, the Structured Stories workers were engaged in a fairly explicit act of meta-reflection at all times. For an ethnographic project concerned with examining journalistic *mindsets* as much as the embedded ideologies that lie at the heart of unthinking, routinized work, this is actually an ideal situation.

It should also be clear that I spent less on-the-ground time with Structured Stories as the project went along, moving from full days in the office at the start of the project to an hour or two I in the morning by the end. This marks a realization that the kind of journalistic labor I was examining at Structured Stories was rather different from the labor I analyzed in Philadelphia newsrooms. The structured stories team was *small*, it was not really part of a larger "organization" in any sense, and perhaps most importantly it was engaged in a constant process of what anthropologist Dominic Boyer has called "screenwork" (Boyer 2014). All of its work, with very few exceptions that I will discuss below, occurred at the interface between the computer screen and the Structured Stories reporter. I was, in short, watching reporters work on computers for almost forty hours a week with very few exceptions. This was remarkably different from the news work I saw in Philadelphia, where reporters rushed out of the office to cover breaking news, engaged in formal and impromptu meetings throughout the day, and socialized constantly with other journalists. Access to the Google Docs and Structured Stories interface, in other words, turned out to be just as important as access to the office environment itself. This also made the one level of access I was explicitly denied—the internal Structured Stories Slack Channel—more of a blow to my overall research than it might have been in a more outward-facing organizational setting. Slack is a form of internal company chat wherein employees who work on computers communicate constantly with co-workers by text. I requested Slack access early in my time at Structured Stories and after a day of deliberation or so, was told that *too much* would be visible to me were I to invade the privacy of the Slack forum.[2] This is an interesting development in the constraints and possibilities of ethnographic research, and while I don't have time to discuss it further here, it is certainly worthy of some meta-reflection by ethnographers doing work in these (increasingly common, screen-oriented) workspaces.

I also think it is worth saying something here about the relationship between this chapter (which is largely ethnographic) and the previous chapters, which have placed the journalistic mobilization of certainty and uncertainty into historical time. This chapter—which looks at a time span of barely a few months—can talk with far less clarity about whether these practices and products will mean much in the grand scheme of journalism history. Indeed, it's arguable that Structured Stories might turn out to be a quiet failure. Nevertheless, my historical research convinces me that the dynamics of computational journalism will serve as an embryo, at the very least, for journalistic mindsets, ideologies, and particular evidentiary practices for decades to come. Whatever else happens in the larger ecosystem of news, the attitudes toward objectivity and evidence mark a real shift and indeed a doubling down on notions of how data can be used to create journalistic truths.

In other words, the summer research project was more successful in examining the formal and explicitly articulated forms computational self-reflection than it was at uncovering the embedded and less explicit ideas at play in daily work of this kind. However, at this point, computational journalism is as much a vanguard idea as it is an actually existing form of journalistic work, and so this level of analysis is not entirely inappropriate. The underlying tensions and social dynamics of a screen-based project like Structured Stories are not entirely opaque—even without Slack access.

Structured Stories NYC in the Summer of 2015

WHAT IS STRUCTURED STORIES?

Structured Stories is so unusual, and its methods and processes so initially unintuitive, that it is worth providing a somewhat schematic definition of what Structured Stories is, how it works, and how it relates to the processes of automation and abstraction I listed earlier as being key to the emerging computational mindset of twenty-first-century digital work. When I told friends and colleagues about the project I was working on that summer, I was often met with stares of bafflement or expressions of confusion about how Structured Stories related in any way to journalism as traditionally understood. "Is this something that comes through an app or on a web page?" I was often asked. What Structured Stories is, then, is not immediately clear.

The key to understanding Structured Stories is to realize that it is a process of creating a database of journalistically relevant news events, themselves comprised most fundamentally of a newsworthy noun and a newsworthy and descriptively accurate verb. In some ways, Structured Stories reverses the process by which algorithms and computers scan traditional eight-hundred-word news stories, looking for relevant metadata and machine-readable text, as Google Adwords does when it looks to sell contextually relevant ads based on search terms and displayed results. Rather than scanning these articles for appropriate nouns and verbs after the story is written, the nouns and verbs are decided upon *first* and then a more traditional story is built around them. These nouns and verbs are linked to two other larger ontological databases on the back end of the Structured Stories CMS: "FrameNet" for actions and various so-called Knowledge Graphs for nouns and other important entities (in the case of Structured Stories, the most important knowledge graph in the summer of 2015 remained Freebase, although that was changing). This database of journalistic events can, when populated with enough entities, link various related events together in a variety of larger semantic webs and event patterns, allowing users themselves to understand how events are connected by manipulating connections in the database, as well as allowing machines to structure a map of relevant linkages in a semi-automated fashion (Fig. 6.1).

The labor of Structured Stories, then, is applying trained journalistic judgment to the process of building a semantic database of newsworthy events and then turning this database into something that might be enjoyed by human readers as well as machines. In the summer of 2015, students and faculty were out to prove that this system could be used to cover a series of ongoing events over the course of multiple weeks, stories that included the status of Uber cars in New York, housing issues related to controversies over public housing vouchers, and police–community relations in the aftermath of the Eric Garner shooting on Staten Island. Imagine that New York City Mayor Bill De Blasio was giving a press conference about the decision to launch a study on the success of Uber in serving minority riders in the outer boroughs of New York City. Structured Story journalists would have to decide upon the newsworthy event that powered the story (e.g., "gave a press conference," "launched a study," "courted controversy," etc.) as well as the relevant noun that was taking the action (e.g., Mayor

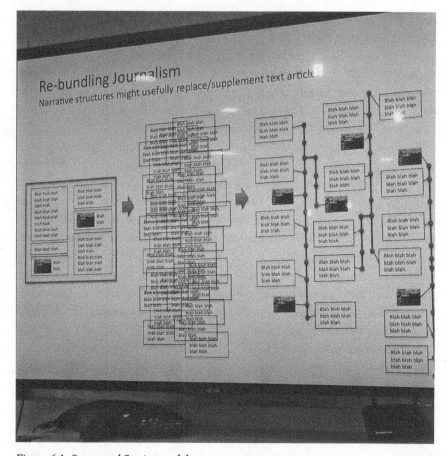

Figure 6.1 Structured Stories model Source: "Understanding Structured Stories," presentation June 16, 2015, New York, NY.

De Blasio, the Department of Transportation, Uber, etc.). As we shall see, making these decisions—particularly the decision about relevant story verbs—was no simple matter, at least in the early days of the experiment. What's more, the decisions made in assembling these databases would turn out to have long running implications for the process by which larger stories and story webs would get built.

THE WEWORK OFFICE ENVIRONMENT

As we will see, most of the Structured Stories work involved sitting in front of a computer. For this reason, it might be easy to assume that the location of the work—in this case, a co-working space on Fulton and Broadway in Manhattan—was extraneous or irrelevant. That is not the case, however; the locale of Structured Stories said much about the larger cultural currents at work in the process of creating a form of database news. It also shaped the day-to-day work itself in some important ways.

Structured Stories rented desk space, and with it obtained shared conference room use, in the WeWork offices at 222 Broadway at the corner of Fulton Street, directly across from the large Fulton Street subway hub downtown. Founded in 2010 in New York, WeWork is a company that provides shared office space to startup companies, freelancers, and small businesses (Guardian US now has its offices at 222 Broadway). The main working area is made up of rows of long wooden desks; a series of glass-enclosed conference rooms rings the primary work area. You can use a web interface to claim open conference-room space to hold meetings and take phone calls. In front of the large co-working space is a common area equipped with a kitchen, with free coffee (available all day) and micro-brew beer (also available all day). If you rent space at WeWork you can either obtain a small private office or, more likely, a chair at one of the long wooden tables (Fig. 6.2). The three Duke students who worked at Structured Stories sat at the very end of a table with their laptops plugged in, and I usually dragged over a free chair to sit with them while they worked. Directly out the large eighteenth-floor window loomed the new World Trade Center building, WTC 1. WeWork seemed invested in creating a sense of community among its various freelancers, and social events were held every Friday, open to all who

Figure 6.2 The WeWork office space

shared office space that week. Arcade games from the 1980s sat in one corner of the office space, though I never saw anyone using them.

The WeWork setup thus resembled the stereotypical Silicon Valley office environment in a number of important ways. It was stylishly designed. It aggressively mixed fun (free beer, the arcade games) with a rather stripped-down office environment (very few people had their own desk or even cubicle walls to separate them from the other workers). This shared space had some interesting effects on the Structured Stories process. Unlike any news project I have ever observed, the three students working on Structured Stories were little more than a pebble in a vast sea of other workers; it was very far, in this way, from a newsroom, where many journalists, editors, producers, and designers are engaged in the collective enterprise of creating a news product. Had I not known Structured Stories was happening, there would have been little if anything to distinguish its journalists from the other white-collar knowledge workers populating the rest of the cavernous hall, aside from their relative youth. Perhaps most importantly, the shared space limited the verbal interaction of the members of the Structured Stories team. Although there was no rule about talking in the office (and indeed, its nature made conversation inevitable) there was definitely a sense in the room that one should not have too many loud conversations that would disturb the other workers. Once or twice early on in the summer, Rachel, Nathasha, and Ishan attempted to hold impromptu editorial meetings, and it was quickly made clear through verbal glances and slightly uncomfortable coughs that this was too much socialization. Ultimately the unwritten rules of the WeWork space, along with the close working quarters, served to turn an already screen-oriented job into even more of one.

THE GOALS OF THE STRUCTURED STORIES EXPERIMENT AND THE DAILY WORK ROUTINE

It is important to remember that the Structured Stories NYC project I examined was, fundamentally, an experiment. The goal was to examine the ways that a structured, computational approach to reporting the news might be applied to ongoing coverage of a series of news stories in a large city. To that end the editorial director of the project, Bill Adair, and the founder of the project, computer scientist David Caswell, hired three Duke students to spend two months in New York reporting several narrative threads in a structured way. Originally, each student chose a story they would work on for the entire summer—city public housing issues, police/community relations, and the judicial primaries—although these foci shifted as the summer went on. To date, most structured and computation reporting had been used for particular kinds of coverage—fact-checking, for instance, or urban homicides. Could this procedure be applied in a more general way to everyday news?

Apart from a first week of training, an average day at structured stories unfolded in a fairly regular way for the two months I engaged in fieldwork. The three reporters would gather at about 9:30 AM for a daily Skype call with either Adair or Caswell, and occasionally both, to go over the events of the previous day, discussing particular problems or issues they ran into, giving general updates of their progress, and so forth. When the call was complete, they would return to their desks and continue the process of turning already-reported stories and facts into structured news information. In the mornings this often meant doing research of the kind that would not be unfamiliar to an average college undergraduate—the dates key recent events occurred, how different structures of city government operated, the longer history of particular issues, and so forth. In the afternoon, the students would turn to the process of turning these stories and facts into structured stories. Occasionally they would reverse the order of this process, engaging in data entry and analysis in the morning and more general research in the afternoon. Even more infrequently, they would leave the office to cover an event, attend a press conference, observe a political protest, and so forth. The three students told me that one of the most important parts of the entire process was finding a way to vary the office routine. In theory, the Structured Stories workers could do nothing but the journalistic equivalent of data entry for eight hours a day. It was therefore important for them to vary their routine in order to break up what was occasionally seen as monotonous work. Usually this variety was provided by research. Only rarely, as I noted above, did it come from undertaking what journalists call "shoe-leather reporting."

Backed up with the research necessary to understand the larger history and context of an issue, turning events into structured stories was the main task the students engaged in during the summer experiment. What, exactly, does this mean? What did these workers *do* in order to facilitate this process?

Let's take a specific example in order to understand the actual emerging journalistic routines at play in the work of Structured Stories. There was a hearing held on regulating Uber at City Hall on July 1, 2015. The Structured Stories reporter responsible for covering Uber would either go to the hearing or, most likely, read about it from a variety of already-reported sources the next day. The reporter would, of course, scan existing news reports about the hearing, but would be particularly interested in uncovering primary source materials—a written statement or press release on the part of the sponsor of a bill, the text of the legislation itself, the formal response from Uber management, any on-the-record comments by government officials, and so on.

At this point, the reporter would open the Google Form that had been designed for the Structured Stories experiment (later, he or she would input information into the user interface directly). The reporter would then spend a significant amount of time thinking about the **story frame** of the **primary event** that formed the core of this news story (sometimes, indeed most of the time, the kind of story I have used as an example here would contain multiple events). By story frame I mean the verb that governed the action of the story, which would initially be chosen from a set of hundreds of suggested frames contained within a database called **FrameNet**,[3] housed at the International Computer Science Institute in Berkeley, California. FrameNet frames often look unusual to human eyes and contain within themselves a wide variety of shaded meanings; for instance, the reporter in the example above considered using "process_ start" as his FrameNet frame but decided against it and used "activity_start" instead. From within the larger umbrella of the FrameNet frame, the reporter then entered his or her own **event frame**, which was a more journalistically specific iteration of the larger FrameNet frame already chosen. The selection of the verb was incredibly important. In Caswell's terms, given during one of the training days in early June, "verbs evoke the frame . . . and the relationship between verb and frame is a term of art in computational linguistics" (Field Notes June 3, 2015).

Following the selection of the verb and the frame, the reporter then decided on the relevant nouns that would occupy the event frame, linking each of *these* to an entity listed in the Freebase Knowledge Graph. Next, and in short order, the reporter would enter a series of bullet points fleshing out the event, a summary statement about the event, link to variety of digital primary sources containing information or evidence relevant to the event, the date and time of the event, and the location of the event (which would contain a universal location code). The ultimate output of this exercise would look something like the following:

[The New York City Council]   [held a hearing]   [about Uber]

which would contain the underlying semantic structure:

[Freebase entity]   [event frame]   [Freebase entity]

which would be ultimately a subset of the larger FrameNet frame "activity_start." One of the things Structured Stories reporters would do over time would be to populate highly semantically general categories like "activity_start" with journalistically relevant event frames like "held a hearing." Also, over time the reporters would generate a list of events—each in turn coded as more or less important to the overall arc of the story—which would flesh out the overall story topic, in this case "Uber in New York City."

Over the longer arc of the two months I observed Structured Stories, I watched three major shifts take place. First, the students gained the ability to enter their data directly into the Structured Stories backend database. Second, they gained some proficiency in identifying the nuances of how to distinguish particular "event frames" from each other and how a variety of subtle nuances could be expressed by choosing different event frames. Finally (and most important), the students became increasingly comfortable in recognizing what constituted an important "event" (in Structured Stories parlance) and how different events were subordinated to other events. Each of these more long-term operational shifts can be seen as the result of a set of specific challenges, questions, dilemmas, and ideological problematics that the Structured Stories workers had to overcome. First, the workers needed to become comfortable with the Structured Stories mandate that they *eliminate* as much color as possible from their journalistic thinking. Second, they needed to gain a better understanding of the difference between *states* and *events* in the context of Structured Stories. Third and finally, they needed to understand the complex way in which the different types of material evidence prioritized by structured journalism interacted with questions of what constituted an initiating journalistic event. I want to analyze each of these problematics in turn before moving, in my conclusion, to a more general discussion of the intellectual underpinnings of computational news reporting in the digital age.

ELIMINATING COLOR: "OFF RAMPS" FOR JOURNALISTIC ANXIETY

All traditional news writing, no matter how terse and factual, strives to incorporate an occasional creative turn of phrase or poetic allusion into its prose. Occasionally, this creative outlet is a headline; more often, it is a clever opening sentence (called the lede sentence by journalists) or some sort of pun. The Structured Stories mandate was different. The goal here was, in the words of one of the team members, to eliminate as much color as possible from the writing and focus only on the most basic facts of the story.

The explanation for this process—eliminate color and find the most important factual events—had both a psychological and operational justification in the context of Structured Stories. Machine language, the kind of language which the Duke students were being trained to model, could not capture all the nuances of natural, human language in any case. However, the Structured Stories process *could* capture the key narrative actions, "the kind which our minds are built to do anyway," in the words of computer programmer Caswell. Structured Stories was all about using language with no color and using language to signal the essence of an event. "I always think to myself when I am trying to drill down to the main event: why did this person write this article at this time," Caswell added as a way of trying to explain the processes he used for shedding color and excess words in his structured pieces (Field Notes June 3, 2015). An example of how this activity could affect the day-to-day construction of a story was encountered early on in the training process when the students and the editorial organizers were discussing a sexual harassment lawsuit filed against an Uber driver by a rider and the way that such lawsuits were impacting larger attempts to regulate Uber in cities. Was "sexual harassment" an existing FrameNet frame, one of the students asked? It was not, one of the editorial directors replied. "Sexual harassment, that's color," he added. "You can specify that it is sexual harassment in the bullet points or in the narrative story that is added on to the basic Structured Story sentence" (Field Notes June 3, 2015).

As might be imagined, the students and Bill Adair initially found this process of eliminating detail and color highly stressful and even a little upsetting. By the second day, it had begun to dawn on all of them how much the core of the Structured Stories process involved violating some basic tenets of what they considered good journalism: sacrificing color, even when it added factual nuance to a narrative; blurring the lines between press releases, governmental statements, and press conferences; occasionally oversimplifying (in their minds) the causal nature of events, and so on. By the end of the training week, a revolt was brewing among the journalism students as they began to balk at the impulse to radically flatten the nuances that they were used to incorporating into a traditional story. At that moment, however, it became clear that the Structured Stories designers had incorporated, deliberately or unconsciously, what I am calling a set of *off-ramps for journalistic anxiety*. By this, I am referring to mechanisms within the Structured Stories process that allowed journalists to engage in activities that corresponded with their own internal notions of "what good journalists did," while completing the core of the Structured Stories tasks. I do not mean to imply that the Structured Stories programmers had tricked these student reporters. Rather, I am referring to the fact that any knowledge-production process involves a multitude of activities and different stakeholders in that process can come to different understandings of the most important values embedded in the different activities while continuing to work together in a productive fashion. This is what organizational sociologist David Stark refers to as *heterarchy* (Stark 2011).

For the purposes of this brief example that I am using to embody a larger point, the most important off-ramp were the bullet points that Structured Stories journalists added to stories after the key nouns, verbs, and event frames had been decided.[4] The bullet points were where journalists linked to primary source documents, added all the color that had been stripped out of the story, filled in the details, and so on—but importantly, the bullet points were created after the primary aspects of the Structured Story had been already decided on. Nevertheless, without exception, every single journalistic participant in the Structured Stories experiment expressed relief to me once they realized that they could conduct more traditional journalistic work in later stages of the story building process. "This [conversation about the bullet points] shows the need to refine how we describe the relationship between the bullet points and the summary [sentence]," Adair noted at the conclusion of a particularly anxiety ridden conversation. "We need to sell it differently to journalists" (Field Notes June 5,2015). Caswell, for his part, referred to the fact that Structured Stories had two audiences. "Bill will kill me here but we're intentionally not trying to engage the reader" he noted, wryly. "No one will sit with their bagel and read Structured Stories. The audience for Structured Stories is a machine." But, in addition to the machine audience that would process the structured language of nouns, verbs, and events, there was also of course a human audience that would read bullet points and click on important links. It is not surprising that the students initially found it far more appealing to write for the second audience than the first.

THE VERBS: STATES VERSUS EVENTS AND THE NUANCES OF THE EVENT FRAME

Perhaps the fundamental epistemological feature of Structured Stories is that it conceives of the universe, including the journalistic universe, as a series of individual events. While the definition of event—a cause and an effect—seems obvious, several important corollaries stem from it. For starters, there is no such thing as a journalistic *non-event*, and all non-occurrences must be described in terms of blockage or as a specific event that keeps another event from occurring. During one of the early training sessions, the students were trying to figure out how to encode Uber's non-compliance with a series of regulations into the Structured Stories framework and were searching for an event frame along the lines of "did not comply." But as Caswell pointed out, "the absence of an event is not an event." Rather, some person or some entity had to note that Uber was not complying with a particular law and say it, as either part of a statement or in a report, for example (Field Notes June 4, 2015).

Related to this is an even more fundamental idea, the idea that Structured Stories cannot describe states of affairs, only events themselves. In the first day of training, a second academic visitor from a journalism school at another university expressed his deep concern that Structured Stories was, in fact, taking journalists back to an earlier era in which they found it hard to integrate discussions of background or the larger context behind news stories into their journalistic work. One of the major developments in modern digital journalism, he argued, was that reporters increasingly engaged in more interpretive work in their writing (see also Fink and Schudson 2014). This background and context, admitted Caswell, was a *state of affairs* rather than *an event* and thus was impossible to include in Structured Stories. "However," argued one of the students who had been listening to the conversation, "you can also link some events to other events, and out of that linking you can get context" (Field Notes June 3, 2015). Rather than simply asserting context, in other words, journalists with Structured Stories are forced to demonstrate its existence step by tiny step until it emerges out of a larger event structure. The way that context is generated here (framed by the users, editors, and computer scientists in almost Latourian terms, though they would never themselves have made that reference), is one of the most important aspects of the Structured Stories project. As I will argue in the conclusion to this chapter, the notion of a larger interpretive and overarching context as capable of being generated by a series of discrete, computable events, is what aligns Structured Stories with larger elements of computational thinking that I discussed in the opening section.

All causes and effects must be summarized as verbs, called event frames, and these event frames needed to ultimately be linked back to the FrameNet Database. This grounding in FrameNet was of fundamental importance for Caswell. "Why do the frames we pick for ourselves have to relate to the 1400 frames in FrameNet?" one of the students asked him. "If we didn't use these frames we'd have a "combinatorial explosion," Caswell replied. If there were too many frames, we'd lose the ability to analyze the story computationally. It would be impossible to find an event frame, impossible to organize the story in the way a computer could understand it. "The benefit to FrameNet is that it provides computational access to the data. It is what gives Structured Stories a rock solid, unmovable base" (Field Notes June 26, 2015). For this reason, reporters simply could not create journalistic event frames out of thin air, even if they drew on frames that they had used before. Rather, they decided that a particular action was the most appropriate for the story, went back and found the best approximation of that event in the FrameNet database, and then further nuanced it as they came up with an event frame that would also describe that action in a slightly more journalistically specific way. All of these factors, along with the general importance of event definitions for the workflow of Structured Stories, led to my informants spending a great deal of time attempting to master the nuances of the FrameNet frame in order to choose the most accurate event frame possible.

THE NOUNS: QUOTES, "TEXT OBJECTS," AND INTENTIONAL ACTORS

If verbs—or rather, the attempt to decide on the proper verbs for news events— were seen as the driving force behind most Structured Stories work, deciding on the proper nouns for particular events was often no less fraught. An important conversation occurred early in the Structured Stories training process, a conversation in which the student journalists attempted to decide the proper noun with which to describe a particular source of evidence for a Structured Story. The conversation began with Adair critiquing the sometimes arcane or complex terminology that Creswell used to describe the Structured Story process.

ADAIR: So what you are calling an "information artifact." It's basically a piece of text used as a noun. Why not just call it a quote?

CASWELL: It's a block of meaning made from text.

ADAIR: Well, I'm pushing to use more common terminology to help sell this to journalists. They won't use it if we keep throwing all these terms at them.

CASWELL: Well, you can't use quote because what this refers to in this particular example is **not** just a quote but also could be a report, a press release, whatever. You can't get too simple or else you lose some of the nuance in what you are referring to.

At this point one of the student journalists interjected with an attempt to find a compromise: "what if we use 'text object' and not information artifact?" she asked. We can see here that the participants, when faced with the simultaneously flat (all objects of evidence in Structured Stories are roughly given equal weight insofar as they are members of a single event frame) and nuanced (it is important for traditional journalists to distinguish between press releases, reports, and quotes, each of which contain within them an embedded understanding of evidence) nature of Structured Stories, were forced to grapple with how they value different nouns in the stories they were writing.

The students spent an equal amount of time, if not more, attempting to decide the noun that might initiate the start of a particular story and whether different nouns meant the same thing or a different thing when applied to the Structured Stories framework. Take, for instance, a press conference that is based on an initial press release that is itself a summary of a governmental report. What is the object that deserves prominence within the Structured Story? What is the most important noun, in other words? Is it a report on industry malfeasance ("an agency compiled a report"), a press release ("a press release documented agency malfeasance"), or a press conference ("the Mayor held a press conference about agency malfeasance")? In general, these are distinctions that journalists pass over quickly as they write their stories in a general narrative framework; for them, the actual distinction between a press conference, report, and press release can be glossed over in the crafting of a journalistic narrative. The nature of Structured Stories, however, forces participants to grapple with these issues in new ways. "Doing this whole process reminds me of high school physics where once you take it you look at the entire underlying structure a different way," one of the student journalists told me (Field Notes June 5, 2015).

One final interesting aspect of the process by which journalists decided on proper Structured Story nouns was that they eliminated consideration of inanimate objects as the cause of particular events. While I am not sure if there was ever a specific policy on this question before I asked, Caswell did have a quick and ready answer when I asked him whether or not the Empire State Building, for instance, could be picked as the primary noun in a Structured Story. "It can't be," he told me. "Structured Stories only allows *intentional objects* to be considered as motivating or action-initiating nouns in an event frame" (Field Notes June 11, 2015). The philosophy of actor-network theory has penetrated enough into journalism research and into the academy in general that I found this decision intriguing. However, I lacked the time to give it a proper follow up. Nevertheless, a question about whether the Empire State Building can be a character in a Structured Story simply demonstrates that decisions about event nouns are not an entirely straightforward process, even if the primary Structured Story focus was on the event verbs.

Computational Thinking and the Objects of Journalism

The final section of this chapter widens our analytical lens to look at three more theoretical aspects of Structured Stories and computational journalism in general. These speculative thoughts attempt, as much as possible, to discern what it is about computational journalism that makes it profoundly different from the forms of news reporting we have discussed in earlier chapters in this book and the ways that these differences serve, perhaps ironically, to ground journalism even more firmly in the world of unproblematic certainty claims. The first point elaborates on the overlap between structured stories and the world of literary narratology and structural linguistics. The second deals with what I call the "second order objectivity" of Structured Stories. The third touches on issues related to professionalism and the possible return of "naïve empiricism" in the early twenty-first century. In essence, I argue, the accumulation of transparent facts and their placement in a database whose objects are defined *within* that database and by their semantic relationships allows journalism to banish *all* uncertainty—truth is grounded in the database itself. These somewhat scattered ideas serve as a prelude to chapter 7, which steps back and looks at the evolution of quantified journalism from the early twentieth century until today.

NARRATOLOGY, STORIES, AND STRUCTURE

What is the relationship between computational journalism techniques and older, more general theories of language and grammar? During my time with Structured Stories in New York, I heard a number of references to ideas of narrative and morphology drawing on the early Russian narratologists and had further conversations on how these complex theories relate back to debates between Vladimir Propp and Levi-Strauss. Obviously, this is not something you hear in most newsrooms. But one interesting aspect of this line of thinking is exactly that—that these connections were specifically invoked by members of the Structured Stories team when they were telling me about their project; "to understand what we are up to you have to understand narratology and the morphology of folktales," one told me during an early training session (Field Notes June 3, 2015). So there is a sense in which these journalists and computer scientists see themselves as part of a particular intellectual tradition, one that relates to fictional narrative as much as it does to stories of the non-fictional kind.

The close ties between literal *stories* and computational journalism can be seen more clearly if we examine perhaps the most successful structured journalism projects, a series of experiments undertaken at the BBC as part of BBC Research and Development (R&D). In the summer of 2016 I conducted a series of interviews with structured journalists at or formerly employed by the BBC, including Jacqui Maher, Tristan Ferne, and Paul Rissen, in an attempt to get a sense of the larger network of computational journalism and how its different pieces related to each other. All three noted that structured mechanisms for organizing narrative data began in **fictional** BBC universes, and was only later adopted by the journalism side of the BBC. Ferne had a long background in BBC R&D (almost twenty years) and the fact that the BBC was primarily an audio and video distribution of non-news content was important to the specific ways that structured news developed under his watch. The original application of structured concepts to BBC content lay in the attempt by the BBC to create web pages for every radio and television program they hosted, at scale, in the earlier days of the commercial internet. The problem was that the BBC produced a tremendous amount of content and while the most watched and prestigious programs had a team to create and maintain a webpage, a great number of programs had no site at all, even one where you could simply get basic information about a show. The solution was structured, linked data (Tristrian Ferne, November 15, 2016)—coming up with a structured data template that would automatically populate static web pages with a select amount of program data (name of the show, name of the episode, air date, host, synopsis, etc.). These early structured data experiments, Ferne told me, helped create a general openness in the minds of a few BBC engineers to notions of structured information, concepts that were then applied to the long-running radio soap opera *The Archers* and the popular cult science fiction show *Doctor Who*.

The Archers is a drama that has been running on BBC radio since 1951 and has broadcast more than 18,000 episodes. Like all soap operas it tells a single, evolving story, one that contains a great many narrative offshoots and important familial relations that change slowly over time. This lead to the creation of what Ferne calls "a new continuity database for drama teams, something they can use for keeping track of what's happened and who's done what," ultimately replacing the paper "story bible" used by the writing and creative staff. These structured databases for fictional universes were not only for the production side, however; as Ferne said, "our vision is for a single common data model that supports production tools and audience-facing services. In this case we have used [a software interface called] Storyarc to provide all the data about storylines, moments and characters" that power a story. Aa described in 2008 blog post:

> the Radio Labs team started to design and build a prototype website for *The Archers* based around the drama's scenes and facets. To start with we created a data model that represented what we thought was important in *The Archers*—including scenes, characters, character relationships (such as marriages or parent-child), locations, storylines and tags. Then we took the daily *Archers* podcast and built a web interface for a production team to use to segment and tag each episode. This allows a user to split the episodes into individual non-overlapping scenes and describe each scene with a title and synopsis and then tag it with the characters, location, storyline, weather and anything else they can think of. (Ferne 2008)

Similarly, Paul Rissen helped build the "Mythology Engine." "The R&D Prototyping team had recently built an internal prototype for BBC Vision called the Mythology Engine," he told me, "a proof-of-concept for a website that represents BBC drama on the web letting you explore our dramas, catch up on story-lines, discover new characters and share what you find . . . So we built a prototype based around the stories of *Doctor Who*." Like *The Archers*, *Doctor Who* is a complex, long-running story with a multitude of character-driven entanglements; unlike *The Archers*, *Doctor Who* relies strongly on technological science-fiction objects to power its stories, necessitating the Mythology Engine to include objects and technological devices as part of its "cast of characters" in a way that was not necessary for *The Archers*. Also unlike *The Archers*, time in *Doctor Who* is a mobius strip, in which narrative developments often create parallel storylines and even universes and where fictional plot points do not necessarily revolve into straightforward linear time. Time, in *Doctor Who*, does not always make sense. "Because of this," Rissen told me with some satisfaction, "we saw *Doctor Who* as the ultimate limit case for a structured narrative concept, one that pushed the vary boundaries of how we could link up people, plot, and objects in a story that did not always move along in a straightforward fashion" (interview with P. Rissen, November 18, 2016).

It was only *after* these structured information experiments with BBC fiction that the engineers at BBC R&D decided to turn their attention to structured journalistic content. Early experiments included structuring a retrospective about the British homefront during World War II (called *Homefront*) and then turning their attention to the structured narrative elements that made up the Greek debt crisis of 2015. Journalism was different from drama," Ferne told me "because it doesn't come with a guaranteed ending or payoff" (interview November 17, 2016). The general concepts, technologies, and underlying mechanisms of the BBC experiments differed little from those discussed in my longer overview of structured journalism experiments in New York. The development of non-fictional, narrative elements at the BBC, however, gives new insight into the complex relationships between *narrative* and *data* that lie at the heart of computational journalism. Structured journalism projects often establish a different relationship to history, drawing on archives and presenting news over the *longe duree*. Context emerges from the manner by which individual elements of a database link up with one another to create the unfolding of time across digital space.

SECOND ORDER OBJECTIVITY

Key to understanding Structured Stories—and this will be explored in the next chapter as well—is the manner in which it re-orders traditional notions of journalistic objectivity while at the same time obscuring the new politics of this objectivity. One of the most important line of thinking in much recent science and technology studies has revolved around the manner by which standards and databases, while seemingly objective, are suffused with their own politics, exclusions, and definitions of "what counts" as a data field (Star and Bowker 2000, D'Ignazio and Klein 2016). For Structured Stories, whose most important "reality" is often the reality provided by its digital databases (i.e., FrameNet and the Wikipedia Knowledge Graph), these insights are of crucial importance. Think about the manner by which a more traditional journalist gathers evidence and then proceeds to link that evidence together in a supposedly objective fashion. Most journalists get information from the world—they conduct an interview, see a document, and watch something happening—and then integrate that information into a larger narrative that becomes the journalistic "story." For structured journalists, on the other hand, the objects that populate different semantic databases serve as the key underlying evidence that is used to construct a story. For the producers of Structured Stories, for example, the most important goal of the journalistic work is to decide upon a verb that links up with a particular event frame, which is linked to the FrameNet database maintained in Berkeley, CA. Any document that is found must have a corresponding reference in a database, as does any character in a story, statement that they make, or action that they take. If something is to be considered "real" for Structured Stories, it must be linked to a digital object populating that database. No database reference, no object. No object, no story.

We can see that this dynamic provides these structured story journalists with a particular notion of objectivity, one that might perhaps be more compatible with a computational, digital era. I call this form of objectivity "second order" objectivity. The ultimate guarantee of the reality of a piece of Structured Stories evidence is its presence in a digital database. This, in turn, keeps us on a surface, digital level of truth, a level where the key factor is that it is represented in a manner that allows it to be integrated with other digital objects, often through computational language. The reality that "counts" for a structured journalist is a reality that can first and foremost be represented as structured data. This structured data can be linked to, cross-referenced, and "proven" to be real. Showing how these objects are encoded in a digital format can compensate for the ultimate uncertainty of "reality." Meaning is thus moved up one level, to the semantic level. Perhaps objectivity is, as well. In either case, uncertainty is eliminated as the line between "fact" and "truth" is rerouted through the database.

THE RETURN OF NAÏVE EMPIRICISM?

Finally, Structured Stories (and structured journalism in general) tells us a great deal about the profession of journalism in the digital age and the possible return of naïve empiricism in the twenty-first century. The larger social context of news events, under the Structured Stories paradigm, emerges not from the scientific method, nor through the application of journalistic judgment and narrative skill. Rather, it is grounded on a series of utterly transparent and discrete events, which themselves are tied into permanent web databases and linked together through computational processes. Is it possible that this might mark the return of early-twentieth-century naïve empiricism (the facts at the most simple level are always transparent)? If this is so, it is also not a coincidence that the contextualization and professional judgment about the *meaning* of these facts are outsourced to the computer rather than to the human being. The post-1920s paradigm of objectivity ran something like this: facts themselves are not simple and are actually indeterminate; to compensate for this a group of professionals must exercise their occupational judgment to probe behind the surface of these facts in order to ascertain both their truth and their meaning. Looking at structured and computational journalism, we see something quite different. The professional judgment of the group, under this view, is hitched to computational processes that supplement occupational practices. Facts themselves are made clear and transparent, and journalism once again doubles down on the certainty it provides by yoking itself to the algorithm.

In sum: the developments discussed in this chapter link the previously discussed notions of a realist ontology (real things exist and we can see them) with the diminution of epistemology (human beings are incapable of stringing these facts together in any objective sense and so we need to rely on computers.) The return of naïve empiricism, and the linking of professional skill to machines and algorithms, may be an important consequence of computational thinking in the digital age. Nevertheless, and even if this is so, how do these developments in computational journalism relate to all the other forms of quantified journalism we have explored thus far? And how do they connect with the larger social, cultural, and political developments of the current moment? Now that we have completed our empirical survey of the use of data in news reporting over the past one hundred years, the final two chapters probe these bigger questions.

7

Three Overview Cases

Varieties of Information in the Digital Age

Religious, reform-minded social scientists. Journalists with an interest in documents and databases. Sociologists who advocate that sociology departments ought to teach students to run a newspaper. Journalists who proclaim their love of the scientific method. Quantitative data journalists. Journalists who transform narratives into structured data. This book has traveled long and winding road, from the early twentieth century to the first years of the twenty-first. This chapter is an attempt to tie these threads together by discussing three "urban mapping exercises" carried out by news organizations in a more schematic and formal manner. Most of them have already been talked about in greater or lesser detail—the SSM, the Detroit Riots survey that won Philip Meyer the Pulitzer Prize, and Structured Stories NYC. I preface the comparative analysis of these projects with a discussion of journalistic practices in the Penny Press and pre-Penny Press eras in the United States. With this comparative overview in mind, we'll be ready for some concluding thoughts on what these different journalistic orientations toward data might be able to tell us about certainty, uncertainty, and democratic life in the digital age.

Comparative Journalism, Comparative Visions of the City

Table 7.1 captures, in summary form, the course I've tried to chart in this book. We can divide the chronology into five periods—the pre-1830s, the post-Penny Press paradigm of reporting, the reform journalism of the progressive era, the precision journalism movement, and the computational journalism movement. We can delve into each of these periods by looking at the material evidence valued by the journalists of the time, the method by which that evidence was gathered and

Table 7.1 **Chronology of journalism in the United States**

	Material	Method	Context	Epistemology
Pre-1830s	Government and business records (documents 1), other newspaper or printed material in circulation (documents 2)	Aggregation, "intelligence"	The printer	The record
The post-Penny Press paradigm	Interviews, observations, documents	"Original reporting"	Elite vs. Jacksonian democracy	The report
Progressive Era	City maps, survey sheets, questionnaires, tables, information graphics	Tablature, counting, classification and coding, visualization	Progressive social movements, public relations firms	Naïve empiricism
Precision journalism	Government databases, reporter generated surveys	Variable-based, social science oriented	Narrative journalism, 1960s urban unrest	Social science
Computational journalism	User traces, previous journalism, semantic lexicons	The algorithm, high level interactivity with users, user control over results	Computer science, Silicon Valley, the turn to new empiricism	Events, linked events as context, machine readable language

evaluated, the larger political and social context against which the journalism was practiced, and the journalistic epistemology underlying each of these.

PRE- AND POST-PENNY PRESS PARADIGMS

As I discussed in chapter 1, the shift from eighteenth-century journalism to the journalism of the 1830s and beyond was accompanied by a change in the forms of evidence drawn on by printers and the other individuals responsible for producing the news. The primary evidentiary forms that were used to put together newspapers in the pre-Penny Press era were often other newspapers, along with business papers, shipping manifestos, and other documents. Government or public documents were rarely, if ever, utilized by printers, but to the degree they were, they represented another form of "paper evidence" that served as a mechanism through which information about society would be gathered into material form. The use of other newspapers as sources— the act of cutting snippets of information from one paper and pasting them into another—is particularly important to keep in mind here; as scholars like Ellen Gruber Garvey (2012) have demonstrated, the process of "cutting and pasting" news from one paper to another did not end with the coming of the penny press in the 1830s. Scholars can trace the spread of information, ideas, and even jokes (Nicholson 2012) from paper to paper and across the Atlantic Ocean, because of the aggregative practices of these early newspaper printers.

The notion of "aggregation" is important; to be less anachronistic, we might also speak of newspapers as "synthesizers of intelligence" rather than as "aggregators," but the basic concept of the relationship between new information, knowledge, and the events in political and economic life is roughly the same. Newspapers in the American colonial era had a largely synthetic function: their primary role was gathering already existing information (contained in documents, records, ledgers, and so on) and ordering it so that it could be quickly and easily grasped by readers. They served as a place where you might go to get relevant information about a particular topic or area of interest. But it is important to note here that the information you found there was not considered "original" even if it was "new to you." This led to a mechanism of evaluation for the sources of news in the pre-1830 journalistic era that differed from the ones that came later. Was the document an accurate representation of events in the world, printers might ask, and could it be folded into the already existing material about a particular topic or topics that might be interesting to a reader? Or, conversely, the addition of a paper item might help create an eclectic mélange of occurrences to amuse the reader. More prosaically, the train of thought was usually not this deep; oftentimes, items were added to a newspaper simply to make sure the printer filled all its available space.

It should be clear that the figure of the *printer* is essential here. Rather than the editor, the reporter, or the storyteller, it was the man (and it was nearly always a man) who operated the literal machinery of newspaper production who dominated the pre-Penny Press era. This development has been thoroughly discussed by Barnhurst and Nerone (2001) and I do not want to repeat their argument—that one key to understanding the development of American journalism can be glimpsed in the shift from "printer papers" to "editor papers"—at length here. For the purposes of this summary overview, it is enough to note that the printer's main job was the physical production of a news object (the newspaper) in a manner that largely dispensed with the value-laden notions of what it meant to "do journalism" common to our modern understanding of what it means to "make news." Printers were less doing journalism, or even making news, than they were simply making newspapers—contradictory and often catch-all documents that contained a plethora of gossip, humor, business ledgers, sermons (Nord 1990), and even actual news. Largely shorn of its normative role, except in retrospective analysis, a newspaper was often simply one of a number of aggregative objects that circulated across the American colonies and Europe from the seventeenth until the nineteenth centuries.

In her monograph *Journalistic Standards in Nineteenth Century America*, Hazel Dicken-Garcia (1989) characterizes the epistemological change that followed in the 1830s as part of a broader shift in American journalism from thinking of news products as *records* to thinking of them as *reports*. The paradigm of colonial printing discussed so far sees information as a record. The post-Jacksonian era would see a re-thinking of the type of information provided by journalists, eventually coming to consider it as a sort of report. In Dicken-Garcia's words, "if information is thought of as a record, its value is principally the same whether it is a week or a year old, and this value may, in fact, increase with time. But if it is regarded as a report, recency is its most valuable quality" (Dicken-Garcia 1989, 54). The insatiable demand for information about the bloody Civil War, she argues, shifted the public appetite for news irrecoverably in the direction of demanding news reports. This demand, in turn, activated a variety of latent potentials in the news production process. Techniques such as the eyewitness observation, the interview, and the cultivation of army officers as sources all emerged from the urban menagerie and later from the battlefields and campgrounds of the war. Technologies also played a role, though primarily a reactive one, with already-existing techniques like photography and telegraphy assuming a more prominent role in the assemblage practices of newspapers.

While Dicken-Garcia describes the role played by technology in news production as a largely reactive affair, it seems clear that macro-changes in material infrastructures also played a role in the transformation of the journalistic record into the journalistic report. In that light, *Journalistic Standards in the Nineteenth Century* makes a subtle argument that the modern newspaper marked the culmination of a lengthy process of *documentary disenchantment*. When printing techniques were expensive, laborious, and time-consuming, "the tedious work of recording information confined printing to the absolutely essential; anything beyond was required to be of a nature that elevated and ennobled mankind . . . a predominant view saw the press as the keeper of the record of human kind and civilization's store of knowledge" (Dicken-Garcia, 117). The phrase "disenchantment of documents" points to a radical change, one in which print was used as much to convey the report (with its trivialities, its eyewitness accounts, and its insider gossip) as it was a record of the activities of government, foreign events, and profit-generating market news.

Rather than printers scouring already existing documentary material, the new focus on currency generated a need to talk to human sources about what happened more recently in time, to haunt the lobbies of police stations and court-houses and society balls, all in an attempt to gather oral evidence about recent events. As I discussed in chapter 1, these interviews were often supplemented (though less often) by direct observations made by journalists themselves. What we are seeing here, in short, is the invention of *original reporting*, or a notion of journalistic behavior that led to a focus on gathering evidence that had never been discovered before, crafting it into a narrative, and circulating that narrative among an insatiably curious, often urban public.

Schudson (1978) has discussed these developments in terms of one further shift: the growing conflict between the emerging urban bourgeoisie aroused in part by the ideologies and reforms of Jacksonian democracy and an older, more mercantile business class previously well served by a class of more document-oriented newspapers. What I mean by this is that the focus on the document never entirely disappeared from journalistic practice, particularly at news organizations that spoke to a more to a business-oriented audience. As before, the journalistic goal was focused less on genuinely new information than it was on procuring "intelligence" about market developments and financial conditions. These papers and practices were forced to co-exist alongside other publications, however, newspapers that would come to dominate the professional self-conception of the journalist (a somewhat shabby figure with a nose for news, concerned with dragging new information out of the darkness and presenting it to the public, as quickly as possible). It marked, in essence, the invention of the modern news paradigm in the United States.

THE MRFM: ATTEMPTING JOURNALISTIC-SOCIOLOGICAL REFORM

The second chapter of this book, then, launches into some orthogonal challenges to that paradigm, challenges that emerge from an unlikely

source: religious reformers looking to advance social policy through the politics and visual display of what at the time could have been called "big data."
What does this proto-sociology have to do with journalism? I focused on the
MRFM in chapter 2 for several reasons. Their story shows just how undiffer-
entiated and hybridized early sociology was in the United States, torn between
reformers, scientists, quantitative data enthusiasts, and publicity men. One
aspect of this hybridized social science was a focus on the journalistic elements of scientific practice, one that sought to gain public attention for social
causes through the gathering and strategic communicative deployment of
quantitative, visual data. Chapter 2 demonstrated that this strategy failed to
make much of an impact on daily newspapers, in part due to technological
challenges but also because the quantitative data favored by social reformers
largely revolved around providing *contextual information* whereas most newspapers approached MRFM reporting by focusing on incidental occurrences
(like speeches or dinners). There was a disjuncture between how journalists
envisioned their reportorial roles and how social reformers thought the press
ought to behave. In short, the MRFM had higher expectations of the power of
the press than the press itself did.

One strategy of social surveyors in general (and the MRFM in particular) was
to use material forms of evidence, collected by them and transformed into pleas-
ing visualizations, to gain space for stories in the daily press. This involved what
we might call a "return to the document," the evidentiary form that had been
largely shuffled aside in the turn to direct observations and interviews as a way
to produce journalistic knowledge. It should be reiterated here that paper forms
of evidence were never entirely abandoned by journalists, especially in the business press. But the utilization of city maps, survey blanks, questionnaires, tables,
and information graphics highlighted the growth of material forms of data collection, categorization, and storage which were well under way outside journalism. The roots of this growth lie further back in the early nineteenth century, but
these practices began to diffuse more generally into ameliorative and knowledge
professions outside of science and the government several decades later. The
MRFM can be seen as attempting a form of materialist ju-jitsu: simultaneously
assuming the role of a quasi-journalistic actor to document poverty, vice, and
religious belief in the twentieth century metropolis and attempting to use a col-
orful form of visual materiality to get information they considered important
into newspapers.

There are several key aspects of this data-gathering *process* to consider here,
aspects of epistemology that intersect with but are distinct from the **material
forms** of the data themselves. First of all, the survey data collected by the MRFM
was primarily gathered by means of simple counting, a counting that tried to
gain an overview of an entire urban population for the purposes of grasping its

moral behavior *in toto*. Volunteers who went house to house or from church to church in the absence of available government data usually did this counting. These results were recorded, put into tables, and turned into a variety of urban maps and pictures documenting social patterns. These maps, and the stories about them, were distributed to news organizations and other reporters, and were sometimes even placed as advertisements in these papers. As chapter 2 showed, however, this strategic use of data did little to affect the overall tenor of news coverage of the MRFM and did not generally lead to stories that were more contextual or focused on broader patterns.

All of these efforts, and their mixed successes, need to be viewed against the backdrop of several larger developments in both politics and the social sciences in the United States. The early twentieth century was the heyday of the US "progressive movement" that attempted, among other things, to use data and empirical scientific evidence to move the country in a particular political direction. While today we think of the Progressives as fundamentally "liberal," it needs to be kept in mind that there was a moralistic, anti-immigrant, anti-vice undercurrent running through all of these scientific initiatives, undercurrents that clearly show themselves in much of the work of the social surveyors. These quasi-scientific tendencies also acted as the backdrop for the emergence of sociology, a science that also possessed an affinity toward the kind of journalism that was reformist, moralistic, contextual, a type of "good journalism" that urban progressives could accept with pride. In chapter 3, I looked at what became of sociology (and journalism) when sociology began to ramp up its criteria for what counted as a science while journalism, at the same time, became more contextual and visually driven. I will turn to these changes in a moment.

For now, I just want to conclude by stressing that the overall epistemology embodied by the work of the social surveyors and the journalists who covered them clearly seems to be a variant of "naïve empiricism"—the generally unproblematic reliance on individual facts and observations to construct scientific reality (Schudson 1978). This view takes the relative clarity and transparency of facts for granted and assumes that data and evidence maintain a straightforward relationship to the social world. Facts exist, they are easy to observe, and what goes on in the social world does not generally affect what counts as genuinely "real." Individuals, when presented with enough accurate data, will come to use that data as a heuristic for both their own behavior and their view of the larger world. This attitude of the piling up of facts can best be summed up by the quote from Charles Dickens' *Hard Times* that could serve as the epigraph to this chapter: "In this life we want nothing but facts, sir! nothing but facts!" This statement captures a particular mindset whose clarity and forcefulness were to be much challenged in the decades ahead.

DATA JOURNALISM AND COMPUTATIONAL REPORTING

By the time the precision journalism movement emerged in the 1960s, a great deal had obviously changed in both empirical professions of journalism and sociology. The love of empirical facts had not disappeared, but the notion of what a fact *was*, as well as how its existence was to be ascertained, had shifted. Journalism had become more contextual, but at the same time it had also become less "scientific," while to be a social scientist now meant to be a member of a professionalized class of largely quantitative researchers who occasionally acted in an advisory capacity to the government. It was against this backdrop that Meyer conducted his Pulitzer Prize-winning Detroit Riots survey, which came to be seen as the prototypical precision journalism endeavor, combining the methods of journalism and social science to uncover the causes of the riots and the motivations of the rioters. Meyer uncovered evidence that contradicted the accepted narrative pointing to either inadequate assimilation of African Americans from the south or the influence of radicals or criminal elements as the cause of the riots. Instead, according to his survey research, the Detroit uprising was largely fueled by feelings that social movement scholars now call "relative deprivation," in which the fuel of unrest is not the lack of material and social progress but rather the paucity of such progress relative to the progress of others.

It is interesting to contrast the material underpinnings of the Detroit survey with the social survey work carried out a few decades earlier. Rather than going about gathering large scale demographic data on their own, reporters made use of existing government databases and conducted stratified random sample interviews of Detroit residents. And rather than relying on activists to feed them statistical information, the reporters themselves were making use of social science techniques on their own. Rather than adopting a proto-big-data approach to statistical evidence, the Detroit Survey was based on what had, by now, become commonly accepted sampling procedures and involved juggling variables in order to obtain statistical validity. Rather than naïve empiricism, the Detroit Survey clearly practiced a form of social science, one that involved invoking the judgment of a professional community in order to guard against individual researcher error. The Detroit surveyors, finally, understood that social data was not evident on its face but needed to be put through a rigorous process of statistical testing in order for the truth to emerge.

Even given all this, the most important differences between the urban work carried out by the social surveyors and the precision journalists may have been less the material at hand or the epistemological underpinnings behind the analysis of that material than the larger occupational groups that the journalists of the 1960s were interacting with, along with the wider political climate they were operating *in*. Social survey work, and the journalism that accompanied it, occurred at a moment of social and epistemological crisis in which the spirit of empirical science was challenging older forms of community and traditional knowledge. There was also a deep sense of crisis that shadowed the work of Philip Meyer, but it was an urban and social crisis that had enveloped many US cities in the 1960s, accompanied by a general scientific disillusionment that stands in sharp contrast to the optimism and scientism of the progressive era. There is an ironic twist here: the underpinnings of social science had become commonplace enough to diffuse into tangentially related knowledge professions such as journalism and news reporting. But at the same time, these underpinnings were starting to become challenged on a number of social and cultural fronts.

Representative of this broader challenge was the emergence of long-form narrative reporting, which I have characterized at the "epistemological other" of precision journalism. It was only in the context of the work of authors like Gay Talese, Norman Mailer, and even Hunter S. Thompson that precision journalism took root. Clearly, journalism was now confident enough to assert a professional autonomy to transmit reality beyond the simple "he said–she said" of political discourse, but the debate about where that autonomy ought to be grounded was in full swing by the 1960s. Should it be located in the mind and creative spirit of the individual reporter? Or should it be centered on the scientific method? To the degree this question was ever conclusively answered, I have argued in this book that it was answered in favor of a scientific, variable-based journalism and a coterminous doubling down on objectivity on the part of the journalism profession. Thus, precision journalism became CAR and data journalism in the 1980s and 1990s.

I've also argued that the methods, epistemologies, and material forms of data did not change in fundamental ways between the invention of precision journalism and the full-flowering of data journalism in the early twenty-first century. While the speed, interactivity and scale of data journalism work did mark a major advance over previous decades, and while social-scientifically inclined news reporting was institutionalized in certain fundamental ways, the underlying thinking behind the practice was still social scientific in nature. True to Meyer's notion of what good journalism ought to be, data journalism used data, filtered through social scientific practices, to craft traditional news narratives, combined with a more professional, robust notion of what "objectivity" was (a bias toward reporting "the truth" rather than giving all sides a hearing). The important (and thus far final) shift in the story I've told does not occur until the invention of computational and structured journalism in the early 2000s.

On to, finally, computational and structured journalism. What are the material objects of evidence that underpin them? I argue in chapter 6 that there are three: an already existing narrative, narrative events, and semantic databases. By already existing narratives I only partially refer to the fact that much of the work of the Structured Stories team, for example, was based on already written news reports and historical accounts, although that notion of aggregation was certainly an important part of the work done by the students in that project. By "actually existing narratives" I also refer to the foundational premise of Structured Stories—that narratives come first and then are transformed into data. These narratives, seen as a unified whole with plot elements, characters, and a dramatic arc, exist first and are then decomposed into both events and semantic data. The second key material element to computational and structured journalism is that very notion of the *event*—the motivating cause of action by which characters make decisions or objects force occurrences to move in particular ways. The characters and the events that encircle them, finally, are linked to already existing semantic databases, which allow these events to exist not as data but as structured data, or data that allows for the building of second-order relationships with other data by virtue of its implicit or explicit categorization structures.

We can see, especially when we compare it to the other cases discussed so far, that by standards of previous material forms those embraced by computational journalism seem much more "digital" or even "immaterial." We need to be extremely cautious in pushing this dichotomy too far, for as decades of research in science and technology studies have shown us, the digital is far from an immaterial state of affairs. Nevertheless, there is something important going on here. It is not as if the products and the basis of computational journalism articles are less materially thick than their data journalism counterparts but rather that the reporters and editors have embraced a flexible version of material evidence and products—what Law and Singleton (2003) have termed "mutable mobiles." Objects in a database are, by their definition, solid enough to exist as structured data, and deeply material insofar they can exist as data at all but are also flexible enough to assume a variety of positions within an overall semantic network. Perhaps even more importantly, the articles or narratives that eventually re-emerge from the transformation of narrative into data are deliberately designed to be as manipulable as possible by the audience. One of the major conceits of structured stories—and this was represented in conversations I had with Caswell and Adair as they started to ponder how they should design the public facing, front end of their website—was that it allowed a great deal of agency for their readers. The "selling point" of structured journalism, to the degree one exists, is that it allows for an extensive level of user interactivity as readers scroll through different epistemological levels of information about a single story or set of stories. If you care deeply about a topic, in other words, you can dive deeper into the information provided, and if you care less, you can skim along the surface. The arrangement of events and actors in a structured sense allows for that kind of product flexibility and thus implies a different notion of materiality, at its root.

Placing these different forms of journalism next to one another allows us, in a fairly fundamental sense, to get a sense of how the objectivity, epistemology, and materiality of journalism have shifted over time, and have shifted in a sense that is not entirely teleological or linear. Despite the growing importance of databases and computational power at the technological level, computational journalism is as much a return to older notions of information and knowledge as it is an extension of data journalism and social science. Facts are transparent and, if deployed properly, can mobilize the public on behalf of "the truth." In the final chapter I turn to more political questions and attempt to tease out what this study might tell us about journalism in a digital age, particularly journalism in what some critics and commentators have labeled our "post-truth" era.

8

Solidarity and Uncertainty

The Dial

On November 8, 2016, I and a few hundred other people gathered in a Brooklyn bar to watch the expected triumph of Hillary Clinton at an election night party. The mood was festive, especially for the many professional women in the room who had waited their whole lives to see a candidate like Clinton at long last ascend to the highest political office in the United States.

The festive atmosphere didn't last long. When we were not staring at each other in growing shock and dismay or looking at one of the television screens that lined the stage area, many of us were furtively glancing at the *New York Times* iPhone app, which just that day had unveiled a "digital dial" that would track the percentage chance each candidate had of winning the presidential race at that exact moment in time. The dial started off the night showing there was greater than 80% chance of a Clinton victory, but quickly began to swing wildly as results came in. One moment it read 60% for Clinton, the next 60% for Trump. As the evening went on, the swings grew less pronounced until the dial finally, shockingly, inevitably settled on "Donald Trump: 100%."

Watching the election dial, to my mind, perfectly captures the state of public life in our age of digital journalism and omnipresent data. How can we have so much information, so much computational power, and yet at the same time so much uncertainty? How can a cold, hard number like "80%" suddenly dissolve under the weight of reality into a swinging needle with no seemingly obvious pattern and no central resting place. Why, for heaven's sake, couldn't the dial *ever sit still*? As it turned out, the "twitchy" nature of the dial was a deliberate choice on the part of the designers to incorporate statistical error into their readings; since there was no way to demonstrate error graphically, the needle would fluctuate around a percentage *within the margin of error* at that particular moment:

> Second, we [the designers] thought (and still think!) this movement actually helped demonstrate the uncertainty around our

forecast, conveying the relative precision of our estimates. In our opinion, having the dial fluctuate a small amount—bound by the 25th and 75th percentiles of simulated outcomes—was more successful at conveying the uncertainty around our forecast than simply listing what those percentiles were. As the night went on, the gauges fluctuated less and less as our forecast became more precise. By the end of the night, the gauges barely moved. (Aisch 2016)

The twitchy dial was purposefully designed to capture uncertainty; it was an embrace of a more feminist style of information visualization (D'Ignazio and Klein 2016) and an attempt to push back against the cold accuracy usually designated by visual data conventions (Kennedy et al. 2016). And it was this statistical uncertainty, according to many observers (and according to my friends at the bar), that caused the greatest anxiety of all.

In this book I have tried to show the many ways that professional journalism, as the twentieth century progressed, became increasingly confident that it could convey reality with a type of scientific certainty, a certainty that grounded itself in large part on the techniques and evidentiary forms of social science. As I conclude, I want to ask whether this growing professional certainty has really been all to the good. While we cannot blame the current state of US politics on journalism alone, it would seem by the evidence all around us that increased professional confidence in journalistic abilities has not led to a better politics. One response, very much a child of the early digital age, was to de-professionalize news reporting. A second response has been to foster community conversation and dialog with different members of an audience. A final response to this has been to double down on the truth. All these of these responses, while not misguided, do not get to the root of the twenty-first-century political malaise, which I describe as the desperate search for certitude among conditions of deep uncertainty.

In this conclusion I want to first revisit the critique of "he said/she said" journalism and, perhaps quixotically, attempt to defend it from its most serious detractors. I will then give an alternate reading of the relationship between journalism and social science, one that uses demonstrable uncertainty as a springboard for getting closer to (but never entirely reaching) the truth. I provide a few examples to show how uncertainty is actually baked into modern journalism's DNA. I conclude by reflecting on the broader dilemmas of uncertainty and certainty and speculating how our common condition of uncertainty might be turned toward progressive political goals.

Humility and Professional Uncertainty: Revisiting the Case of the View from Nowhere

In chapter 4, I documented how Philip Meyer's case against traditional reporting was grounded in an argument against "value free" or "all sides could be right" reportage. "Old-fashioned objective reporting needed no anchor," Meyer argued. "It merely bobbed along the surface of the news like a Ping-Pong ball floating down a mountain stream. Interpretation requires a reference point. One must begin with a pre-judgment, a position of some kind" (Meyer 1973, 8). First and foremost, this is a claim of increased professional capacity on the part of journalism—journalism *can* venture to interpret events and *can* render judgments as to the certainty of events, because it is a professional class of intellectual workers that possesses the ability to do so. Alongside the rise in precision and data journalism is a corresponding rise in the professionalism of reporters. We should note that this view of its professionalism is at odds with many standard histories of the occupation, which often view journalism as increasingly colonized by technology, economic incentives, or state power over the course of the twentieth century.

Why did "all sides could be right" reporting exist in the first place? There are many convincing explanations. One argues that there were economic imperatives in monopoly media markets to not offend the political sensibilities of potential readers and thus make sure the claims of "their side" were included in news stories. Arguments indebted more to political science see journalism as inherently dominated by elite sources, such as government officials, who help set the parameters of acceptable debate against which a diversity of neutral sources can be included. What all of these arguments have in common is that they cast "all sides" reporting in such a negative light that it becomes obvious that journalism has nothing to lose by leaving it behind.

Is there any way to see "all sides could be right" styles of journalistic discourse as in any way a positive thing? Perhaps we could mount an argument that it was part of a style of journalism that *recognized and understood its own limits, a journalism that was, in some sense, more humble*. Why, after all, would a profession with questionable methods, working under a deadline, and dealing with a variety of self-interested actors in complex situations be at all capable of ascertaining the exact truth of a situation? More than that: how would journalists possess any special insight into the motivations or internal states of mind of any of the people they talked to? The best case for journalism that *refuses* to take a stand is that it represents a journalism that understands its own limitations.

This is, in effect, an anti-professional argument. We are long past the days, however, when journalism can be placed back in its pre-professional bottle, nor would we want to do so even if we could. I am not endorsing this argument on behalf of a certain style of neutral journalism. Indeed, the way to create a more nuanced and uncertain journalism is not to make it *less* like a science or a social science, but *more* so. Science, after all, has a somewhat paradoxical way of demonstrating certainty, one that is in fact powered by the open acknowledgement of *uncertainty*.

Data and Doubt

In a 2017 article for *The Atlantic*, Ed Yong grapples with how the movement toward "open science" could be used by an anti-scientific Congress to demean and defund science research. Yong quotes Christie Aschwanden, a science reporter at FiveThirtyEight: "it feels like there are two opposite things that the public thinks about science," she tells Yong. "[Either] it's a magic wand that turns everything it touches to truth, or that it's all bullshit because what we used to think has changed . . . . The truth is in between. Science is a process of uncertainty reduction. If you don't show that uncertainty is part of the process, you allow doubt-makers to take genuine uncertainty and use it to undermine things." These thoughts align with the work of STS scholar Helga Nowotny (2016), who argues in *The Cunning of Uncertainty* that "the interplay between overcoming uncertainty and striving for certainty underpins the wish to know." The essence of modern science—at least · in its ideal form—is not the achievement of certainty but rather the fact that it so openly states the provisionality of its knowledge. Nothing in science is set in stone. It admits to often knowing little. It is through this, the most modern of paradoxes, that its claims to knowledge become worthy of public trust.

What this scientific attitude requires is the ability of human beings to live comfortably in the heart of this paradox. Would it be possible for professional journalism to embrace this type of paradoxical uncertainty as well? We have already seen evidence of data journalists' attempts to build uncertainty into the very nature of election forecasting and the concomitant anxiety this uncertainty twitch in the "prediction dial" caused users. All election forecasting is an exercise in uncertainty mapping; there has never been a FiveThirtyEight result that gave a candidate a 100% chance of winning an election. The difficulty lies in the tendency of partisan human beings to interpret uncertainty as a formal prediction about a particular outcome.

There are other examples of journalism attempting to capture more fully the radical uncertainty of everyday life. As discussed in chapter five in the third edition of *Precision Journalism*, Philip Meyer discusses the manner by which science is grounded in what it does not know and openly acknowledges this fact before going on to discuss how those lessons can be applied to CAR. The *New York Times* regularly includes a feature "What We Don't Know" alongside its stories of high-profile mass casualty events, like public school shootings or terrorist attacks. The "Upshot," perhaps more than any other *Times* feature, seems to embrace uncertainty at its very core, hewing close to a more social science approach of nuanced evidence and hedged factual claims. Increasingly, data journalism is concerned with building admissions of uncertainty and lack of knowledge into the design of visual displays. In my call for journalism to embrace a more con-textualized version of uncertainty I am *not* trying to claim that such a vision is entirely unknown to the press at the moment, nor that it would be contrary to much of what journalism is already doing. There are already existing procedures and media practices that could be invoked and drawn on for lessons.

My problem, rather, is with the increasingly sharp-edged press rhetoric that openly proclaims American journalism to be the heir to an Enlightenment tra-dition of truth, fact, and a knowable external reality and implicitly or explicitly contrasts that occupational value system with the emotional, the ideological, or the post-modern sensibilities of politicians, academics, or rural Trump support-ers. I lack the space in this conclusion to fully spell out the recent politics of this rhetorical turn (for that see, in part, Graves 2016), but I do think that the elec-tion of George W. Bush and the utter mendacity by which that administration pursued the Iraq War in terms of its own press strategy is a key development in recent journalistic history. A central moment—perhaps *the* central moment—took place when an anonymous Bush advisor (later revealed to be Karl Rove) told the *New York Times* mockingly that journalists were members of the "reality-based community."

> He told me that guys like me were "in what we call the reality-based community," which he defined as people who "believe that solutions emerge from your judicious study of discernible reality." I nodded and murmured something about Enlightenment principles and empiricism. He cut me off. "That's not the way the world really works anymore." He continued, "We're an empire now, and when we act, we create our own reality. And while you're studying that reality—judiciously, as you will—we'll act again, creating other new realities, which you can study too, and that's how things will sort out. We're history's actors . . . and you, all of you, will be left to just study what we do. (Suskind 2004)

It was not a great step for journalists to proudly accept the reality-based commu-nity label as a point of pride. As I have tried to show over the course of this book, this has been the general trajectory of professional American journalism for the past one hundred years. The trouble lies when the rhetoric of scientific certainty is only embraced halfway; science is, in the end, a discipline of uncertainty and even humility. It is not a becoming posture for a more methodologically uncertain, provisional, off-the-cuff intellectual discipline like journalism to proclaim itself more scientific than science itself.

Solidarity in Uncertainty

From Thomas Hobbes on, many political philosophers have understood the future orientation of humanity to lie at the root of the modern condition. What distinguishes human beings from animals, Hobbes argues, is not their use of reason but rather the manner by which their minds are perennially preoccupied with the future and the relationship between the future and the present. Hobbes' genius was to see this future-oriented uncertainty as the mainspring of two different impulses—the commercial impulse to achieve a secure future via industry and the political impulse to seek refuge from uncertainty by embracing the Leviathan, or the absolute sovereign (Michaelis 2007). Future thinkers like Spinoza and Hume, on the other hand, saw "productive uncertainty" (Vergary 2014) as a mechanism by which human freedom could be strengthened—by removing humankind's gaze from the metaphysical heavens and turning it toward the very real task of living together in a modern, limited political state.

Uncertainty, of course, can have deeply negative consequences. As Nowotny dryly puts it, "on a superficial level, at least part of the western world seems to have entered a phase in which uncertainty as an enduring feature of life is losing the allure of being mainly a carrier of opportunities. As the collective mood swings, not for the first time, uncertainty becomes associated with threat" (Nowotny 2016, 4). Although her book was written before the full implications of the recent populist upsurges in the United States and Europe became clear, the specter of Hobbesian uncertainty looms in the background of Nowotny's analysis. Reduction of uncertainty, anxiety, and fear through the embrace of ethnic nationalism, soothing populist rhetoric, or even the leviathan itself is always an option.

Having come to professional maturity—as I hope this book has shown—by honing its drive for greater factual certainty, and temperamentally opposed to the leviathan in all its forms, it is natural that journalism would react to current conditions of uncertainty by doubling down on its claims to be objective. This is, in the end, a noble professional goal—who would not want one's job to be that of driving out darkness with the light of transparent truth and clear, cold, quantifiably certain facts? What is good for the profession may not always be good for the polity however. At the very least, more confident professional certitude and loud proclamations about "the truth" may not be the only solution to the United States' democratic crisis. In embracing a more humble, provisional, and uncertain journalism, and by using the open acknowledgement of the unknown as a spur to gain further (always provisional) knowledge, there is no guarantee that a more progressive, human, or equitable politics will inevitably emerge, of course. Better journalism alone is incapable of curing what ails us. Nevertheless, as the great philosophers of uncertainty Joel and Ethan Coen have put it, "we can't ever really know what's going on. So, it shouldn't bother you. Not being able to figure anything out." If anything can be said to characterize the human condition, the one thing that unites us, our common state of casting about blindly in the half-darkness is as good a candidate as any. Journalism has a part to play, however small, in turning our uncertainty into something that brings us closer together, rather than something that drives us apart.

On Objects, Objectivity, and Method

In the summer of 2008, as I was completing my first round of research in the newsrooms of the struggling *Philadelphia Inquirer* and *Daily News* (Anderson 2013a), I was discussing with one of the few *Daily News* employees who could code his vision for the future of the news industry. There needed to be a greater and more strategic use of newspaper archives, he told me. What's more, he had a particular notion of how these archives might intersect with the *place* a story occurred.

> Say you're walking down the street with your iPhone or your mobile device. One of the things newspapers could do that no one else has the resources to do is to tell you the news story that's happened recently at the very place you're in. You could use geo-location for that. But that's not all we could do. We could find a way to share **every** single news story that's ever happened in a place by drawing on our archives. Say you walk into an intersection where a politician gave an important speech or there was a good restaurant or a famous murder. We could tell you that too even if it was fifty years ago. And we could link to the story. And we could sell ads off that too. (Field Notes June 10, 2008)

This radical vision of news reporting as drawing on *structured data*—the notion that journalism could live at intersection between static archives and dynamic, consumer-oriented location services—seemed radically new to me and much different from the ideas I was hearing from other journalists in 2008. At the same time, however, many newsroom journalists were unwilling to engage in far more common digital-era practices such as linking out to other websites in order to justify their claims to factual knowledge. When mentioning another website or noting a piece of government data housed in an online archive, the journalists of 2008 seemed largely incapable of placing a <html=> tag in their news stories in order to send readers to that information via a hyperlink, something I had learned to do in 1996 when building my first ever university-hosted home page. Sometimes journalists blamed their CMS (Anderson and Kreiss 2013), other times they claimed that the economics of the news industry mitigated against sending readers "away" from their news websites (De Maeyer 2014), but in both cases there seemed to be a great deal of professional resistance to the idea of linking in news stories.

To my mind, what united both of these disparate findings was that they both involved questions of what "objects of evidence" journalists considered to be appropriately truthful and journalistic (Anderson and De Maeyer 2015). Was deploying a hyperlink in order to buttress an evidentiary claim something journalists ought to do? Should journalists integrate news archives and other forms of structured data into their stories? These questions, in turn, raised further questions about the *materiality* of journalistic evidence and the manner by which material affordances intersected with journalistic *epistemologies* and *professional cultures* in order to create particular forms of news reporting. In other words, journalistic pretensions to knowledge (what journalists could claim to know about public life) were in part influenced by the way they assembled network chains of evidence to buttress particular notions of journalistic expertise—and there were material, epistemological, and professional elements to these network chains (Anderson 2013b).

When data journalism emerged as the next big thing in news reporting in 2012 or so (Anderson 2013c) I thought about it in a way that was based on my earlier thinking about hyperlinks and news archives. Data journalism seemed to offer a plethora of new objects of evidence for journalists to consider—from large numbers of documents to statistics to online databases and data visualizations to structured information—and somehow integrate into their traditional reporting practices. What was more, many of these new evidentiary objects had a particular materiality (particularly documents and databases) and made new epistemological claims (they were quantitative) in ways that challenged some fundamental reporting practices, practices which were still largely based on oral and qualitative evidence. These are the origins of this book, which proposes to analyze how "data" is (or is not) creating new "journalistic cultures of truth" and in turn changing how journalists understand objectivity and their professional role in public life.

I've concluded that there are four essential requirements if we are to properly understand the role played by data in news reporting, requirements that can be said to more generally apply to the emergence and evolution of "cultures of truth" writ large. Our research must discuss the materiality of evidence. It must consider the epistemologies of professional groups. It must be comparative; that is, it must go beyond journalism and compare journalism to other kinds of professional knowledge production. Finally, it must approach these materialities and epistemologies *historically*, i.e., it must consider how they change over time.[1]

Here, I demonstrate the importance of the historical-sociological perspective through my outline of the chapters and intertwined arguments contained in this volume. First, we should consider the manner by which news stories are facilitated by the integration of certain forms of material evidence into the production of journalistic knowledge. Integrating these evidentiary forms depends in turn on the underlying occupational schema through which journalistic knowledge workers assess the meaning and relevance of that evidence. That assessment takes place against the backdrop of a dynamic, intra-professional process whereby different knowledge groups interact with others in a process of legitimating their knowledge claims about the world. The ultimate success or failure of the knowledge claims in turn relates to the interactions between *journalism* and *its public*—how journalists understand the public they serve, how journalistic actions call different publics into being, and how the public responds to the authority claims that journalists deploy.[2] In putting forward this model, I also discuss each of these three frameworks—comparative and historical materiality and epistemology—by reviewing some of the most important literature about each of them and tying this literature into journalism scholarship.

What methods and perspectives, then, ought we use to assess the historical evolution of professional knowledge? My model begins with the objects of evidence journalists use to construct what they consider to be empirically objective narratives and news stories. Different patterns of evidence collection and the journalistic assessment of the "truth affordances" of these evidentiary forms help lay the groundwork for a variety of news stories that integrate time, context, and explanation in different ways (Tenenboim-Weinblatt and Neiger 2017; see also Barnhurst 2011). The manner by which these objects of evidence are integrated depends, in turn, on the underlying occupational schema through which journalistic knowledge workers assess their meaning and relevance. This assessment should take place within a *comparative* professional context, a context in which particular knowledge groups interact with others as part of a process of legitimating empirical claims about the world. The ultimate success or failure of these knowledge claims, finally, is grounded in the relationship between *journalism* and *its public*—how journalists understand the citizens they purport to inform and how the public responds to the authority claims that journalists deploy.

THE HOLY TRINITY OF NEWS OBJECTS: OBSERVATION, DOCUMENTS, AND INTERVIEWS

This model starts with the notion of "objects of evidence." What does this mean, and what are the objects of evidence most valued by journalists? To answer this question, I first turned to the professional literature about how journalists ought to conduct basic reporting. In sources as diverse as an introductory college lecture in basic "news reporting and writing," (Fieldwork, November 2007), an online syllabus for budding citizen journalists (McGill 2006), a guide for elementary school students about the nature of news (Niles 2005), and a faculty handbook for the assessment of journalism and mass communication programs, the "holy trinity" of valid news objects is repeated over and over again: "observation, interviews, and documents" (McGill 2006). "There are three main ways to gather information for a news story or opinion piece," writes the guide to journalism for middle-school children. "Interviews: talking with people who know something about the story you are reporting. Observation: watching and listening where news is taking place. Documents: reading stories, reports, public records and other printed material" (Niles 2005). For budding journalists on college campuses, the instructions are similar. A rubric for assessing the "core competencies and learning objectives" for journalism students lists the very first basic skill as "gathering information through interviewing, observation, and the use of documents, printed and computerized, to write fair and balanced news stories" (Niles 2005).

Interviews

Taking documents, sources, and direct observations—journalistic objects of evidence—as a starting point, I want to briefly turn to an overview of how the journalism studies and communications literature has analyzed each of them as part of a larger ensemble of news-work practices, practices that shed light on the state of journalistic knowledge production. We can begin with the notion of the interview, the key evidentiary form in modern news. Perhaps inspired by larger sociological questions about the uncertain methodological status of qualitative opinion research (Lee 2008), the history of the "news interview" has received a significant amount of attention in the journalism studies literature. The news interview, according to a basic definition in the *International Encyclopedia of Communication*, is marked by its focus "on matters related to recent news events, its highly formal character, and its [management] primarily through questions and answers" (Clayman 2008, 2510). At the heart of this vein of scholarship is the argument that the interview has a history. In Schudson's language, "interviewing, all but unknown in 1865, had become a common activity for reporters in the 1870s and 1880s, was widely practiced by 1900, and was a mainstay of American journalism by World War I" (Schudson 1995). Not only does the interview have a chronological history, however, it can also be examined cross-culturally. The overview of the diffusion of the news paradigm between 1850 and 2000 by Høyer and Pöttker (2005) is perhaps the most ambitious and wide-ranging example of this type of analysis. Credit for launching this strain of comparative research belongs to Chalaby (1996), with his work on the Anglo-American origins of journalism and his argument that the interview is an Anglo-American invention. More than simply a historical and cultural artifact, the interview also has material and technological underpinnings. Lee (2004), along with other scholars working broadly in the tradition of science and technology studies, has documented the importance of technological artifacts and recording technologies in the emergence of the interview in sociological research.

In a tradition of news access research running from Gans (1980) and Tuchman (1978) to Schlesinger (Schlesinger and Tumber 1994) and Cottle (2007) empirical evidence documents that "the mass media in the United States look to [interviews with] government officials as the source of most of the daily news they report" (Bennett, 1990, 103). Most of the research on the emergence of the news interview has thus focused on its relationship to changes in the political sphere and the increased professionalization of the journalistic field vis-à-vis politics. In historical terms, a pattern of deference to public officials and the verbatim regurgitation of official government transcripts was slowly replaced, first in the United States and England and later elsewhere, by an increasing attempt to gather news via the formal interrogation of the powerful (Schudson, 1995; Chalaby, 1996; Clayman 2008). Sociologically speaking, these public officials continue to exercise a great deal of control over the general shape and contours of the news agenda through their placement inside key nodes of discursive reporting networks, even as the journalist–politician relationship has grown more confrontational.

The history of how interviewing evolved as a practice that also came to implicate the so-called "man on the street," or the "vox pop" (Montgomery 2008), has been studied less. Once again, the bulk of the literature on interviews with "ordinary people" (Palmer 2017) are primarily housed in disciplines outside journalism, such as sociology, anthropology, and oral history (Feldstein 2004). The most intriguing analyses in these fields tends to take a macro perspective, pointing toward large-scale social changes such as the emergence of the "interview society" and "the spread of the interview into new areas as indicative of the spread of the modern temper" (Riesman and Benney 1956, 229). Research on the American radio show *Vox Pop*, which in the 1930s established the "voice of the people" as a legitimate object of discourse by turning its attention to the "forgotten man on the street" (Hilmes and Loviglio, 2002, 91), provides some empirical evidence for these larger social changes. In his discursive analysis of the four general types of interviews (which include the "experiential interview," or the interview with a non-expert, non-public figure, justified on the basis of that person having witnessed or experienced a particular event), Montgomery argues that "to focus on the political interview as if it were typical of news interviewing in general is supported neither by the history of the journalistic interview nor justified by a survey of current broadcasting practice" (Montgomery 2008, 261).

Documents

Through this brief overview of research on the news interview, we can see that is a particular form of journalistic evidence that has its own pattern of cultural diffusion that intersects with a combination of sociological, political, technological, and organizational factors. It is, in short, *a news object with a history.* Less attention has been devoted to the evidentiary form the news interview replaced (or, at the very least, strongly supplemented): the document. One way to better understand the interview is to understand how printers and publishers used "paper" as journalistic source material from the colonial period up through and beyond the so-called Penny Press era, and how oral forms of evidence overtook these documentary practices. Not that the use of documents by journalists ever entirely went away, of course. While the growth of oral forms of evidence gathering was related to the increased consumption of news by the newly urbanized middle and working classes, "documents and data" remained important sources of journalistic knowledge production, particularly for the financial and political elite. The earliest material category of news "evidence" in the centuries following the diffusion of printing technology was, indeed, the document, both in the form of other news media (magazines, broadsheets, and other newspapers), as well as in the form of letters, publicity documents and, eventually official and quasi-official government reports. How were these different objects of evidence used to report (indeed, to "aggregate" the news) and how did journalists understand what these sources meant to those who used them? While much of the discussion of document use in journalism is scattered across various media histories, it has not generally been analyzed as a specifically material form of news in the same manner as the interview (but see also Gitelman 2014; Kafka 2012for this mode of analysis outside journalism).

Key to the understanding of paper documents advanced here is the development in journalism of a new and shifting relationship toward material evidence, an attitude that helped reorder the evidentiary value of the human beings, paper documents, and news reporters that together made up the journalistic story. The beginnings of this shift can be traced to, first, the growth of the Penny Press and the related emergence of the "spectacle" of the urban city center in the early to mid-nineteenth century, and then to the shifting news practices of battlefield correspondents during the Civil War. Whereas most printers were once content to *aggregate* the news through the collection, cutting, and pasting of paper, the Penny Press began to *report* the news by increasingly relying on human sources to provide the latest information on events. Following some brief but intriguing remarks by Hazel Dicken-Garcia in her monograph *Journalism Ethics in the Nineteenth Century* (1989), I contend that it is helpful to think of this shift from "paper to people" as part of a broader transformation of American journalism from understanding news products as records to understanding them as reports. The key shift here lies at the nexus between materiality, time, and the larger structures and cultures of newsgathering. Far more than in research on the interview, research on the history of "the document" is an interdisciplinary effort. Pondering the nature of documents in journalism takes us into the primordial soup of news itself—to printing, to the public sphere, and to paper. In discussing documents, we verge perilously close to those vast oceans of book history and medium studies. The role of documentation (and assorted terms like inscription devices, traceability, and immutable mobiles) also rests at the heart of science and technology studies (see, for instance, recent work on "paperwork" [Kafka 2009] and "the epistemology of documents" [Sokolov 2009], which combines medium history and technology studies in an overview, quite literally, of paper [Vismann 2008]).

While the analysis of documents is interdisciplinary, there is less research on the use of documents in journalism. An exception can be found in the scholarship on investigative reporting, of which work by Ettema and Glasser (1998) remains the classic example. In an early paper (a revised version of which eventually became chapter 7 of their book *Custodians of Conscience* [1998]) Ettema and Glasser discussed the "epistemologies of investigative reporting," drawing a connection between the manner in which an anonymous "tip" is rendered as a *material* form and the eventual accumulation of supporting journalistic evidence by which that tip is turned into news (Glasser and Ettema 1984). While the framework for their analysis is obviously indebted to Tuchman (1978), there are tantalizing hints of a more materialist perspective shot throughout the paper. In discussing the collection of investigative evidence, Ettema and Glasser quote a journalist who refers to the importance of "paper, documents, signatures, recordings, anything that captures the fact, that certifies the fact. So, always the first question I ask after some preliminary stuff is there any more paper on this? If there's not, I've got a lot more work to do. I would have to skip the paperwork and go directly to interviews." (16) Later, Ettema and Glasser refer to the "weight" of evidence a material property that serves to justify the further pursuit of the story; a "hierarchy of evidence, based on weight" (Glasser and Ettema 1984, 20).

Direct Observations

There is a great deal of scholarship on the journalistic interview. There is less on documents and even less on the third journalistic object of evidence, the eyewitness report (for evidence that editors prefer elite sourcing over direct observation see, in particular, Pedelty 1995). Closely tied to the field of cultural studies, visual culture, and the idea of "eyewitness news," direct observation is perhaps most notable for the fact that it is the ugly stepchild of journalistic practice. Comedy news shows like *Saturday Night Live, The Daily Show*, and *The*

Colbert Report induce laughter by drawing attention to the idiosyncratic journalistic tendency to ask the "man on the street" to describe events that reporters
themselves have just witnessed. In a more serious fashion, John Durham Peters
has contributed a philosophically inclined perspective on witnessing, arguing
that the experience of the eyewitness captures many of the most important vec-
tors of modern communication, standing, as it does, between the experience of
something and its translation into semiotic discourse (Peters 2001). In a more
properly sociological vein, concerns about the relationship between the eyewitness, the broadcast, and the truth of an event runs though the pioneering work
of Lang and Lang (1973) to the theory of media events (Dayan and Katz 1992),
and beyond.

It is Barbie Zelizer, however, who has done the most to deepen our understanding of the role that the "eyewitness account" has played in journalism.
Indeed, the uneasy journalistic status of the eyewitness is a thread that runs
through her work, from *Covering the Body* (Zelizer 1992) to more recent articles
on the firsthand witness of news events (Zelizer 2007) In *Covering the Body*,
Zelizer interrogates the authority of the eyewitness account by documenting how
journalists compensated for their uncertain status as witnesses to the Kennedy
assassination both through narrative reconstruction and by marginalizing unau-
thorized storytellers. In her 2007 article "On Having Been There: Eyewitnessing
as a Journalistic Keyword," Zelizer typologizes and historicizes eyewitnessing.
She argues that while the epistemological difficulties associated with eyewitnessing have remained constant, the practice itself has gradually moved from
existing as a kind of report toward being institutionalized in a specific role, a role
eventually both buttressed and problematized by technology (Zelizer 2007).
Despite Zelizer's path-breaking work, however, research on the journalistic status of the "direct observation" remains sparse, particularly when compared to
the work already done on the history of the news interview and even the news
document. Also lacking is a comparative analysis of the first-person account
similar to that which Chalaby has provided for the interview. Currently, analysis
of direct observation proceeds as if the status of eyewitnessing was broadly the
same across cultures and nations and under all circumstances. But is this actually
the case? Was there a "diffusion" of the practice of journalistic direct observation in the same manner in which there was a diffusion of the lede, the inverted
pyramid, and the interview (Høyer and Pöttker 2005)? To date, we do not know.

Objects and Objectivity

This brief literature review brings to the surface a fundamental conceptual distinction: the difference between *the study of journalistic objectivity* (as a norm, an
attitude, an ideology, a professional state of mind) and *the study of news objects*
(the underlying raw materials of the news process that are woven together to

create "the news"). When I first started to plan this book, my grand goal was to construct a history of journalism that dispensed with considerations of objectivity and focused solely, or at least primarily, on journalistic objects themselves. As should be clear by now, this attempt was a failure. Whether or not this was a conceptually bad idea, it was simply untrue to the historical, archival, and ethnographic evidence I discovered as I conducted my research. I quickly understood that it is impossible to understand how journalists have used particular pieces of material evidence to construct news stories without considering how journalists have understood what these news objects are capable of doing and how these understandings relate to larger dynamics of power, authority, gender, race, and class. Less a history of the objects of journalism, then, this book became a history of the circular process through which different forms of material evidence intersect with different journalistic conceptions of what that evidence meant and how material evidence makes journalistic reportage appear to be more truthful, contextual, and factual.

The question of journalistic objectivity—its historical origins, its sociological purposes, its occupational meanings, and its normative validity—stands as the beating heart of journalism scholarship. It is everywhere because it obviously marks the focal point of a vast system of scholarly and social concern; and it is nowhere because its very importance and prevalence have tended to obscure its normative development. Objectivity, argues Hackett (2008) should be defined as "a set of [journalistic] practices and ideas, such as a stance of "neutrality" or 'balance' in relation to the people and events being reported" (Hackett 2008, 3349). Or in Schudson's more expansive definition (2001),

> [the] objectivity norm guides journalists to separate facts from values and to report only the facts. Objective reporting is supposed to be cool, rather than emotional, in tone. Objective reporting takes pains to represent fairly each leading side in a political controversy. According to the objectivity norm, the journalist's job consists of reporting something called "news" without commenting on it, slanting it, or shaping its formulation in any way (150).

Journalists have used objectivity as a discursive shield to defend their occupation from assault, while critics have likewise used it as a hammer to pound journalism for its embrace of an impossible ideal (Cunningham 2003; Carlson 2015). Journalism historians have located the primal origins of objectivity in a variety of domains, ranging from shifts in the political system to economic commercialization to technological impact (Kaplan 2006; Tuchman 1972). For many scholars, newsroom objectivity has often served as a theoretical stand-in for questions of journalistic professionalism, with the growth of objectivity seen as analytically equivalent to the rise of journalists as a professional class (Dicken-Garcia, 1989). But as noted elsewhere, a generation of historical and, particularly, comparative journalism research has demonstrated in convincing fashion that "objectivity cannot be seen as the only occupational norm to both emerge from and buttress the professional project, and in some cases, it may not even be the most important norm" (Anderson and Schudson 2008, 93). While objectivity has served as a rhetorical weapon in struggles over journalism's special status, and while it remains an important sociological marker of the rise of journalistic professionalism, scholars should not commit the analytical shortcut of automatically equating the presence of one particular type of objectivity with the emergence of a professional class.

Alongside these historical and sociological studies of objectivity, however, a second strand of communications research is visible. This strand is concerned less with "objectivity" as a mental state, a professional practice, or a literary form, and is more interested in the study of the *objects* that go into making the news and the historical processes by which these objects are rendered appropriately journalistic. This ties in with the discussion of documents, interviews, and observations here. This strand of communications scholarship possesses some clear affinities with recent research in STS, and in particular, actor-network theory (ANT). Most of the extant ANT-inspired newsroom research deals either with the manner in which new technologies is integrated into newsrooms (Loon and Hemmingway 2005; Plesner 2009) or the way that news organizations innovate (Schmitz-Weiss and Domingo 2010). I would argue that the implications of ANT as a method for understanding the production of news lie far beyond either technological adoption or newsroom innovation; in particular, ANT is a highly appropriate lens through which to analyze a media universe in which "news facts" emerge, circulate, and dissolve.

This focus on news objects also helps turn our gaze to a comparative dimension. One of the most important and neglected studies by ANT founder Bruno Latour is his most recent analysis of the workings of the French legal system (Latour 2010b). By comparing the socio-material processes of knowledge construction in both the legal and scientific arenas, Latour sheds light on what objectivity has meant in *both* domains. In Latour's ethnographic analysis, scientists actually behave in far less "objective" a manner than their legal counterparts, who must rely on a particular shared "bodily attitude" ("passion is the least appropriate term to describe the attitude of judges in the course of a hearing") (204) to compensate for the uniform textuality of their evidentiary objects. ANT-influenced journalism studies would pay as much attention to the objects of journalism as they do to the framing and social construction of reality by journalistic institutions. They would take heterogeneous news objects seriously. In studying the assemblage of these news objects, they would pay attention to the way in which bits and pieces from the social, the technical, the conceptual, and the textual are fitted together" (Law 1992, 381) to form news stories, news networks, and news organizations.

This, at least, was my train of thought when I started this book. But I want to reiterate, before proceeding to the third element of my analytical framework, that the notion of a resolutely object-oriented analysis of journalism worked better as a conceptual schema than as an analytical practice. Latour aside, it is nearly impossible to isolate "the object" as an analytical category without considering how the object is understood. This is why we must take both the variety of journalistic objects of evidence *and their cultural, political, organizational, and social embeddedness seriously.* We must consider both journalistic objects and journalistic objectivity. The fact that objects and culture are inevitably intertwined should have become clear over the course of this book.

One way to understand the intersection between materiality and culture is to consider empirical knowledge professions, not in isolation, but as part of a more dynamic system of expertise (Abbott 1991; Eyal and Hart 2010; Colins, and Evans 2007). This constitutes the third plank of my analytical lens: the need for a comparative perspective that looks at the ways different occupations tasked with generating "knowledge" divide the world up into domains of what might be known and by whom. This type of disciplinary comparative work is relatively common in the science and technology studies and sociology of knowledge literature. *Questions of Evidence* (Chandler, 1994) inaugurates a cross-disciplinary conversation about "what counts" as legitimate evidence and why and how what counts varies from knowledge regime to knowledge regime; unofficial sequels to that work might include books like *Things That Talk* (Daston 2007), *An Inquiry Into Modes of Existence* (Latour 2013), *Making of the Law* (Latour 2010b), and A *History of the Modern Fact* (Poovey 1998). Books as different as *Trust in Numbers,* Porter' (1995) s cross-disciplinary history of statistics and Umberto Eco's *The Infinity of Lists* (2009) continue these conversations in a variety of domains. *Objectivity* (Daston and Galison 2007) is a seminal work in this regard, providing a materially and visually indebted history of scientific objectivity that dialogs well with the literature on journalism (and indeed, directly does so in some of Galison's future work (Galison, 2015)..

From within journalism studies, on the other hand, these types of cross- disciplinary comparisons have been rare. One example of this type of work would be Michael Schudson's PhD dissertation, *Origins of the Idea of Objectivity in the Professions* (1990) which compared the rise of objectivity in journalism with its development in the legal profession during the nineteenth and early twentieth century. This example is instructive both for its rarity and for the fact that the comparative element was entirely dropped when the dissertation became the book *Discovering the News* (Schudson 1978). Most studies of journalism consider journalism alone to be enough of an analytical object. This book is an argument that we need to expand our epistemographic horizons and bring other knowledge practices into our conversations about the news.

In his comparison between the objectivity of journalism and the objectivity of science, Galison (2015) notes that "journalistic arguments over objectivity engage more directly with the politics of the moment" than scientific disputes, which engage more directly "with the production of knowledge." A different way to phrase this would be that journalism, as opposed to science and even social science, is heavily dependent on the public as both a subject of analysis and a source of professional legitimation. The final argument that underpins my analytical framework is that we must consider, in any history worthy of the name, both the relationship of journalism to its audience and to its public and the way in which that relationship changes over time. The way journalists understand the relationship between data, quantification, and visualization and the public, as we have seen, is far from being static.

Notes

Chapter 1

1. For a longer discussion of the materialist–genealogic method employed by this book, see the appendix, "On Objects, Objectivity, and Method."

Chapter 2

1. Just as an example of one particular methodological flaw, the census conflated occasional employment with full employment, meaning that a respondent counted as a "worker" even if he or she had not been regularly employed for many years (Bales 1991, 71). Beyond this basic methodological opacity, the question of how to correlate even nominal employment with actual poverty and wealth was a contested question, with the answer usually depending more on the respondent's ideological predispositions than on actual evidence. The political parties in Britain did not collect detailed information about wages and poverty, and official government statistics, such as those used to document the application of the Poor Law, were shoddy and unreliable (Bulmer, Bales, and Sklar 1991, 18–19).

Chapter 3

1. The *AJS* began publishing in 1895, the *ASR* in 1936. Thus, the early citations in this analysis all come from the *AJS*.
2. In a 2012 piece in *Journalism*, Susana Salgado and Jesper Strömbäck (2012) contend that the category of "interpretive journalism" is a fraught one, subject to a variety of meanings and definitional shades that render it problematic as an analytical category for political communication research. This is correct as far as it goes. They also usefully propose more conceptual clarity that, they argue, can help scholars compare their research findings about the role (and rise?) of interpretation in news. Once again, this is a useful exercise. However, Salgado and Strömbäck also treat the notion of "journalistic interpretation" as an ahistorical concept, neglecting the variety of different meanings journalists and editors themselves have attributed to interpretive journalism since at least the 1930s. Without an understanding of journalists' own visions for contextual, analytic news, political communications researchers risk only focusing on half the story.

Chapter 4

1. The first third of this section draws heavily on an interview I conducted with Phillip Meyer on January 16, 2015, as well as on his 2012 memoir *Paper Route*. While transcribing the interview I was interested to see how closely his memories in the interview tracked the sentiments in his memoir. Quite often, the stories and anecdotes were virtually identical.
2. By "counter-sorter," Lancaster means simply computers.
3. At the time he wrote the overview, Chaffee was an assistant professor in the UW-Madison school of journalism. He had studied at Stanford University under Wilbur Schramm, and returned there in 1981 as a full professor. Chaffee was well regarded both at Stanford and in the larger field of political communication research and journalism, and it is interesting to see this glimpse of his work as a younger (and perhaps angrier?) man.

Chapter 5

1. Meyer's article on game theory for *Playboy* must go down as one of the oddest examples of data-driven journalism in the canon. Commissioned by the men's magazine to write about how game theory could be applied to picking up women, the married and buttoned-up Meyer—lacking much recent experience in the dating department—reworked real-life courtship situations with his wife Sue, providing her with pseudonyms or simply referring to her as a "leggy redhead."

Chapter 6

1. See, for example, works as different as Hayles (1999) and Turner (2006) for different versions of this argument.
2. The relevant part of the message from the Structured Stories leadership read as follows: "we need a few places where we can have our own space and private conversations and one of those is Slack. It is both our email system and our CMS, so I'm not comfortable with you having access. If you were hanging out with a writer for the *New York Times*, do you think he/she would give you open access to the *Times* email and CMS? Uh, no. If there's an occasional document or message that you hear about and want access to, let me know. But I can't let you simply sign in to our system in the same way no other news organization would." This is an interesting commentary about how journalists (and indeed, all ethnographic subjects) view their side of the access equation, particularly when the social interaction ethnographers observe is rendered in what Bruno Latour would call "inscribable" form; that is, written and permanent.
3. FrameNet describes itself this way: "The FrameNet project is building a lexical database of English that is both human- and machine-readable, based on annotating examples of how words are used in actual texts. From the student's point of view, it is a dictionary of more than 10,000 word senses, most of them with annotated examples that show the meaning and usage. For the researcher in Natural Language Processing, the more than 170,000 manually annotated sentences provide a unique training dataset for semantic role labeling, used in applications such as information extraction, machine translation, event recognition, sentiment analysis, etc." https://framenet.icsi.berkeley.edu/fndrupal/about.
4. There were other off-ramps as well. Picking the correct event frame actually involved a great deal of editorial judgment; "deep dives" were a type of Structured Story that allowed reporters to go into greater depth about events that they found particularly important. For the sake of space, however, I focus here on the importance of bullet points as an example of the heterarchy of values in the Structured Story process.

Appendix

1. A final framework to consider would be that these studies ought to be internationally comparative, that is, they ought to look at countries and epistemological cultures that lie outside the United States and even outside "the West." With luck, other scholars will broaden and even challenge these findings as they launch more comparative projects on data journalism and journalistic epistemologies.
2. For an important alternate perspective on the relationship between journalism and its public see Ryfe 2016.

Primary Sources and Archives

Bureau of Social Service of the Presbyterian Church in the United States (1912) *Sociological and Religious Survey of Seventy American Cities*. New York, NY.

Charles Stelzle Papers. ca. 1889–1941. Rare Book and Manuscript Library, Columbia University.

Chronicling America: Historical Newspaper Database, Library of Congress. Available at http://chroniclingamerica.loc.gov. Accessed May 3, 2018.

Columbia University Graduate School of Journalism to the Russell Sage Foundation. March 20, 1965. "Proposal for a Training Program in Social Science and the Mass Media." Folder 1317, Box 139, Series 11. Rockefeller Archive Center.

Ferne, T. Interviewed by C.W. Anderson in London, UK, November 15, 2016 and November 17, 2016.

James Byrne to the Russell Sage Foundation. June 17, 1970. Mass Media and the Social Sciences Project. Folder 464, Box 55, Series 5. Subseries 7. Rockefeller Archive Center.

Messages of the Men and Religion Forward Movement, Volume VII: The Church and the Press (1912).

Meyer, P. Interviewed by C.W. Anderson in Chapel Hill, North Carolina, January 13, 2016.

Paul Lancaster to the Russell Sage Foundation. August 3, 1971. Social Science in the Professions Project. Folder 1317, Box 139, Series 11. Rockefeller Archive Center.

Philip Meyer Collected Papers, Rockefeller Foundation Archives. Folder Box 139, Series 11. Rockefeller Archive Center.

Philip Meyer to Russell Sage Foundation. September 1, 1971. Social Science in the Professions Project. Folder 1317, Box 139, Series 11. Rockefeller Archive Center.

Philip Meyer to Hugh Cline. September 7, 1971. Social Science in the Professions Project. Folder 1317, Box 139, Series 11. Rockefeller Archive Center.

Report on the Russell Sage Program in Journalism and the Behavioral Sciences at the Graduate School of Journalism, Columbia University, for the Academic Year 1967–68. January 19, 1969. Folder 1317, Box 139, Series 11. Rockefeller Archive Center.

Rissen, P. Interviewed by C.W. Anderson in London, UK, November 18, 2016.

Ross, S. Interviewed by C.W. Anderson in New York, NY, August 22, 2016.

Russell Sage Foundation (1918). *The ABCs of Exhibit Planning*. New York, NY.

Social Sciences in the Professions, Russell Sage Foundation Archives. Folder Box 139, Series 11. Rockefeller Archive Center.

Sociology in the Professions Project. March 23, 1965. "Re: Columbia Journalism Proposal." Russell Sage Foundation. Folder 1317, Box 139, Series 11. Rockefeller Archive Center.

Steven E. Chafee to the Russell Sage Foundation. April 2, 1966. Mass Media and the Social Sciences Project. Folder 464, Box 55, Series 5. Subseries 7. Rockefeller Archive Center.

University of Wisconsin School of Journalism to Russell Sage Foundation. May 22, 1965. "Proposal For a Social Science Reporting Program." Folder 464, Box 55, Series 7, Subseries 7, Record Group S61. Rockefeller Archive Center.

W. Phillips Davidson to Orville Brim. May 15, 1967. Social Science in the Professions Project. Folder 1317, Box 139, Series 11. Rockefeller Archive Center.

Waite, M. Interviewed by C.W. Anderson in Lincoln, Nebraska, January 7, 2016.

Bibliography

Abbott, A. 1991. *The System of the Professions*. Chicago, IL: University of Chicago Press.

Abbott, A. 1999. *Department and Discipline: Chicago Sociology at 100*. Chicago, IL: University of Chicago Press.

Abbott, A. and Sparrow, J.T. 2008. Hot War, Cold War: The Structures of Sociological Action, 1940–1955. In Calhoun, C. (ed.) *Sociology in America*. Chicago, IL: University of Chicago Press, 281–313.

Aisch, G. 2016. Why We Used Jittery Gauges in Our Live Election Forecast. Online at https://www.vis4.net/blog/posts/jittery-gauges-election-forecast/. Accessed April 11, 2017.

An Independent Journalist. 1909. Is an Honest and Sane Newspaper Press Possible? *American Journal of Sociology* 15(3): 321–334.

Anderson, C.W. 2013a. *Rebuilding the News: Metropolitan Journalism in the Digital Age*. Philadelphia, PA: Temple University Press.

Anderson, C.W. 2013b. What Aggregators Do: Towards a Network Concept of Journalistic Expertise in the Digital Age. *Journalism: Theory, Practice, Criticism* 14(8): 1008–1023.

Anderson, C.W. 2013c. Toward a Sociology of Computational and Algorithmic Journalism. *New Media and Society* 15(7): 1005–1021.

Anderson, C.W. 2015. Between the Unique and the Pattern: Historical Tensions in Our Understanding of Quantitative Journalism. *Digital Journalism* 3(3): 349–363.

Anderson, C.W. and Kreiss, D. 2013. Black Boxes as Capacities for and Constraints on Action: Electoral Politics, Journalism, and Devices of Representation. *Qualitative Sociology* 36: 365.

Anderson, C.W. and de Maeyer, J. 2015. Objects of Journalism and the News. *Journalism: Theory, Practice, Criticism* 16(1): 3–9.

Anderson, C.W. and Schudson, M. 2008. Objectivity, Professionalism, and Truth Seeking. In Hanitzsch, T. and Wahl-Jorgensen, K. (eds.) *The Handbook of Journalism Studies*. Mahwah, NJ: Lawrence Erlbaum, 88–101.

Asimov, I. 1951. *Foundation*. New York, NY: Gnome Press.

Baack, S. 2015. Datafication and Empowerment: How the Open Data Movement Re-Articulates Notions of Democracy, Participation, and Journalism. *Big Data and Society* July–August: 1–11.

Bales, K. 1991. Charles Booth's *Life and Labour of the People in London 1889–1903*. In Bulmer, M.T., Bales, K., and Kish Sklar, K. (eds.) *The Social Survey in Historical Perspective*, 103–117.

Barnhurst, K.G. 2011. The Problem of Modern Time in Journalism. *KronoScope* 11(1–2): 98–123.

Barnhurst, K.G. 2016. The Interpretive Turn in News. Online at http://www.academia.edu/11321792/The_Interpretive_Turn_in_News. Accessed March 11, 2017.

Barnhurst, K.G. and Mutz, D. 1997. American Journalism and the Decline in Event Centered Reporting. *Journal of Communication* 47(4): 27–53.

Barnhurst, K.G. and Nerone, J. 2001. *The Form of News: A History*. New York, NY: The Guildford Press.

Bartlett, H. 1928. The Social Survey and the Charity Organization Movement. *American Journal of Sociology* 34(2): 330–346.

Bateman, B. 2001. Make a Righteous Number: Social Surveys, the Men and Religion Forward Movement, and Quantification in American Economics. *History of Political Economy* 33: 57–85.

Bennett, W. 1990. Toward a Theory of Press–State Relations in the United States. *Journal of Communication* 40: 103–127.

Bennett, W.L. and Paletz, D.L. 1994. *Taken by Storm: The Media, Public Opinion, and US Foreign Policy in the Gulf War*. Chicago, IL: University of Chicago Press.

Boczkowski, P. 2004. *Digitizing the News*. Cambridge, MA: The MIT Press.

Boyer, D. 2014. *The Life Informatic: Newsmaking in the Digital Era*. Ithaca, NY: Cornell University Press.

Brinkley, A. 2010. *The Publisher: Henry Luce and His American Century*. New York, NY: Vintage.

Bulmer, M.T., Bales, K., and Sklar, K.K. 1991. *The Social Survey in Historical Perspective*. Cambridge, UK: Cambridge University Press.

Burawoy, M. 2005. For Public Sociology. *American Sociological Review* 70(February): 4–28.

Burdick, E. 1964. *The 480*. New York, NY: McGraw-Hill Education.

Bush, V. 1945. *Science—The Endless Frontier: A Report to the President by Vannevar Bush, Director of the Office of Scientific Research and Development, July 1945*. Washington, DC: United States Government Printing Office.

Cairo, A. 2014. Gorgeous Infographics. *Fortune Magazine* (March 1938 issue). Online at http://www.thefunctionalart.com/2014/07/gorgeous-infographics-from-fortune.html. Accessed April 1, 2018.

Carey, J. 1978. A Plea for the University Tradition. *Journalism Quarterly* 1978: 846–855.

Carey, J.W. 1965. The Communications Revolution and the Professional Communicator. *Sociological Review* 13(1): 23–38.

Carlson, M. 2015. The Many Boundaries of Journalism. In Carlson, M. and Lewis, S. (eds.) *Boundaries of Journalism: Professionalism, Practices, Participation*. New York, NY: Routledge, 1–18.

Carroll, G. and Huo, Y. 1986. Organizational Task and Institutional Environments in Ecological Perspective: Findings from the Local Newspaper Industry. *American Journal of Sociology* 91(4): 838–873.

Chalaby, J.K. 1996. Journalism as an Anglo-American Invention: A Comparison of the Development of French and Anglo-American Journalism, 1830s–1920s. *European Journal of Communication* 11: 303–326.

Chambers, C. 1971. *Paul U. Kellogg and the Survey: Voices for Social Welfare*. Minneapolis, MN: University of Minnesota Press.

Claussen, D. 1998. National Print Media Coverage of the Men and Religion Forward Movement, 1911–1917. Paper submitted to the Religion and Media Interest Group, AEJMC Convention Baltimore, Maryland, August 5–8, 1998.

Clayman, S. 2008. Interview as Journalistic Form. In *International Encyclopedia of Communication*. Oxford, UK: Wiley-Blackwell.

Coddington, M. 2014. Clarifying Journalism's Computational Turn: A Typology for Evaluating Data Journalism, Computational Journalism, and Computer-assisted Reporting. *Digital Journalism* 3(3): 331–348.

Coddington, M. 2015. *Gathering Evidence of Evidence: News Aggregation and the Production of Journalistic Knowledge*. PhD Thesis, University of Texas-Austin.

Cohen, S., Li, C., Yang, J., and Yu, C. 2011. Computational Journalism: A Call to Arms to Database Researchers. In *Proceedings of the 5th Biennial Conference on Innovative Data Systems Research*. Sailorman, CA: ACM.

Collins, H. and Evans, R. 2007. *Rethinking Expertise*. Chicago, IL: University of Chicago Press.

Columbia Journalism Review. 1979. Journalism and Social Science: Continuities and Discontinuities, by Gerald Grant. In Gans, H.J., Glazer, N., Gustield, J.R., and Jencks, C. (eds.) *On the Making of Americans: Essays in Honor of David Riesman*. University of Pennsylvania Press.

Cottle, S. 2003. *Media Organisation and Production*. New York, NY: SAGE.

Cottle, S. 2007. Ethnography and News Production: New(s) Developments in the Field. *Sociology Compass* 1(1): 1–16.

Cunningham, B. 2003. Toward a New Ideal: Rethinking Objectivity in a World of Spin. *Columbia Journalism Review* July–August 2003: 24–33.

Curtis, S. 2001. *A Consuming Faith: The Social Gospel and Modern American Culture*. Columbus, MO: University of Missouri Press.

Danzger, M.H. 1975. Validating Conflict Data *American Sociological Review* 40(5): 570–584.

Daston, L. (ed.). 2007. *Things That Talk: Object Lessons from Art and Science*. Cambridge, MA: The MIT Press.

Daston, L. and Galison, P. 2007. *Objectivity*. Cambridge, MA: The MIT Press.

Dayan, D. and Katz, E. 1992. *Media Events: The Live Broadcasting of History*. Cambridge, MA: Harvard University Press.

Deegan, M. 1990. *Jane Addams and the Men of the Chicago School*. New York, NY: Transaction Publishers.

Devine, E. 1909. Results of the Pittsburgh Survey. *American Journal of Sociology* 14(5): 660–667.

De Maeyer, J. 2014. Citation Needed: Investigating the Use of Hyperlinks to Display Sources in News Stories. *Journalism Practice* 8(5): 532–541.

De Maeyer, J., Libert, M., Domingo, D., Heinderyckx, F., and Le Cam, F. 2015. Waiting for Data Journalism: A Qualitative Assessment of the Anecdotal Take-up of Data Journalism in French-speaking Belgium. *Digital Journalism* 3(3): 432–446.

Dicken-Garcia, H. 1989. *Journalism Ethics in 19th Century America*. Madison, WI: University of Wisconsin Press.

D'Ignazio, C. and Klein, L. 2016. Feminist Data Visualization. Online at http://www.academia.edu/28173807/Feminist_Data_Visualization.

DuBois, W.E.B. 1967 [1899]. *The Philadelphia Negro*. New York, NY: Shocken Books.

Dunbar-Hester, C. forthcoming. *Hacking Community: The Politics of Inclusion in Open Technology Cultures*. Princeton, NJ: Princeton University Press.

Eco, U. 2009. *The Infinity of Lists*. London, UK: Rizzoli.

Epstein, J. 2000 [1973]. *News from Nowhere: Television and the News*. Lanham, MD: Ivan R Dee.

Ettema, J.S. and Glasser, T.L. 1998. *Custodians of Conscience: Investigative Journalism and Public Virtue*. New York, NY: Columbia University Press.

Eyal, G. and Hart, B. 2010. How Parents of Autistic Children became "Experts on Their own Children": Notes Towards a Sociology of Expertise. Keynote Address, BJS Annual Conference. *Berkeley Journal of Sociology* 54: 3–17.

Feldstein, M. 2004. Kissing Cousins: Journalism and Oral History. *Oral History Review* 31: 1–22.

Felgenhauer, N. 1971. Precision Journalism. In Dennis, E.E. (ed.) *Magic Writing Machine*. Eugene, OR: University of Oregon, School of Journalism, 71–83.

Fenton, F. 1910. The Influence of Newspaper Presentations Upon the Growth of Crime and Other Anti-Social Activity. *American Journal of Sociology* 16(3): 342–371.

Ferne, T. 2008. Archers: An Everyday Story of Web Development. Online at http://www.bbc.co.uk/blogs/radiolabs/2008/08/archrs_an_everyday_story_of_we.shtml. Accessed April 2, 2017.

Finnegan, C. 2005. Social Welfare and Visual Politics: The Story of Survey Graphic. Online at http://newdeal.feri.org/sg/essay01.htm.

Fink, K. and Anderson, C.W. 2015. Data Journalism in the United States: Beyond the Usual Suspects. *Journalism Studies* 16(4): 467–481.

Fink, K. and Schudson, M. 2014. The Rise of Contextual Journalism, 1950s–2000s. *Journalism: Theory, Practice, Criticism* 15(1): 3–20.

Fishman, M. 1978. Crime Waves as Ideology. *Social Problems* 25(5): 531–543.

Foucault, M. 1980. Power/Knowledge: Selected Interviews and Other Writings, 1972–1977. New York, NY: Vintage.

Fried, A. and Ellman, R. (eds.). 1969. *Charles Booth's London*. Online at http://booth.lse.ac.uk/static/a/4.html.

Friendly, M. 2008. *A Brief History of Data Visualization*. Online at http://www.datavis.ca/papers/hbook.pdf.

Galison, P. 2015. *Journalist, Scientist, Objectivity*. Online at http://galison.scholar.harvard.edu/files/andrewhsmith/files/petergalison_journalistscientistobjectivity_final.pdf. Accessed March 31, 2017.

Gans, H. 1979. The Messages Beyond the News *Columbia Journalism Review* January: 40–45.

Gans, H. 1980. *Deciding What's News: A Study of CBS Evening News, NBC Nightly News, Newsweek, and Time*. New York: Vintage.

Gans, H. 2015. Public Sociology and Its Publics. *American Sociology Review* 47(1): 3–11.

Garvey, E.G. 2012. *Writing With Scissors: American Scrapbooks from the Civil War to the Harlem Renaissance*. New York, NY: Oxford University Press.

Gillespie, T., Boczkowski, P., and Foote, K. 2014. *Media Technology: Essays on Communication, Materiality, and Society*. Cambridge, MA: The MIT Press.

Gitelman, L. 2014. *Paper Knowledge: Toward a History of Documents*. Durham, NC: Duke University Press.

Glasser, T.L. and Ettema, J.S. 1984. On the Epistemology of Investigative Journalism in collected proceedings of the Association for Education in Journalism and Mass Communication conference, Gainsville, Fl, June 1–3, 1984.

Graves, L.D. 2016. *Deciding What's True: Fact-Checking Journalism and the New Ecology of News*. New York, NY: Columbia University Press.

Greenwald, M.W. and Anderson, M.J. (eds.). 1996. *Pittsburgh Surveyed: Social Science and Social Reform in the Early Twentieth Century*. Pittsburgh, PA: University of Pittsburgh Press.

Grey, D. 1966. Supreme Court Headlines: Accuracy vs Precision. *Columbia Journalism Review* July: 26–29.

Hackett, R.A. 2008. Objectivity in Reporting. In Donsbach, W. (ed.) *The International Encyclopedia of Communication*.

Hammack, D. and Wheeler, S. 1994. *Social Science in the Making: Essays on the Russell Sage Foundation*. New York, NY: The Russell Sage Foundation.

Harrison, S.M. 1930. Development and Spread of Social Surveys. In Eaton, A. and Harrison, S.M. (eds.) *A Bibliography of Social Surveys*. New York, NY: Russell Sage Foundation, 1–7.

Hayles, N.K. 1999. *How We Became Posthuman: Virtual Bodies in Cybernetics, Literature and Informatics*. Chicago: University of Chicago Press.

Haskell, T.L. 1977. Power to the expert! *New York Review of Books*. October 13. Online at http://www.nybooks.com/articles/1977/10/13/power-to-the-experts/.

Hennock, E.P. 1991. Concepts of Poverty in the British Social Surveys from Charles Booth to Arthur Bowley. In Bulmer, M., Bales, K., and Kish Sklar, K. (eds.) *The Social Survey in Historical Perspective, 1880–1940*. Cambridge: Cambridge University Press, 189–216.

Herbst, S. 1993. *Numbered Voices: How Opinion Polling Has Shaped American Politics*. Chicago, IL: University of Chicago Press.

Herbst, S. 1998. *Reading Public Opinion*. Chicago, IL: University of Chicago Press.

Hess, S. 1981. *The Washington Reporters*. Washington, DC: Brookings Institution Press.

Hilmes, M. and Loviglio, J. 2002. *Radio Reader: Essays in the Cultural History of the Radio*. London, UK: Routledge.

Holavaty, A. 2005. A Fundamental Way Newspaper Websites Need to Change. Online at http://www.holovaty.com/writing/fundamental-change/. Accessed March 8, 2017.

Høyer, S. and Pöttker, H. 2005. *Diffusion of the News Paradigm 1850–2000*. Göteborg, Sweden: Nordicom.

Hsieh, H. and Shannon, S. 2005. Three Approaches to Qualitative Content Analysis. *Qualitative Health Research* 15(9): 1277–1288.

Igo, S. 2008. *The Averaged American: Surveys, Citizens, and the Making of a Mass Public*. Cambridge, MA: Harvard University Press.

IRE. n.d. IRE: A History. Online at http://www.ire.org/about/history/.

Jacobs, R. 2009. Culture, the Public Sphere, and Media Sociology: A Search for a Classical Founder in the Work of Robert Park. *American Sociologist* 40(3): 149–166.

Johns, E. 1942. The Newspaper and Society: A Book of Readings, by George L. Bird; Frederic E. Merwin [Review]. *American Journal of Sociology* 48(2): 274.

Johnstone, J.W.C. 1982. Who Controls the News? *American Journal of Sociology* 87(5): 1174–1181.

Kafka, B. 2009. Paperwork: The State of the Discipline. *Book History* 12: 340–353.

Kafka, B. 2012. *The Demon of Writing: Powers and Failures of Paperwork*. Cambridge, MA: The MIT Press.

Kaplan, R.L. 2006. The News about New Institutionalism: Journalism's Ethic of Objectivity and Its Political Origins. *Political Communication* 23(2): 173–185.

Karpf, D., Kreiss, D., Nielsen, R.K., and Powers, M. 2015. The Role of Qualitative Methods in Political Communication Research: Past, Present, and Future. *International Journal of Communication* 9: 1888–1906.

Kellogg, P. 1912. The Spread of the Survey Idea. *Proceedings of the Academy of Political Science in the City of New York* 2(4): 1–17.

Kennedy, H., Hill, R.L., Aiello, G., and Allen, W. 2016. The Work that Visualisation Conventions Do. *Information, Communication, and Society* March: 1–21.

Kinneman, J.A. 1946. Newspaper Circulation from Small Metropolitan Centers. *American Sociological Review* 11(2): 150–155.

Kreiss, D. 2012. *Taking Our Country Back: The Crafting of Networked Politics from Howard Dean to Barack Obama*. Oxford, UK: Oxford University Press.

Kreiss, D. 2016. *Prototype Politics: Technology-Intensive Campaigning and the Data of Democracy*. Oxford, UK: Oxford University Press.

Lamble, S. 2001. Computer Assisted Reporting, Phil Meyer, and the Emperor's New Clothes. *Ejournalist* 1(2): 1–10.

Lang, K. and Lang, G.E. 1973. Television Hearings: The Impact Out There. *Columbia Journalism Review* November: 52–57.

Lang, K. and Lang, G.E. 2004. The Unique Perspective of Television and Its Effect: A Pilot Study. In Peters, J.D. (ed.) *Mass Communication and American Social Thought Key Texts (1919–1968)*. Lanham, MD: Rowman & Littlefield, 328–337.

Lannoy, P. 2004. When Robert Park Was (Re)Writing the City: Biography, the Social Survey, and the Science of Sociology. *American Sociologist* 35(1): 34–62.

Latour, B. 2010a. Coming Out as a Philosopher. *Social Studies of Science* 40(4): 599–608.

Latour, B. 2010b. *The Making of Law: An Ethnography of the Conseil d'Etat*. Cambridge, UK: Polity Press.

Latour, B. 2013. *An Inquiry Into Modes of Existence: An Anthropology of the Moderns*. Cambridge, MA: The Harvard University Press.

Latour, B., Jensen, B., Venturini, T., and Grauwin, S. 2012. The Whole Is Always Smaller Than Its Parts: A Digital Text of Gabriel Tarde's Monads. *British Journal of Sociology* 63(4): 590–615.

Law, J. 1992. Notes on the Theory of the Actor-Network: Ordering, Strategy and Heterogeneity. *Systems Practice* 5(1992): 379–393.

Law, J. and Singleton, V. 2003. This is Not an Object. Online at http://www.comp.lancs.ac.uk/sociology/papers/Law-Singleton-This-is-Not-an-Object.pdf.

Lee, R.M. 2004. Recording Technologies and the Interview in Sociology. *Sociology: The Journal of the British Sociological Association* 38: 1–16.

Lee, R.M. 2008. David Riesman and the Sociology of the Interview. *Sociological Quarterly* 49: 285–307.

Lengermann, P. 1979. The Founding of the American Sociological Review: The Anatomy of a Rebellion. *American Sociological Review* 44(2): 185–198.

Lengermann, P. and Niebrugge, G. 2007. *The Women Founders: Sociology and Social Theory, 1830-1930*. Long Grove, IL: Waveland Press.

Lenthall, B. 2008. *Radio's America: The Great Depression and the Rise of Modern Mass Culture*. Chicago, IL: University of Chicago Press.

Lepore, J. 2015. Are Polls Ruining Politics? *New Yorker*. Online at http://www.newyorker.com/magazine/2015/11/16/politics-and-the-new-machine. Accessed April 7, 2017.

Lewis, S. 2015. Introduction to Special Issue of Digital Journalism: Journalism in an Era of Big Data: Cases, Concepts, and Critiques. *Digital Journalism* 3(3): 321–330.

Lewis, S. and Usher, N. 2013. Open Source and Journalism: Toward New Frameworks for Imagining News Innovation. *Media, Culture, and Society* 35(5): 602–619.

Linch, G. 2010a. Computational Thinking and the New Journalism Mindset. Online at http://www.greglinch.com/2010/05/computational-thinking-and-the-new-journalism-mindset.html. Accessed October 22, 2016.

Linch, G. 2010b. Rethinking our Thinking. Online at http://www.greglinch.com/2010/04/rethinking-our-thinking.html. Accessed October 22, 2016.

Linder, R. 2006. *The Reportage of Urban Culture: Robert Park and the Chicago School*. Cambridge, UK: Cambridge University Press.

Loon, J.V. and Hemmingway, E. 2005. Organizations Identities and Technologies in Innovation Management: The Rise and Fall of Bi-media in the BBC East Midlands. *Intervention Research* 1(2): 125–147.

McGerr, M. 2005. *A Fierce Discontent: The Rise and Fall of the Progressive Movement in America, 1870-1920*. Oxford, UK: Oxford University Press.

McGill, D. 2006. Largemouth: A Citizen Journalism Syllabus. Online at http://www.mcgillreport.org/largemouthsyllabus.htm.

Meyer, P. 1969. Playing for the Upper Hand. *Playboy*. April 1969.

Meyer, P. 1973. *Precision Journalism: A Reporters Guide to Social Science Methods*. Bloomington, IN: Indiana University Press.

Meyer, P. 1979. *Precision Journalism: A Reporters Guide to Social Science Methods*. 2nd ed. Bloomington, IN: Indiana University Press.

Meyer, P. 1991. *The New Precision Journalism*. Bloomington, IN: Indiana University Press.

Meyer, P. 2002. *Precision Journalism: A Reporter's Guide to Social Science Methods*. 4th ed. New York, NY: Rowman & Littlefield Publishers.

Meyer, P. 2009. The Straw Man: A Rejoinder to Lamble. Online at https://www.unc.edu/~pmeyer/Emporer3.html. Accessed April 7, 2017.

Meyer, P. 2012a. *Paper Route: Finding My Way to Precision Journalism*. Chapel Hill, NC: iUniverse.

Meyer, P. 2012b. Precision Journalism and Narrative Journalism: Toward a Unified Field Theory. Online at http://niemanreports.org/articles/precision-journalism-and-narrative-journalism-toward-a-unified-field-theory/. Accessed April 7, 2017.

Michaelis, L. 2007. Hobbes's Modern Prometheus: A Political Philosophy for an Uncertain Future. *Canadian Journal of Political Science* 40(1): 101–127.

Molotch, H. and Lester, M. 1974. News as Purposive Behavior. *American Sociological Review* 39(1): 101–113.

Molotch, H. and Lester, M. 1975. Accidental News: The Great Oil Spill as a Local Occurrence and National Event. *American Journal of Sociology* 81(2): 235–260.

Montgomery, M. 2008. The Discourse of the Broadcast News Interview. *Journalism Studies* 9: 260–277.

Morris, A. 2015. *The Scholar Denied: W.E.B. DuBois and the Birth of Modern Sociology*. Berkeley: University of California Press.

Mosco, V. 1980. What's Black and White and Split Down the Middle? *Columbia Journalism Review* January: 1–3.

Musson, A.E. 1959. The Great Depression in Britain, 1873–1896. *Journal of Economic History* 19(2): 199–228.

National Science Foundation. 1994. The National Science Foundation: A Brief History. Online at https://www.nsf.gov/about/history/nsf50/nsf8816.jsp. Accessed April 5, 2018.

Nicholson, B. 2012. You Kick the Bucket; We Do the Rest! Jokes and the Culture of Reprinting in the Transatlantic Press. *Journal of Victorian Culture* 17(3): 273–286.

Nietzsche, F. 2013 [1887]. *On the Genealogy of Morals*. London, UK: Penguin Classics.

Niles, R. 2005. What is Journalism? Online at http://www.robertniles.com/journalism/.

Nord, D. 1990. Teleology and the News: The Religious Roots of American Journalism. *Journal of American History* 77(1): 9–38.

Nowotny, H. 2016. *The Cunning of Uncertainty*. London, UK: Polity Press.

Palmer, R. 2017. *Becoming the News: How Ordinary People Respond to the Media Spotlight*. New York, NY: Columbia University Press.

Parasie, S. and Dagiral, E. 2012. Data-driven Journalism and the Public Good: Computer-assisted-reporters and Programmer-journalists in Chicago. *New Media and Society* 15(6): 853–871.

Park, R. 1915. The City: Suggestion for the Investigations of Human Behavior in the City Environment. *American Journal of Sociology* 20(5): 577–612.

Park, R. 1923. The Natural History of the Newspaper. *American Journal of Sociology* 29(3): 273–289.

Park, R., Burgess, W., and McKenzie, R. 1925. *The City*. Chicago: University of Chicago Press.

Pedelty, M. 1995. *War Stories: Culture of Foreign Correspondents*. London, UK: Routledge.

Peters, J.D. 2001. Witnessing. *Media, Culture & Society* 23: 707–723.

Plesner, U. 2009. An Actor-network Perspective on Changing Work Practices: Communication Technologies as Actants in Newswork. *Journalism: Theory, Practice, Criticism* 10(5): 604–626.

Pocock, J.G.A. 1970. James Harrington and the Good Old Cause: A Study of the Ideological Context of His Writings. *Journal of British Studies* 10(November): 30–48.

Pocock, J.G.A. 1981. The Machiavellian Moment Revisited: A Study in History and Ideology. *Journal of Modern History* 53(March): 49–72.

Polsby, N. 1967. The Boys of Boise: Furor, Vice and Folly in an American City, by John Gerassi [Review]. *American Journal of Sociology* 72(6): 691.

Pooley, J. 2011. Another Plea for the University Tradition: The Institutional Roots of Intellectual Compromise. *International Journal of Communication* 5: 1442–1457.

Pooley, J. and Katz, E. 2008. Further Notes on Why Sociology Abandoned Mass Communication Research. *Journal of Communication* 58(4): 767–786.

Poovey, M. 1998. *A History of the Modern Fact: Problems of Knowledge in the Sciences of Wealth and Society*. Chicago, IL: University of Chicago Press.

Porter, T.M. 1995. *Trust in Numbers: The Pursuit of Objectivity in Science and Public Life*. Princeton, NJ: Princeton University Press.

Potter, Z. 1915. *The Social Survey: A Bibliography*. New York, NY: Russell Sage Foundation.

Powers, M. 2011. In Forms that are Familiar and Yet-to-be Invented: American Journalism and the Discourse of Technologically Specific Work. *Journal of Communication Inquiry* 36(1): 24–43.

Putney, C. 2003. *Muscular Christianity: Manhood and Sports in Protestant America, 1880–1920*. Cambridge, MA: Harvard University Press.

Riesman, D. and Benney, M. 1956. Asking and Answering. *Journal of Business of the University of Chicago* 29: 225–236.

Ross, D. 1992. *The Origins of American Social Science*. Cambridge, UK: Cambridge University Press.

Royal, C. 2010. The Journalist as Programmer: A Case Study of the *New York Times* Interactive News Technology Department. Paper presented at the International Symposium For Online Journalism. Austin, TX.

Ryfe, D. 2016. *Journalism and the Public*. Cambridge, UK: Polity Press.

Salgado, S. and Strömbäck, J. 2012. Interpretive Journalism: A Review of Concepts, Operationalizations and Key Findings. *Journalism* 13: 144–161.

Schlesinger, P. and Tumber, H. 1994. *Reporting Crime: The Media Politics of Criminal Justic*. Oxford, UK: Clarendon Press.

Schmitz-Weiss, A. and Domingo, D. 2010. Innovation Practices in Online Newsrooms as Actor-Networks and Communities of Practice. *New Media and Society* 12(7): 1156–1171.

Schudson, M. 1978. *Discovering the News: A Social History of American Newspapers.* New York, NY: Basic Books.

Schudson, M. 1990. *Origins of the Ideal of Objectivity in the Professions: Studies in the History of American Journalism and American Law 1830-1840.* Cambridge, MA: Harvard University Press.

Schudson, M. 1992. *Watergate in American Memory: How We Remember, Forget, and Reconstruct the Past.* New York, NY: Basic Books.

Schudson, M. 1995. Question Authority: A History of the News Interview. In *The Power of News.* Cambridge, MA: Harvard University Press, 269–283.

Schudson, M. 2001. The Objectivity Norm in American Journalism. *Journalism* 2: 149–170.

Schudson, M. and Fink, K. 2014. The Rise of Contextual Journalism: 1950–2000. *Journalism* 15(1): 3–20.

Seyb, R. 2015. What Walter Saw: Walter Lippmann, the *New York World*, and Scientific Advocacy as an Alternative to the News-Opinion Dichotomy. *Journalism History* 41(2): 58–72.

Shalloo, S. 1940. News and the Human Interest Story, by Helen McGill Hughes; Backgrounding the News: The Newspaper and the Social Sciences, by Sidney Kobre. *American Sociological Review* 5(4): 663–664.

Shapin, S. and Schaffer, S. *The Leviathan and the Air Pump: Hobbes, Boyle, and the Experimental Life.* Princeton, NJ: Princeton University Press.

Sigelman, L. 1973. Reporting the News: An Organizational Analysis. *American Journal of Sociology* 79(1): 132–151.

Silver, N. 2014. What the Fox Knows. Online at https://fivethirtyeight.com/features/what-the-fox-knows/. Accessed March 30, 2018.

Skinner, Q. 2012. *Visions of Politics: Hobbes and Civil Science.* Cambridge, UK: Cambridge University Press.

Smith, G.S. 2000. *The Search for Social Salvation: Social Christianity and America, 1880–1925.* Lanham, MD: Lexington Books.

Sokolov, A.V. 2009. The Epistemology of Documents (a Methodological Essay). *Automatic Documentation and Mathematical Linguistics* 43: 57–68.

Solovey, M. and Pooley, J. 2011. The Price of Success: Sociologist Harry Alpert, the NSF's First Social Science Policy Architect. *Annals of Science* 68: 229–260.

Star, S.L. and Bowker, G. 2000. *Sorting Things Out: Classification and Its Consequences.* Cambridge, MA: The MIT Press.

Stark, D. 2011. *A Sense of Worth: Accounts of Dissonance in Economic Life.* Princeton, NJ: Princeton University Press.

Steinmetz, G. 2008. American Sociology before and after World War II: The (Temporary) Settling of a Disciplinary Field. In Calhoun, C. (ed.) *Sociology in America.* Chicago, IL: University of Chicago Press, 314–366.

Stezle, C. 1926. *Son of the Bowery: The Life Story of an East Side American.* New York: George H. Doran Company.

Stonbely, S. 2013. The Social and Intellectual Context of the U.S. "Newsroom Studies," and the Media Sociology of Today. *Journalism Studies* 1–17.

Stouffer, S. 1949. *The American Soldier, Volume I: Adjustment during Army Life.* Princeton, NJ: Princeton University Press.

Stray, J. 2010. Computational Journalism: A Reading List. Online at http://jonathanstray.com/a-computational-journalism-reading-list. Accessed October 22, 2016.

Suchman, E. 1953. Understanding Public Opinion, by Curtis D. MacDougall. *American Sociological Review* 18(2): 218–219.

Suskind, R. 2004. Faith, Certainty, and the Presidency of George W. Bush. *New York Times Magazine.* October 17, 2004.

Tenenboim-Weinblatt, K. and Neiger, M. 2017. Temporal Affordances in the News. *Journalism: Theory, Practice, and Criticism* 19(1): 37–55.

Toff, B. 2015. The Blind Scorekeepers: Journalism, Polling, and the Battle to Define Public Opinion in American Politics. PhD Dissertation, University of Wisconsin-Madison.

Tuchman, G. 1972. Objectivity as Strategic Ritual: An Examination of Newsmen's Notions of Objectivity. *American Journal of Sociology* 77(4): 660–679.

Tuchman, G. 1973. Making News By Doing Work: Routinizing the Unexpected. *American Journal of Sociology* 79(1): 110–131.

Tuchman, G. 1978. *Making News: A Study in the Construction of Reality*. New York: Free Press.

Turner, F. 2006. *From Counterculture to Cyberculture: Stewart Brand, the Whole Earth Network, and the Rise of Digital Utopianism*. Chicago, IL: University of Chicago Press.

Turner, F. 2015. *The Democratic Surround: Multimedia and Liberalism from World War II to the Psychedelic Sixties*. Chicago, IL: University of Chicago Press.

Turner, F. and Hamilton, J.T. 2009. Accountability through Algorithm: Developing the Field of Computational Journalism. Online at: http://dewitt.sanford.duke.edu/images/uploads/About_3_Research_B_cj_1_finalreport.pdf. Accessed November 12, 2013.

Turner, S. 1994. The Pittsburgh Survey and the Survey Movement: An Episode in the History of Expertise. In Greenwald, M.W. and Anderson, M.J. (eds.) (1996) *Pittsburgh Surveyed: Social Science and Social Reform in the Early Twentieth Century*. Pittsburgh, PA: University of Pittsburgh Press, 35–49.

Usher, N. 2016. *Interactive Journalism: Hackers, Data, and Code*. Champaign-Urbana, IL: University of Illinois Press.

Vergaray, A.R. 2014. *Rethinking Uncertainty: Spinoza and Hume on Shaping. Uncertain Secular Futures*. Unpublished Doctoral Dissertation. Virginia Polytechnic Institute and State University.

Vincent, G. 1905. A Laboratory Experiment in Journalism. *American Journal of Sociology* 11(3): 297–311.

Vismann, C. 2008. *Files*. Palo Alto, CA: Stanford University Press.

Wahl-Jorgensen, K. forthcoming. *Emotions, Media, and Politics*. Cambridge, UK: Polity Press.

Weeks, A. 1916. The Mind of the Citizen III. *American Journal of Sociology* 21(4): 501–520.

Williams, B. and Delli Carpini, M. 2011. *After Broadcast News*. Cambridge, UK: Cambridge University Press.

Wilner, I. 2006. The Man Time Forgot. *Vanity Fair*. Online at http://www.vanityfair.com/news/2006/10/henry-luce-briton-hadden-rivalry.

Wing, J. 2006. Computational Thinking: A Vision for the 21st Century. *Communications of the ACM* 49(3): 33–35.

Wing, J. 2008. Computational Thinking and Thinking About Computing. Online at http://www.cs.cmu.edu/afs/cs/usr/wing/www/talks/ct-and-tc-long.pdf. Accessed October 27, 2016.

Wirth, L. 1947. Consensus and Mass Communication. *American Sociological Review* 13(1): 1–17.

Wolfe, T. 1972. Birth of the New Journalism: An Eyewitness Report by Thomas Wolfe. *New York Magazine*. February 14, 1972.

Yarros, V.S. 1899. The Press and Public Opinion. *American Journal of Sociology* 5(3): 372–382.

Zelizer, B. 1992. *Covering the Body: The Kennedy Assassination, the Media, and the Shaping of Collective Memory*. Chicago, IL: University of Chicago Press.

Zelizer, B. 2007. On "Having Been There": "Eyewitnessing" as a Journalistic Key Word. *Critical Studies in Media Communication* 24: 408–428.

Index

Note: page numbers followed by *f* and *t* refer to figures and tables respectively. those followed by n refer to notes with note number (and chapter number, when necessary.)